# Consorting and Collal
## Education Market riace

Education Policy Perspectives Series

# Consorting and Collaborating in the Education Market Place

*Edited by*

## David Bridges and Chris Husbands

 The Falmer Press

(A member of the Taylor & Francis Group)

London • Washington, D.C.

**UK**    The Falmer Press, 4 John Street, London WC1N 2ET
**USA**   The Falmer Press, Taylor & Francis Inc., 1900 Frost Road, Suite 101, Bristol, PA 19007

---

© D. Bridges and C. Husbands 1996

First published in 1996

**A catalogue record for this book is available from the British Library**

**Library of Congress Cataloging-in-Publication Data are available on request**

ISBN 0 7507 0449 7 cased
ISBN 0 7507 0450 0 paper

Jacket design by Caroline Archer

Typeset in 10/12 pt Times by
Graphicraft Typesetters Ltd., Hong Kong.

*Printed in Great Britain by Burgess Science Press, Basingstoke on paper which has a specified pH value on final paper manufacture of not less than 7.5 and is therefore 'acid free'.*

# Contents

*Contents*

# Chapter 1

# The Education Market Place and the Collaborative Response: An Introduction

*David Bridges and Chris Husbands*

The Conservative Government's educational 'reforms' of the 1980s and 1990s sought deliberately to introduce market relations into educational services at all levels. The 'LEA monopolies' of schooling (Flew, 1991) were eroded by the introduction of a grant-maintained sector, by the provision of assisted places to widen access to independent schools and by the creation of City Technology Colleges. The sometimes voluntary and sometimes enforced delegation of financial management from LEAs to schools put LEA services in a competitive relationship with other providers of, for example, advisory, training and personnel services, for which schools would now pay directly. In some authorities, LEA departments became indeed service providers for other sections of the same LEA (Morris, 1994).

Similarly, as a result of the Education Acts of 1980, 1986 and 1988, schools were put in a competitive relationship with regard to the recruitment of pupils. They were allowed to accept pupils up to the limits of their physical capacity and were funded on the basis of their success in attracting them. The power of local education authorities to shield less popular schools from some of the consequences of parental choice (and indeed their capacity to intervene in such schools with a view to improving their popularity) were first curtailed and then effectively abolished. The comprehensive re-organizations of the 1960s and 1970s were challenged by those provisions of the 1988 Education Reform Act which allowed schools to 'opt out' of local authority control and seek direct funding as grant-maintained schools, and which encouraged commercial sponsors to create new City Technology Colleges: diversity of provision in the supply side of the market was seen as an essential component of the rhetoric of choice. For all schools, the national publication of examination results, the publication of annual reports with information about absenteeism and other matters determined by the Government and the imposition of a system of regular inspection accompanied by published reports were designed to inform the demand side of the market, as parents were placed in the role of service consumers (Bridges, 1994). These developments also heightened the competitive ethos which, on the market model, was intended to provide a spur to individual institutional development.

Some commentators have observed of course that, as far as schools are concerned, the application of market principles has been far short of what any serious ideological commitment would require (Tooley, 1994). While employing the rhetoric of the market place, the Conservative administration has in fact imposed the heaviest centralized controls that the school system in England and Wales has ever experienced: a national curriculum; national assessment requirements in which the roles of independent examining boards are steadily eroded; a national system of staff appraisal and pupil records of achievement; the acquisition by the Secretary of State of enormous regulatory powers which can be exercised without even reference back to Parliament; and a more regular policing of schools' conformity to these requirements by the Office for Standards in Education (OFSTED). These newly centralized powers, of course, are additional to an established system of national pay settlements for teachers and national controls over the formula for the funding of schools, so the sense in which market forces have been released in the school system is a pretty limited one. Headteachers and governors have a sense that government has successfully delegated to them the blame for educational shortcomings whilst retaining to itself the main instruments of power through which those shortcomings can be addressed. Nevertheless, the changes which have been introduced, particularly in respect of admissions, have fragmented the identity of the education-service provider and heightened the competitive relations between schools.

In higher education, the abolition of the binary divide between universities and polytechnics in 1992, the replacement of block grants by largely formula-driven funding, the introduction of selective funding for research based on an assessment of prior performance and the introduction of published quality assessments of teaching have produced similar pressure towards competition. The universities already stood in something closer to a market relationship with each other in their recruitment of students. The time is probably not far off when they will be charging differential fees related to different services and reputations. In the research field universities act very much like, and indeed in competition with, private companies in tendering and competing for research and development contracts. Indeed the competition sometimes extends to relations between units within the same university — a scenario which has prompted a definition of the modern university as 'a series of individual faculty entrepreneurs held together by a common grievance over parking' (Kerr, 1973, p. 16).

The response of educational organizations to initiatives designed to institutionalize competitive market relations has, however, been not entirely in line with the ideological expectations. This book describes one of the somewhat paradoxical consequences of the development of the education market place: the development of collaborative relations and infrastructures between what are in significant respects competing institutions. In some cases these have taken the form of relatively loose networks linking individuals (as, for example the Collaborative Action Research Network and the Cambridgeshire Secondary Education Trust described here by Bridget Somekh and Sylvia West, respectively) in others more formally defined and structured consortia of institutions (as, for example represented here by Education 2000, The Hertfordshire Project and the Eastern Region Teacher Education Consortium).

The contributors to this book, who are in many cases active agents in the development of these collaborative or consortial relationships, describe and analyse their responses to the market place and consider the implications of collaborative, including consortium, relationships for the future development of education. The contributors come from a variety of institutions and address the issue from a variety of perspectives, but they are concerned with the answers to some common questions: Why do and why should competitive institutions collaborate? What forms does such collaboration take? Under what circumstances is collaboration most likely to succeed — or to fail? What are the implications of collaboration for the development of education?

We are particularly interested in exploring two related issues. The first is to consider the strategies which schools and other institutions adopt in their relationships with each other in the educational market place. We are interested in the patterns of collaboration and consortium which are emerging in different ways and in different areas. In historical or empirical terms we are interested simply in documenting and describing patterns which are emerging. At a more conceptual level, we are interested in addressing the question of what constitutes 'rational' behaviour in the educational market place — in finding out why it is that schools collaborate rather than compete and over what matters.

The second set of issues is less concerned with description and more concerned with analysis. Some collaborations persist. Some do not. Some collaborations are perceived either by those involved or those observing from outside to be successful. Others are not. In most cases, the balance between 'success' and 'failure' is more jagged, less well defined than this, as indeed are the criteria of success or failure themselves. We are interested, then, in trying to establish what functional or ethical aspirations these collaborations set out to satisfy, the conditions under which they succeed in satisfying these aspirations and, most generally of all, what implications these arrangements might have for the future development of the educational market place.

We have divided the contributions into two sections, which roughly correspond to the two sets of issues which our contributors address. In the first section, we offer a series of descriptions, often by participants in the sorts of collaborative arrangements which schools and higher education institutions have entered into since the 1988 Education Act. Chris Husbands analyses the background to the development of collaboration between schools and outlines the variety of different types of collaboration which appear to be emerging. Husbands argues that the motives for collaborative relationships are complex, and that the development of collaborative arrangements can either derive from a rejection of market-driven philosophies or an attempt to 'manage' a more rational and, in economic terms, 'perfect' market.

Most of the chapters in the first section describe the development of different collaborative arrangements. Linda Hargreaves draws on research work with rural primary schools to explore the ways in which collaboration can become a condition of the survival of the small rural primary school given the shifting curriculum demands. A series of contributions trace the development of collaborative networks or consortia, identifying the aims of the original collaborating schools as well as some of the tensions which were experienced in the process of developing collaborative relationships. The chapters bring out the wide range of purposes for which collaboration was established, as well as some of the different qualities of consortium or collaborative relationships which emerged. Mike Harbour and Ron Wallace both explore the development of cross-phase networks of first, middle and upper schools in Lowestoft and south-east Bedfordshire. In both cases, the networks, although springing from different impulses, allowed the schools to develop a shared identity and common purposes which were to define them in their relationships with outside bodies.

Peter Upton, Sylvia West, Lynne Monck and Chris Husbands all write about secondary-school networks. Here the focus is more explicitly on the collaborative consortium as a tool in the search for some model of school improvement via staff development. Again, the internal structures of the consortium involve some 'prime movers' amongst school staff who play a highly significant role in developing relationships and who come to value the consortium highly, whilst other staff remain more peripheral to the development of the consortium. A common theme of all these contributions is the way in which the consortium becomes a 'shell' within which the participating institutions develop a common identity 'against' outsiders, within which participating staff have an opportunity to articulate shared values for which the consortium is seen as providing a location. For Peter Upton, the collaborative network both provides a locus for an extended model of staff development and a management and professional challenge in terms of the management of roles and relationships both within individual schools and across the network. Working with a group of fairly isolated secondary schools, where there were clear role definitions and strong senses of institutional identity, Upton argues that the construction of consortium was never easy but that it had, eventually, considerable power to shift staff cultures in the schools. Monck and Husbands are able to trace the contribution of a possibly unique set of circumstances to staff development and educational change amongst the State and private schools in the 'garden city' of Letchworth. The Education 2000 Project on which they draw was, at its fullest expression, about the involvement of the whole community in the renewal and reshaping of learning in schools via information technology and curriculum review. Monck and Husbands are clear about the principles which underpin the Education 2000 model of change, and suggest that the strains which recent national policy has placed on the model have left their marks on the schools involved in the Letchworth Project. Nonetheless, their conclusion is that collaborative approaches to change in the Project have wider, positive implications for the schools involved. Sylvia West, writing from the perspective of a group of heads striving to locate a new identity and 'grammar' of local management presents the issues of collaborative networking as a feature of post-modern crises of authority and ideas in schooling and society. For all these contributors, the key issue is the way in which collaborative networks shift the sense of 'boundary' for participants in and across schools.

The final contribution in this first half of the book widens the focus and demonstrates the ways in which schools — either in groups or individually — have begun to form highly significant collaborative relationships with outside institutions. Michael Barber and Michael Johnson examine the collaboration for school-improvement work undertaken from the University of Keele. In the Keele 'Two Towns Project', the collaborating stakeholders include urban secondary schools, the local education authority, two local universities and the local Training and Enterprise Council.

The chapters in the second section of the book examine the second set of issues, relating to the conditions under which successful consortia operate and some of the difficulties which can confound unsuccessful consortia. Ann Bridgwood explores the development of curriculum working groups under the umbrella of TVEI consortia in the later 1980s and the ways in which these groups created new curriculum approaches and management structures in schools. Bridget Somekh explores the issues raised for teacher and school development by the existence of a much looser network — the Collaborative Action Research Network. In Somekh's account, as in Bridgwood's there are important insights into the pressures on individual teachers who are extensively involved in collaborative activity deriving from their role in their own institution at the same time as their responsibilities to individuals in other institutions with whom they are brought into contact by virtue of the collaborative networks.

David Bridges explores the experience of consortia in higher education where the nature of competition between institutions is often more sharply focused than between schools and the pressures on those closely involved in consortium development are correspondingly greater. His chapter identifies some of the practical benefits of consortium collaboration, not least in giving institutions more clout on a national stage than they may have individually and in providing support for innovators in the institutional context. At the same time it raises questions, more directly than Somekh or Bridgwood, about who actually experiences the consortium ('the consortium people'?), whose interests are served by the consortium activity and the extent to which consortium activity offers a substitute for, or offers real leverage on, institutional change. It argues in conclusion that the possibilities for collaborative activity between competing institutions are increased in proportion to the extent that their characters and priorities are differentiated.

Both Mike Fielding and Harry Gray take a wider perspective. For Fielding, the values of collaborative consortia are problematic, and need to be underpinned by a commitment to the values of community which recent educational reforms have prejudiced. Gray's chapter, from the perspective of organizational psychology explores the conditions under which consortium relationships appear to be most successful and to isolate the key organizational variables in the generation of successful consortium working.

All of the contributors to this collection exhibit a combination of educational and social idealism with political and economic realism. Though they articulate it in different ways, they share a deep-seated commitment to education as a public service which is owed to all pupils within the period of compulsory schooling and to all those able to benefit from continuing and higher education. They identify part of the professionalism of their engagement in this public service as requiring that they should give priority to that action and those policies demanded by a broad view of what is in the best interests of students of whatever age. Individual educational institutions are not ends in themselves but the means to the provision of the best, most comprehensive, public-education service that society can afford. The contributors to this volume share a conviction that such provision requires a broader vision on educational provision than that provided by the self-interested pursuit of whatever is beneficial to an individual institution. Not only this, but that vision can best be advanced by active collaboration between individuals and through inter-institutional structures between institutions which are in partnership in the educational service.

This kind of vision is tempered by a recognition of the realities of competition for reputation and resources in the educational market place. Some collaborations are, after all, designed merely to advantage one group of institutions in their competition with others; in education as in commerce a consortium may operate as a purely self-interested group established to resist for example, the downward pressure on pricing (perhaps also on quality) which the free reign of market forces would enforce; some consortia offer a forum for 'busy' but unproductive work which substitutes for the 'real' work needed in the institutional context.

The contributors to this volume show themselves to be well versed in these political realities, but not yet reduced by them to the pessimism and cynicism that underpins the market ideology. Like very many of their colleagues in the public-education service they continue to find meaning and motivation in notions of community, collegiality and collaboration, underpinned, perhaps, by the conviction articulated by the eighteenth-century Scottish philosopher, David Hume, that:

> So far from thinking, that men have no affection for anything beyond themselves, I am of opinion, that tho' it be rare to meet with one, who loves any single person better than himself; yet 'tis as rare to meet with one, in whom all the kind affections, taken together, do not overbalance all the selfish. (Hume, 1969, Bk III, p. 538)

## References

BRIDGES, D. (1994) 'Parents: Customers or partners?', in BRIDGES, D. and McLAUGHLIN, T. (Eds) *Education and the Market Place*, London, Falmer Press.

BRIDGES, D. and McLAUGHLIN, T. (Eds) (1994) *Education and the Market Place*, London, Falmer Press.

FLEW, A. (1991) 'Education services: Independent competition or maintained monopoly?', in GREEN, D.G. (Ed) *Empowering Parents*, London, Inner London Education Authority, Health and Welfare Unit.

HUME, D. (1969 first pub. 1739) *A Treatise on Human Nature*, Harmondsworth, Penguin.

KERR, C. (1973) *The Uses of the University*, Cambridge, Massachusetts, Harvard University Press.

MORRIS, G. (1994) 'Local education authorities and the market place', in BRIDGES, D. and McLAUGHLIN, T. (Eds), *Education and the Market Place*, London, Falmer Press.

TOOLEY, J. (1994) 'In defence of markets in education provision', in BRIDGES, D. and McLAUGHLIN, T. (Eds), *Education and the Market Place*, London, Falmer Press.

*Part 1*

*Mapping the Development of Collaborative Networks*

*Chapter 2*

# Schools, Markets and Collaboration: New Models for Educational Polity?

*Chris Husbands*

### Introduction

The hallmark of the Conservative Governments' social policy between 1988 and 1994 was the introduction into social provision of market-led concepts such as competition, purchaser–provider distinctions and the empowerment, in a variety of ways, of consumers. In education the transformation was rapid: professional and essentially bureaucratic modes of managing a largely stable system were replaced by marketized relationships within a competitive, unstable and increasingly fragmented system. The introduction of market-led reforms redefined both the institutional structure of the education system and the task of management within it. Schools were encouraged to think of themselves as competing businesses, providing services and purchasing support and supply systems as they required them. However, whilst the injection of market forces into the system imposed on schools elements of the discipline of competition, there were powerful countervailing pressures in the professional culture of schooling and in the logic of the market place which encouraged schools in a variety of ways to collaborate or to form formal and informal consortia. This chapter explores the logic of the market-led structure of schooling which was created by Conservative legislation between the 1988 Education Reform Act and the 1993 Education Act, and the ways within the structure in which schools were establishing collaborative relationships with other schools. It concludes by exploring some of the managerial and structural implications of the new structures.

### Educational Structures and Educational Change: The Dynamics of the Market

In the early 1990s, the public education service in England and Wales was experiencing a turbulence it had scarcely experienced before in a century and a quarter's history. The implementation of the 1986, 1992 and 1993, and, most significantly the 1988 Education Acts meant that within the space of a few years, the structure of the education service was reshaped, the working practices of school teachers significantly altered, and the assumptions, working practice and management of schools and colleges were transformed. The hallmarks of this turbulence are well known and have been explored widely (e.g., Chitty, 1993; McClure, 1991). In some respects, the turbulence was based on the progressive centralization of control over the educational service through the introduction of a national curriculum (DES, 1987), regular testing (TGAT, 1987), and a new model of school inspection based on a standard inspection instrument (OFSTED, 1993). At the same time, the legislation of 1988–1993 fragmented the educational service by the introduction of market-led competitive forces into the educational system: parents were to be conceptualized as consumers and schools as producers, competing to sell their wares in the market place. The central legislative instrument for the development of the educational market place was the 1988 Education Reform Act. Local Education Authorities (LEAs) were required by the Act to devolve the management of funding to their schools, and, whilst 'there is nothing intrinsically competitive about LMS, this government's gearing of the formula is in effect a voucher system designed to reinforce the accumulation of pupil numbers' (Ranson, 1992, p. 171). As a result first of the 1986 Education Act and more particularly of the 1988 Act, LEAs were no longer able to limit admissions numbers to schools, but obliged to allow successful schools to expand to the limits of their physical capacity. In consequence, at a time of stable or falling rolls, especially in secondary schools, schools would be required to compete for pupils/funding against each other. In urban areas, new types of school — City Technology Colleges — were to be established outside the control of LEAs and, at least in intention, on the basis of large-scale industrial and commercial sponsorship. The CTCs were intended to raise the quality of schooling in urban areas largely through the mechanism of competition. Finally, schools were given the option of balloting the parents of current pupils on opting out of LEA control to grant-maintained (GM) status. The creation of the GM option was self-consciously an attempt to stimulate local choice and progressively to differentiate between schools, further entrenching the concept of local markets. Policy initiatives in the early 1990s further advanced the concepts of an educational market place, the principles of which were enunciated in the 1992 White Paper Diversity and Choice (DFE, 1992): the process of opting-out was made simpler, and all school governing bodies were required to consider the possibility of opting-out at least annually. The process by which GM schools might change their character — for example by introducing academic selection as an admission requirement was made simpler. In 1993, the Technology Schools Initiative was constructed as a route by which schools could bid for funds to enhance technology provision and was seen as a further step towards the internal differentiation of schools. Crucially, from 1992 onwards under the Citizens Charter Initiative schools outcome performance indicators, public-examination results, staying-on rates and truancy indicators, were published in local and national league tables.

The emphasis on market-led choice and competition which characterized Conservative government policy after 1988, and perhaps particularly between 1990 and 1994 marked a sharp break with the policies of the post-war period. Constitutionally, the structure of the educational service in England and Wales throughout much of the twentieth century has been characterized as a national service, locally administered. The Education Act of 1902 established in local authorities a model of educational governance which remained essentially in place for most of the century. The changes in educational structure following the 1944 Act, the expanding educational provision of the 1960s and 1970s and particularly the development of comprehensive education all tended to reinforce and entrench the control of local education authorities over schooling in their areas. John Tomlinson has characterized the post-war period, and particularly the period from the end of the 1960s to the end of the 1980s, as one of corporatism in educational management (Tomlinson, 1994, pp. 5–7), in which local authorities sought to manage their services as an integrated, interdependent and managerial whole. However, as Stewart has argued, the traditions of professional administration which characterized the corporate LEAs of the 1960s and 1970s, 'were built for the conditions of the era of growth. As growth has turned to constraint, as society faces change, as consensus is replaced by challenge . . . those traditions are themselves questioned' (Stewart, 1986, p. 37).

The corporate model was challenged from a number of sources, but most potently, from the free-market Right. Throughout the 1960s and 1970s, a number of small free-market and right-wing pressure groups such as the Institute of Economic Affairs (IEA), and later Centre for Policy Studies (CPS) urged the Conservative party to abandon the corporatist consensus and adopt educational and other policies based on nineteenth-century free-market anti-statism. The democratic effectiveness and accountability of local government had been questioned by research carried out for the Redcliffe-Maud Commission (Redcliffe-Maud, Lord and Wood, 1974), but, increasingly in the later 1970s, 'the argument that carried most weight with some central politicians was that LEAs, and their accomplices in the education establishment had failed to deliver education, of appropriate quality' (Cordingley and Kogan, 1993, p. 20). Following the election of Margaret Thatcher's Conservative Government in 1979, the number of New Right pressure groups mushroomed and their influence on government markedly increased. One of the central planks of the New Right pamphlet campaign was the application to educational policy of essentially economic principles of the market place. Local education authorities were characterized as local education monopolies (Flew, 1987) supplying a product (education) to consumers (parents, rather than pupils). Government was urged to develop strategies to break local monopolies. Such policies were seen as being desirable both in themselves — as part of a wider assault on the power of the local and national state — and as a means of dismantling what Flew and others saw as the progressive education ideas which had been generated by comprehensive and other reforms of the 1960s (Flew, 1987, Lawlor, 1989).

### Shifting Structures: LEAs, Schools and the Market Place

The general tendency of policy, then, between 1988 and 1994 was towards the establishment, entrenchment and promotion of what Legrand and Bartlett have described as a 'quasi-market'. The characteristics of a quasi-market include the replacement of monopolistic with competitive, though non-profit-making providers of a service, based on an ear-marked budget (Legrand and Bartlett, 1993, pp. 2–3). The effectiveness of a quasi-market is seen by Legrand and Bartlett to depend largely on the degree of competition between the service providers, and the willingness of customers to exercise choice between providers, but the market remains a quasi-market since the consumers themselves do not spend currency directly in the market. In education, the quasi-market was developed through mechanisms by which control of schools was progressively, and in most cases decisively removed from local education authorities, in which schools increasingly competed with each other for pupils and in which there was considerable policy support for the development of a diversity of provision within the state education system. These changes were implemented 'in order to bring about an improvement in the quality of education by creating a system in which high quality provision is financially rewarded. The idea has been that such a system of rewards works best when decision-making is decentralised' (Bartlett, 1993, p. 125). A series of evaluation reports and commentaries have suggested that at the level of implementation many of the policy initiatives which embodied the market-led principles were flawed: grant-maintained schools and CTCs were largely seen as exceptionally weak vehicles for the development of alternative models of schooling or the widening of choice. Parents were generally found to be — with some exceptions — less enthusiastic about the attractions of choice between schools than with the quality of schooling in their nearest schools (see Whitty, Edwards and Gewirtz, 1993; Halpin, Fitz and Power, 1993). Indeed, Bartlett's own analysis of the quasi-market in an English LEA suggested that the implementation of the quasi-market was only partially achieved. However, if policy details were flawed, then the wider concept of an educational marketplace was influential in two important respects: the role of the LEA and the concept of the autonomous school.

The place of the LEA in the educational market place shifted markedly between 1988 and 1993 (Edwards, 1991). The 1988 Act redefined, but did not in many respects fundamentally question the central role of the LEA; Heller and Edwards listed seventeen separate statutory functions of the LEA in place following the 1988 Act (Heller, 1992, pp. 20–1), and the then Secretary of State insisted that 'there will be much innovative work to be done by LEAs'. In an influential paper in 1989, entitled *Losing an Empire: Finding a Role*, the Audit Commission (Audit Commission, 1989) identified continuing roles for the LEA in a more pluralist environment, as leader, partner in school and college development, planner of future facilities, provider of information, regulator of quality and banker channelling local funds. Ranson, indeed suggested that several of his study LEAs welcomed the new role envisaged for them in the 1988 Act, which allowed them to take a more strategic view of their role than had hitherto been the case. But the pluralist model of the LEA was quickly undermined both by further centrally driven changes and by the gathering pace of local developments. The privatization of school inspection transferred to private inspectorial teams formal responsibility for regulation of quality; the creation of the Funding Agency for Schools as a channel for funding for grant-maintained schools required LEAs to share responsibility for planning future school places in many LEAs. The 1993 Education Act (Clause 266) removed the requirement for local authorities to have an education committee leaving LEAs with what Tomlinson has described as residual functions (Tomlinson, 1994, p. 1); indeed, the combined effects of legislative change between 1988 and 1994 undermined the very concept of an educational service in place of a looser, more fluid educational market place.

A key characteristic, then, of the new market place is that 'schools . . . are all becoming increasingly autonomous. That is clearly true for those that opt for grant-maintained status, but it is not very different for schools that are fully involved in LMS . . . Consequently it is at the school level that most of the important decisions about priorities will be made . . .' (Bolton, 1993, p. 8). The effective privatization of decision-making in the context of an educational market place had a series of consequences. Locally, the relationships between schools and their LEAs were effectively marketized: since funding was formula-driven and schools held budgets which had hitherto been controlled centrally both LEA and GM schools were able to buy services as they wished either from LEA suppliers or from elsewhere. In the area of professional support and guidance as in the area of local purchasing, the effect on LEAs was in effect to transform them into business units concerned with the efficient and effective supply of services to autonomous institutions and in many cases to create internal markets within LEAs. More generally, such developments raised more fundamental questions about the governance of education: 'there is no reason in principle why a state education service need have within it bodies such as LEAs. Quite a substantial number of other countries run wholly respectable national educational services that get on quite well without them'. However, Bolton went on to argue that it is surely a triumph of hope over experience to expect that such self-interested, isolate, fragmented decisions made in thousands of separate institutions will add up to a sensible, effective and efficient national school system', so that in practice 'some kind of regional or local administration is needed for something as complex as a public education service. [But] whether or not those arrangements should contain some element of local democracy is open to debate' (Bolton, 1993, pp. 7–9). Other commentators drew a similar conclusion; for example, Tomlinson suggested that in spite of the rapid changes in educational management, there remained 'pragmatic and functional arguments' for the maintenance of a tier of government able to 'provide critical external advice and external support for the professional development of staff, the development of the curriculum and organisational development'. In addition, the 1992 White Paper Diversity and Choice, recognized that there were limitations to the notion of the autonomous school:

3.5   There are, however some functions that even autonomous schools cannot carry out for themselves. For example, someone has to calculate the levels of current and capital funding and pay relevant grants to schools. Schools use of public funds needs to be subject to scrutiny an audit. These tasks currently fall to the Department for Education. As the number of GM schools grows, it will become increasingly inefficient and inappropriate for these essentially executive tasks to be performed by the Secretary of State. (DFE, 1992)

Tomlinson's model and the 1992 White Paper model offer different sets of perceptions about the developmental needs of the educational service against an increasingly marketized system. Tomlinson's core responsibilities of an intermediate tier are largely concerned with the development of curriculum quality and the nature of the teaching force, whereas the White Paper appears to see such issues as unproblematic: the only residual issues which cannot be addressed by individual competing schools are those to do with the statutory requirement to provide adequate school places. Tomlinson concedes (p. 12) that 'it has been suggested that entrepreneurs will arise to provide this [professional development] function', but suggests that 'it cannot be sufficient that the school buy what they need in the market place . . . to rely on external agencies whose chief objective is to sell their wares is in principle unsatisfactory'. There are difficulties with both sets of propositions from the perspective of an emergent educational market. The free marketeer would argue that the provision of additional school places and the development of a variety of provision in schooling can indeed be left to the market: as new places are needed, additional schools would be developed to meet the need or popular schools would expand. In the same way, the provision of external advice could, from a free-market perspective be left to external, market-oriented agencies: schools would buy services as they needed them. Tomlinson's proposal that 'even very effective schools do not and cannot always know what they need to be able to make the next significant advance' can be countered from a free-market perspective by arguing that given the dynamics of the market, the consequences of competition with other institutions would of necessity force schools to recognize developmental needs. In the free-market model, the market provides a structural context for school-level decision-making; no other intermediate framework is needed. In practice the situation does not differ widely between the quasi-market defined by Tomlinson's case for an intermediate tier and the White Paper's residualization of LEA functions. In both, the relationships between schools are defined by the logic of the market place so that either by internal needs-identification or by the pressures of operating in a shifting external context schools buy in services and goods they require, whilst relationships between schools and their LEAs are increasingly marketized. What is at issue is not the nature of marketization — implicitly acknowledged by all commentators in the wake of the 1988–1994 legislation — but the extent to which there are irreducible, non-marketizable relationships between schools and authorities. There is considerable professional disagreement about this. Working with senior managers in three differing LEAs, Cordingley and Kogan found that there were only two LEA functions — the provision of sufficient school places and provision for pupils with special needs — which all three LEAs regarded as irreducible functions of the LEA. Across the range of other services and needs — from strategic planning to the specification of capital programmes to quality assurances and INSET — there were those in all three LEAs who argued that the dynamics of the market could replace the professional/bureaucratic model.

## Models of Collaboration: Purchasing, Professionalism and Partnership

The development of a variety of school consortia collaborating for a variety of purposes and in a variety of ways can be traced to a number of causes, including the collapse of corporatist models of educational governance and the marketization of relationships between schools and other statutory or community agencies. The latter is the economic accompaniment of the increasingly articulated professional and educational autonomy of the school. The extent of marketization and the nature of consortium relationships differ sharply precisely because LEAs have evolved different responses to the changed governance of education and because of the different nature, extent and pace of the movement to GM status in different parts of England and Wales. Moreover, if marketization and the consequent fragmentation of the educational service provide the broad context for the development of consortium approaches, the construction of consortium relationships has also been accompanied by an articulation of a commitment to contrasting educational management values. Consortium and collaboration in the educational market place is seen by some as reiterating a commitment to the concept of an educational service and to the professional or educational values, for example, of community or comprehensive education. At a time when public policy and institutional structures are seen to imply quite different structures and values, consortium relationships are seen as collaborative and hence an antidote to the market driven, competitive pressures imposed on schools by the dynamics of the market.

Reviewing the literature on school cooperation in the wake of the developing education market place, a variety of models, and equally a variety of impulses towards collaboration can be identified. The models can be characterized in a number of ways, based on the extent to which they assume long-term commitment from the school, the extent to which they involve a variety of staff at different levels of schooling and the extent to which they involve the pooling of a school's developmental resources. I characterize three broad models: purchasing models, professional interchange models, and partnership models, and the three can be regarded as sitting at different points along a continuum:

| Loose | | Collaborative |
| Association | - - - - - - - - - - - - - - - - - - - - - - - - - - - - - - - - - - | |
| Development | | |

| **Purchasing** | **Professional Interchange** | **Partnership** |

These are, however, heuristic models rather than exclusive categories: some schools may be involved in a variety of consortia arrangements for different purposes and for different lengths of time; some consortia may serve multiple purposes.

For many schools, the marketization of professional relationships and the assumptions of purchasing powers following the implementation of LMS and

GMS have involved significant internal management transitions. The notion of collaborating schools as *purchasing consortia* can be directly traced to the development of the market, and particularly the development of the school as a purchasing unit in a buyer-driven market for support services. Cordingley and Kogan analyse a variety of models for educational governance including what they describe as multi-purpose public purchaser models and single purpose public purchaser models (Cordingley and Kogan, 1993, pp. 36–7). At the level of school consortia, the distinction is helpful in a quite different context, in distinguishing between loose and tight models of purchasing consortia. Viewed in crudely economic terms, it is clear that consortium approaches to the purchase of educational supplies and equipment, or the purchase of educational services (e.g., consultancy, in-service support) produce economies of scale to purchasers and strengthen the negotiating position of the consortium. The distinction to be made is between single purpose purchasing either for specific items or over a period of time for generic types of items, and multi-purpose purchasing. Levacic and Woods demonstrate a range of advantages of cooperation, including not only economies of scale and shared management costs but also risk-pooling and the avoidance of wasteful competition. They have explored and documented a range of purchasing relationships between schools and have shown how increasingly 'school partnerships . . . co-operate over a range of services, but they distinguish between "long term stable and formal collaborative relationships between a group of schools which have usually enunciated a set of principles and aims which reflect the values placed on co-operation as a mode of interaction", and arrangements more like clubs which members join for specific but limited purposes' (Levacic and Woods, 1994, pp. 70, 72). In the latter case, relationships between the consortium members are looser, fewer individuals in each institution are likely to be involved and the impact on other relationships between the collaborating schools is likely to be weak. Moreover, purchasing relationships at the level described co-exist with competitive relationships across other activities. Caddy, for example (1989) cites the example of the bursar of Eggbuckland School in Plymouth who has a shared appointment with the school's feeder primary schools, and provides financial advice to their heads and governors.

A second model of consortium relationships, whilst being consequent on the marketization of relationships between schools and between schools and LEAs is more clearly concerned with the development of *professional interchange* between schools. As schools become increasingly autonomous and as relationships with other schools at institutional level become characterized by competition, some of the assumptions of professional exchange which characterized LEA-controlled structures begin to suffer strain; it has, for example, become less common for LEAs to provide INSET opportunities which bring together headteachers or heads of department or subject coordinators for extended collaborative development. As in-service funds have moved to school level, professional development has become increasingly school-centred and school-led. Consortium arrangements provide an opportunity if not to reconstruct the professional interchange of an earlier era then at least to exchange ideas and practice. Relatively loose associations at headteacher level are most common, bringing together groups of headteachers in an area or in

LEA groups. Such area groupings have in some instances become negotiating units between the LEA or other external and community agencies, such as Training and Enterprise Councils and schools, and in areas where there are significant numbers of GM schools, associations of GM headteachers have proved a vehicle for interchange on development. What appears to be less common are arrangements which permit such professional, collaborative interchange at lower-management levels: indeed, in many cases the devolution of in-service and development funds to schools and the promotion of school-led and school-centred INSET have, except in the case of specific projects (see Bridgwood, elsewhere in this collection), reduced the scope for teachers to work collaboratively with teachers in other schools. A distinction, then, can be drawn between collaborative relationships for policy or strategic purposes, involving senior managers, where the effective purpose is the exchange of market information and, on the other hand from a market perspective less desirable collaboration over service delivery and development. There are exceptions to this general position. Both before and after the development of the 1988–1994 legislation, some consortia existed for what can be described as service delivery: for the provision of sixth-form education in areas where individual schools had relatively small sixth forms, or for curriculum provision in small rural primary schools (Prestage, 1993). In the case of collaboration over shared sixth forms, there are paradoxes in which schools agree to collaborate in some areas of activity whilst competing in other areas — for example, over admissions from feeder primaries. Both in this case and in the case of collaborative development in small primary schools, what is effectively happening is that competing institutions see that their own wider position in the market place is served by an agreement to collaborate in one or two defined areas: in short, the agreement to collaborate makes competition more broadly possible. In economic terms, the collaboration makes the competition more perfect: for example, allowing all secondary schools in an area to offer sixth-form provision.

The third model for consortium development can be described as *partnership development*. The defining characteristic of partnership models of collaboration is that the institutional collaboration is across a range of institutional activities, for an extended time period and involving staff at a variety of institutional levels. In this model of consortium collaboration, relationships between individual schools across a number of areas of activity are extremely close. As has already been noted, Ranson suggests that LEAs welcomed the 1988 Act for the opportunity it gave them to concentrate on strategic management and service development rather than day-to-day administration. Under the first variant of the partnership model, a structure for collaboration is established between schools and the LEA. This model is far from a reassertion of the corporatist model of the LEA: as, for example Garrett, Logan and Maden (1994) and Hutchinson and Byard (1994) show, in partnership collaboration, the LEA fulfils an enabling role, providing services to a variety of schools both LEA and GM. The key to the partnership model — which distinguishes it from the purchasing models identified earlier — is that rather than identifying LEAs as providers and schools as purchasers, the nature of the provision is jointly developed — a process described in detail for Enfield by Hutchinson and Byard (1994). In Oxfordshire, the Oxfordshire Quality Schools Association 'is an association of schools . . . [whose] policy and development is to be in the hands of a board of management to include teachers, headteachers, education officers, inspectors, governors and members from the Education Committee. . . . [based on] joint-management of joint-provision' (Stephens and McConnell, 1994). All the examples so far adduced depend on a close relationship between a cluster of schools and an LEA, or, put more generally, a close relationship between a cluster of schools and an external agency. A priori, there is no reason why this should be with an LEA; indeed the LEA functions described in the case studies from Warwickshire, Oxfordshire and Enfield — or those in Ranson's case studies of Manchester or Kent (Ranson, 1992) — are authority functions. Elsewhere in this volume, Peter Upton describes a model of close partnership between a cluster of GM schools which suggests that in a more thoroughly marketized and balkanized educational service formal agreements between schools, possibly involving bought-in external agencies might form the basis for continued and thorough collaborative work.

Consortium or collaborative relationships can be established at a variety of organizational levels for a variety of purposes and for varying lengths of time. Relatively loose relationships are most likely to be those where the relationship between institutions is at a single management tier, for short periods of time or for a single purpose, whilst tight relationships will involve staff from a variety of management levels over the longer period of time across multiple areas of a schools activity. Collaborative relationships, viewed from the perspective of the educational quasi-market can in some instances derive from professional disenchantment with the values of the market place — collaboration is seen as better than competition — or they can implicitly involve the acceptance both of the existence of the market place and its values — the exchange of market information is seen as a condition of the creation of a more perfect market. However, relatively loose collaborative relationships would be more likely to follow from the former values and relatively tight relationships from the latter.

## New Models for Local Governance?

A key issue is the extent to which school collaboration and school consortia provides a model for 'new forms of local governance' (Tomlinson, 1994), and whether local collaborative consortia can assume those functional responsibilities which are regarded even within Cordingley and Kogan's study LEAs as irreducible functions. Here, the position is unclear. Consortia of schools are, almost by definition, unstable. They are driven by either instrumental perceptions of the benefits of cooperation over competition or in an environment of competition or by an institution's relationship with a single project. It follows from this that the values which underpin any consortium are implicit, deriving from the activity as much as they are explicitly explored. It is too early in the development of the nascent quasi-market to be clear about whether school consortia can persist with adequate stability to discharge functional responsibilities in relation to wider issues over and beyond purchasing responsibilities or service delivery and development. Barr, for example, has argued that the development of market-led reforms in education is most likely to increase educational inequality (Barr, 1993, p. 376), and it is largely for this reason that Bogdanor argues that the persistence of effective strategic LEAs is an essential element in the continued development of the market in education (Bogdanor, 1991). As the dynamic of competition becomes more firmly entrenched, it may be that schools judge that the instrumental benefits of collaboration are maximized through loose and flexible relationships which contribute to effective competition and the efficient workings of the quasi-market by providing for the exchange of market information. In this case school collaboration becomes an element in the development of the market rather than a countervailing force. On such a model, school collaboration has weak potential to assume the residual functions which Tomlinson identifies: schools will continue to need a framework agency or authority (Tomlinson, 1994).

Nonetheless, there are powerful impulses towards the maintenance of consortia and local collaborative networks. Schools will continue to become more autonomous. Some of the reasons for this derive directly from the continued development of devolved and market-driven financial management systems including LMS or GMS and the extension of compulsory competitive tendering. Other reasons relate more closely to the educational functions of the school. In particular, the process of school-development planning against the background of a less tightly prescribed national curriculum will provide an internal dynamic, at least in urban areas, towards a more sharply differentiated educational system with increased specialization and diversity amongst schools. The policies will exaggerate the extent to which the individual school is conceptualized in financial terms as a cost centre and purchaser of contracted-out services. In this context, as Stewart Ranson has already demonstrated, LEAs have become more sharply focused on strategic management, formal quality assurance and the provision of services (Ranson, 1992, pp. 164–6). Increasingly in LEAs, the relationship between the authority and schools is a commercialized one, in which schools — whether locally managed or grant-maintained — buy services from the authority. In this environment, as we have seen, there are clear managerial premiums to be gained by schools agreeing for purchasing purposes — whether of supplies such as exercise books and computer hardware, or managerial functions such as personnel or payroll management, or consultancy advice on school management and curriculum issues — to form associations or cartels. In an increasingly diverse educational structure, such consortia have the potential to develop into an important managerial link.

### References

AUDIT COMMISSION (1989) *Losing an Empire: Finding a Role — the Future of the LEA*, London, Audit Commission.

BARR, N. (1993) *The Economics of the Welfare State*, London, Weidenfeld and Nicholson.

BARTLETT, W. (1993) 'Quasi-markets and education reforms', in LEGRAND, J. and BARTLETT, W. (Eds) (1993) *Quasi-Markets and Social Policy*, London, Macmillan.

BOGDANOR, V. (1991) 'Where will the buck stop', *Times Educational Supplement*, 14, June.

BOLTON, E. (1993) 'Imaginary gardens with real toads', in CHITTY, C. and SIMON, B. (Eds) *Education Answers Back: Critical Responses to Government Policy*, London, Lawrence and Wishart.

CADDY, M. (1989) 'A combined effort', *Education*, 15 December.

CHITTY, C. (1993) *The Education System Transformed*, London, Lawrence and Wishart.

CORDINGLEY, P. and KOGAN, M. (1993) *In Support of Education: Governing the Reformed System*, London, Jessica Kingsley.

DES (1987) *The National Curriculum 5–16: A Consultation Paper*, London, HMSO.

DFE (1992) *Choice and Diversity: A New Framework for Schools*, White Paper July 1992, Cmnd. 2021, London, HMSO.

EDWARDS, P. (1991) *The Changing Role, Structure and Style of LEAs*, Slough, NFER.

FLEW, A. (1987) *Power to the Parents: Reversing Educational Decline*, London, Sherwood Press.

GARRETT, J., LOGAN, P. and MADEN, M. (1994) 'The enabling LEA: A Warwickshire case study', in TOMLINSON, J.R.G. and RANSON, S. (Eds) *School Co-operation: New Forms of Local Government*, pp. 168–79.

HALPIN, D., FITZ, J. and POWER, S. (1993) *Grant Maintained Schools: Education in the Market Place*, London, Kogan Page.

HELLER, H. (1992) *Policy and Power in Education: The Rise and Fall of the LEA*, London, Routledge.

HUTCHINSON, G. and BYARD, I. (1994) 'A new partnership in Enfield', in TOMLINSON, J.R.G. and RANSON, S. (Eds) *School Co-operation: New Forms of Local Governance*, pp. 121–40.

LAWLOR, S. (1989) *Away with the LEAs: ILEA Abolition as a Pilot*, London, Centre for Policy Studies.

LEGRAND, J. and BARTLETT, W. (Eds) (1993) *Quasi-markets and Social Policy*, London, Macmillan.

LEVACIC, R. and WOODS, P. (1994) 'New forms of financial co-operation', in TOMLINSON, J.R.G. and RANSON, S. (Eds) *School Co-operation: New Forms of Local Governance*, pp. 66–80.

McCLURE, S. (1991) *Education Reformed: The Education Reform Act and After*, London, Macmillan.

McCONNELL, E. and STEPHENS, J. (1994) 'Oxfordshire schools in partnership', in TOMLINSON, J.R.G. and RANSON, S. (Eds) *School Co-operation: New Forms of Local Governance*, Harlow, Longman, pp. 155–67.

OFSTED (1993) *Handbook for the Inspection of Schools*, London, HMSO.

PRESTAGE, M. (1993) 'Dorsets four-site saga', *Times Educational Supplement*, 7 May.

RANSON, S. (1992) *The Role of Local Government in Education: Assuring Quality and Accountability*, Harlow, Longman.

REDCLIFFE-MAUD, LORD and WOOD, B. (1974) *Local Government Reformed*, Oxford, Oxford University Press.

STEWART, J. (1986) *In Search of the Management of Education*, Luton, Local Government Management Board.

TGAT (1987) *National Curriculum: Task Group of Assessment and Testing — A Report*, London, HMSO.

TOMLINSON, J.R.G. (1994) 'The case for an intermediate tier', in TOMLINSON, J.R.G. and RANSON, S. (Eds) *School Co-operation: New Forms of Local Governance*, pp. 1–18.

WHITTY, G., EDWARDS, A. and GEWIRTZ, S. (1993) *Specialisation and Choice in Urban Education*, London, Routledge.

*Chapter 3*

# Collaboration: A Condition of Survival for Small Rural Schools?

*Linda Hargreaves*

### Clustering: At Best an Incomplete Alternative?

These words from the Audit Commission (1990, p. 25) illustrate the view that close collaboration between small primary schools was of limited survival value. This is a fairly unique view based on the commissioners' assessment that collaboration was generally 'insubstantial'. The three-school cluster cited as an example of an impoverished spread of expertise could be regarded as rich with its specialists in the arts, science, the humanities and special needs. It lacked specialists in mathematics and technology only, but mathematics was an area of high confidence amongst generalist primary teachers, whilst technology experts were scarce throughout the primary sector (Wragg *et al.*, 1989; Bennett *et al.*, 1992). It seems reasonable to assume that the Government's funding of large-scale in-service programmes for primary teachers in science, technology and mathematics was indicative of concern about profiles of staff expertise in large urban, as well as in small rural, primary schools.

In contrast to the views of the Audit Commission, cluster formation was being reported favourably elsewhere. Bell and Sigsworth (1987) and Keast (1987) reported positive collaborative developments during the 1980s. The Curriculum Council for Wales (1989) supported clustering for the exchange of staff, the joint purchase of equipment and sharing the burden of document preparation. Galton *et al.* (1991) found clustering to have generally beneficial effects in reducing teachers' professional isolation, extending children's peer groups, increasing the range and availability of resources and, with appropriate support strategies, improving the quality and range of curriculum provision. Hopkins and Ellis (1991) noted the importance of high-quality leadership and coordination, good channels of communication and the firm commitment from the staff involved, and called for further investment in cluster formation. Meanwhile, practitioner reports of managing collaborative groups (Deeks, 1991) represented first-hand testimony to their value. Deeks, however, saw the imposition of the National Curriculum, national assessment, appraisal, and local financial management as a threat to cooperation through erosion of schools' ownership of the educational process. He envisaged ways in which clusters could face these changes and concluded that the 'future for small schools will be much brighter if effective clustering does take place' (p. 30).

In this chapter, I shall try to show that close collaboration can be a complete alternative, but that this state can be achieved neither rapidly nor effortlessly, despite the impression given in the Government's invitation to small schools to 'go grant-maintained with other schools' and form a GM cluster (DFE, 1994). The chapter will draw on research funded by the Economic and Social Research Council between 1992 and 1994 into the Implementation of the National Curriculum in clusters of Small Schools (INCSS). The INCSS project set out to examine a framework of cluster development which emerged from the national evaluation of the Education Support Grant (ESG) provided between 1985 and 1991 to improve the quality or extend the range of the curriculum in rural schools (see Galton *et al.*, 1991: *The Rural SCENE Project*).

Before going further two definitions are needed: a 'small school' in the present context is one with fewer than 100 pupils on roll; 'cluster' is used to refer to any group of two or more small schools which have agreed to cooperate with each other whether this is primarily for children's social development, joint financial benefit, teachers' professional development, the sharing of resources, or a combination of these.

## Cluster Development

The Rural SCENE project team (Galton *et al.*, 1991) visited small schools in fourteen LEAs in 1989–90, and encountered many different types of cooperative cluster. These clusters varied in: size, from two to twenty schools; format, from exclusively small schools to those including large secondary schools; and age, from long-established to newly created. A very wide range of attitudes towards collaboration was also found since well-established groups were still relatively rare and many small schools resisted collaboration because clustering was seen as an open invitation to LEAs to amalgamate schools, particularly where closure programmes were a recent memory. Sometimes collaboration was unthinkable in view of long-standing inter-village feuds, and even where headteachers were keen to collaborate, governors remained highly sceptical about its effects on their inadequate budgets and its implications for impending local financial management.

The SCENE case studies showed that the benefits of clustering were neither instantly nor easily achieved, and the most effective clusters in curriculum enhancement had been formed generally before the ESG projects began. The case studies showed that different kinds of support for curriculum development were appropriate at different stages in the life of a cluster. Thus clusters which had been newly created at the beginning of the ESG projects did not benefit from the same curriculum support strategies which were effective in longer established clusters. From these observations, a framework of cluster development was constructed which attempted to link curriculum support strategies to specific phases of clustering (Galton, 1993; Galton *et al.*, 1991). Three general phases of cluster development and three main curriculum-support models were identified from amongst the case studies. As the evaluation proceeded, a framework relating curriculum support with cluster maturity emerged as shown in Figure 3.1.

| Main curriculum support strategy | New clusters (1–2 years)* | Established clusters (2–4 years)* | Mature clusters (after 4–5 years)* |
|---|---|---|---|
| Generalist support | Initiation $H_1$** | $H_2$ | |
| Specialist support Outsider Insider | $D_1$ A | Consolidation $J_1$ A L | A L |
| Self-development | N | $D_2$ $H_3$ N | Reorientation $J_2$ N |

*Figure 3.1: Curriculum support and cluster development framework*

Notes:
The letters refer to the main case-study pilot projects.
* These times are approximate and they refer to active clusters. The nominal existence of a cluster for five years does not necessarily imply maturity.
** Where a letter appears twice, that project had both cluster and support categories going on simultaneously. Letters with suffixes show progression during the projects.

The shaded cells in Figure 3.1 show an ideal path from the initiation of clustering to the point where a cluster is an independent entity which can determine its own development and direct its energies towards improving children's learning. The first phase of cluster development identified in the SCENE project was the initiation phase in which schools were just beginning to form clusters, or where they had been meeting for sports fixtures, or shared the costs of educational visits but did not communicate on curriculum matters. In this early stage, it was difficult for schools to identify any *common* curricular priorities or resource needs which could be set at a higher priority than each school's own individual priorities or needs. In many cases schools needed help in identifying their own curricular priorities because curriculum evaluation was not taking place within schools at that time. Attempts at resource sharing or joint-purchasing were premature and short-lived and the success of collaboration was determined by the teachers' perceptions of the personal costs versus benefits to them and their school. The second phase of cluster development was that of consolidation when, having identified and worked on individual priorities, the schools could identify common foci and share specialist advisory teachers who organized common themes such as 'water', 'light and colour', 'communications', or 'the Tudors'. With the help of advisory teachers, resource sharing was possible because topics could be coordinated. Thus the schools now had access not only to a wider range of resources but also enjoyed the professional support of other teachers working on related topics. Gradually, benefits were perceived to outweigh costs and energy devoted to cluster building could be turned to cluster function in terms of enhancing children's learning. The schools could now begin to share workloads and formulate joint policies.

Very few clusters had reached this point however and moved to the re-orientation phase, having integrated and internalized cluster concerns alongside their own school needs. Attempts by LEAs committed to principles of ownership, to initiate new clusters at this level of cluster development guaranteed neither effective collaboration nor any extension of the range or quality of the curriculum. In clusters which had evolved to this stage, however, there were regular cluster staff meetings, common cluster policies and curriculum documents, and moves towards joint cluster governors' groups and the construction of cluster development plans. Key features of the re-orientation phase were: the implicit cluster cohesion which allowed individual schools to opt in or out of cluster activities without posing a threat to the cluster identity; and the support and involvement of governors and parents, in cluster activities. The INCSS project set out to refine, or reject, this cluster development framework and to see whether clustering assisted schools introducing the National Curriculum at Key Stage 2.

## Cluster Levels and the Implementation of the National Curriculum

The INCSS project was based in three LEAs selected for their contrasting traditions and policies with respect to small schools. LEA1 had no specific policy on small schools although some self-help clusters of small schools had established themselves and one had been in existence since 1975. LEA2 had pioneered small schools' clustering in the 1970s only to withdraw support for the scheme in the mid 1980s. Some clusters had continued on a self-help basis, however. LEA3, which had taken part in the earlier ESG project, had a very positive policy on small schools which included the allocation of funds for cluster activities, active encouragement of governor involvement in cluster development and an inspector keen to promote clustering.

In Autumn 1992, a questionnaire about cooperation between small schools was sent to ninety primary schools with between sixty and ninety children on roll in these LEAs. Nine small schools representing various levels of cluster involvement were selected for year-long case studies following consultation with LEA inspectors and headteachers. Fifty-three schools responded to the questionnaire and of these 89 per cent belonged to a cooperative group. The questionnaire responses were used as the basis for the construction of a cumulative cluster score for each school which took into account its various cooperative links, the frequency of joint activities and the existence of shared documentation, for example. Certain features, such as headteachers' meetings and joint sports events were common to all the schools and so scored zero, whilst the existence of cluster development plans received a higher weighting because this discriminated between schools and implied close collaboration. 40 per cent of the schools had completed a cluster-development plan, 21 per cent were planning one and 34 per cent had none. There was considerable variation across the three LEAs however with 75 per cent of schools in LEA3 having a complete cluster development plan compared with only 18 per cent in LEA1.

The distribution of the cluster scores revealed four levels of cooperation, in contrast to the three phases of the SCENE model. This result was checked using a second approach in which school cooperation profiles were prepared which grouped

**Cluster levels**

|      | 1     | 2 | 3 | 4  |
|------|-------|---|---|----|
| LEA1 | x (x) | x |   |    |
| LEA2 | x     | x |   | x  |
| LEA3 |       |   | x | xx |

*Figure 3.2: Distribution of questionnaire returns and case-study schools by cluster levels and LEA*

*Note:*
One LEA1 case-study school (x) did not complete a questionnaire and was placed subsequently on the basis of interview responses.

inter-school links under three headings: 'coordination', 'people' and 'activities'. The profiles were sorted visually using a Q-sort technique and, again four groups emerged. Two of the groups, which we called cluster levels III and IV below, largely confirmed the characteristics of the consolidation and re-orientation phases identified in the SCENE project, but it appeared that the original initiation phase needed to be divided into two levels: a pre-clustered state and an initiation phase. The case studies provided examples of schools in clusters at each level and these will be described next. Figure 3.2 shows how they were distributed by LEA and cluster level.

The uneven distribution of the schools from each LEA across the framework revealed that LEA1's schools were grouped in levels I and II whilst LEA3's were in levels III and IV, with LEA2 represented at levels I, II and IV. Whilst the finding that the LEA3 schools were in the higher levels of clustering was not surprising in view of that LEA's support and guidance for small schools, the results also showed that neither the long-established self-help clusters in LEA1, nor the large (twelve to twenty schools) cross-phase cooperative groups had moved to the levels of inter-school involvement characteristic of cluster levels III or IV in which collaboration was more formalized through the existence of many joint policies.

*Cluster Level I: Pre-clustered Schools*

**Cluster level I**

| Governors | • | some involvement in own school activities |
| Heads | • | regular meetings with heads of other schools |
| Teachers | • | occasional joint INSET courses |
| Coordination | • | little or no joint plans or documents |
| Activities | • | fairly regular sports events |

All of the cluster level I schools were attached, if loosely, to at least one cooperative group of schools. The nature of the cooperation varied however. Two schools belonged to several different cooperative groups at that time, including one which was very long-standing, and did have some pooled finances and did run occasional workshops for teachers, governors and children. It was very much a headteachers' support group and whilst the school's teachers were not well informed of its activities, the parent governor was unaware of its existence. In another level I school, the teachers clearly valued their links with a local group set up to moderate assessments of children's work. The headteacher described it as 'mildly subversive'. What was clear in each case was the headteacher's confidence that they were well-equipped to deal with Key Stage 2, as one headteacher stated early in the project:

> There's a . . . small school self-help group locally . . . who have got themselves set up in response to the National Curriculum and said things like, 'We can't possibly manage to have all the resources necessary, either human or material, so we have to get together'. I didn't take that view. I thought then and I still think now that a small school with the right staff can do the job . . . so I haven't felt the need to get involved. (Headteacher)

In order to cover the range of specialist expertise needed, these schools variously drew on community expertise, used part-time teachers and job-share arrangements to expand the number of teachers (a strategy common to all the schools), and 'those teachers who feel it's worthwhile' could draw on the cooperative support groups. The personal costs: benefits basis of involvement was clear. The notion of mutual benefit in sharing expertise was outweighed by visions of the potential difficulties of supply cover, disruption of classes or governors' supposed views:

> . . . that possibility exists. But then I think my Governors rightly, would feel there ought to be some kind of *quid pro quo*. And if I was going over to work with one school, they ought to come to us. And if that's not possible, well then the whole system starts to look a little bit rocky. (Headteacher No. 21)

It is worth pointing out here that governor involvement in their own schools was higher in the lower-cluster levels particularly on educational visits. Two significant factors contributed no doubt to the self-sufficiency of these schools. They were well-resourced, having recently purchased new books, schemes or equipment, and, more significantly perhaps, they did not detect competition from other local schools. All of the schools had competitive, sports contacts with other schools and the heads were in regular contact with other heads, sometimes through impromptu 'on the touch-line' meetings, which one headteacher found more useful than formal meetings.

The level I schools, then, were associated with at least one cooperative group but showed negligible commitment to other small schools. Participation was an individual matter for the teachers concerned and governors were not necessarily aware of inter-school links.

*Cluster Level II: Initiation*

The main features of the cluster level II schools are summarized below.

**Cluster level II**

| | |
|---|---|
| Governors | • regular involvement in own school activities |
| | • occasional meetings with governors from other schools |
| Heads | • regular meetings with heads of other schools |
| Teachers | • occasional joint INSET meetings |
| | • occasional visits to other schools |
| | • have led an INSET session |
| | • occasional joint teachers' support meetings |
| Coordination | • cluster development plan in planning stage |
| | • shared policy in one or two curriculum areas |
| | • other shared policy statements in planning stage |
| Activities | • occasional joint children's workshops |

The cluster level II schools had more regular links with other small schools' groups. One headteacher listed five different group affiliations including two small schools' groups, one of twelve and one of three schools. Again decisions to participate in cluster activities were a matter of individual choice however, 'I'm sure it's very useful if you're a meetings person' (teacher 12). The social aspects of the groups were valued however whilst meetings with an agreed agenda or the suggestion of any more formal commitment were rejected:

> We don't get involved with other schools and their development plans; I know there's some schools that do. (Headteacher No. 12)

Thus although positive about the value of collaboration, it seemed likely that this school's multiple membership of school groups, some very large, militated against the development of active commitment to any of the groups. This limited the opportunities for any mutual trust to be built up between the schools and a year later when a second round of interviews were carried out there had been two setbacks. One was the breakdown of an earlier cluster agreement not to admit children earlier than they would enter their nearest school: 'If we all stick with that, then all's hunky dory. If not all hell breaks loose' (Headteacher No. 12). The second was the failure of the schools' moderation exercises: 'We've tried to set up some system of looking at pieces of work in order to gauge at what level these are at National Curriculum. It was hopeless, absolutely hopeless, nobody agreed. We met twice and nobody agreed' (Headteacher No. 12). Although both the chair of governors and the head foresaw a bleaker future after full LMS, the potential of closer links with other small schools was not seen as a useful option.

The other cluster level II school was part of a geographically elongated and scattered cluster of eight schools which had formed in 1989 to deal with the National Curriculum assessments. The cluster headteachers met three times a term and were beginning to share responsibility for digesting the ever-increasing load of official documents.

> We were all reading the same documents and quite often we come together (and say) . . . the seven of us, 'Does anyone understand what it is saying?' So we feel that perhaps seven people are wasting their time when perhaps one could read it, report back in terms of the relevant points or even do us a *précis* of the document. (Headteacher No. 23)

The cluster had just completed an audit of staff expertise with a view to identifying cluster-inset needs and had also had a year's 'A' allowance from the LEA for a teacher to work alongside other teachers on mathematics and to help develop school mathematics policies. This had resulted in some schools sharing mathematics schemes and policies. By the second round of the project, the cluster was making strenuous efforts to increase governor involvement more by holding joint meetings for governors at each school on a rota basis. By the end of the case study period, cooperation had replaced competition in this cluster and the schools were rapidly trying to formulate a shared admission policy to cope with an influx of children from the nearest town. '. . . we're passing children on to one another now. And the co-operative side of it is tremendous' (Headteacher No. 23).

### *Cluster Level III: Consolidation*

In the case-study schools, the major difference between levels I and II, and III and IV was the pervasiveness of commitment to *one* collaborative group. By level III, the schools had moved well beyond counting the costs of cluster involvement and were convinced of its benefits which included shared curriculum documents, increased confidence, stability, continuity and trust.

**Cluster level III**

| | |
|---|---|
| Governors | • regular involvement in own school activities |
| | • meetings with governors from other schools 2–5 times a year |
| | • involved in joint cluster activities |
| Heads | • regular meetings with heads of other schools |
| Teachers | • regular joint INSET meetings |
| | • visit other schools |
| | • lead INSET session |
| | • joint teachers' support meetings 2–5 times a year |
| | • work alongside teachers from other schools |
| Coordination | • cluster development plan in preparation |
| | • shared policy in 3 or 4 curriculum areas |
| | • other shared policy statements in preparation |
| | • shared financial arrangements |
| Activities | • fairly regular joint classroom-based activities |

Clusters in this LEA were expected to produce cluster development plans to show how the funding would be used, but there was wide variation amongst the clusters. As the inspector pointed out:

> Some of our clusters are very good at it and some aren't . . . Some of them actually have a cluster development plan which they specify or update at the beginning of each year and from that also identify individual institutional needs as well as the cluster's. Some of them have their own individual school development plans. They use that to help them to put together a cluster so that the school development plan supports the cluster development plan. Some of them, it might be on a framework, based on a framework which has been partly provided by the county. Some of them it might be two sheets of A4 . . . (Inspector)

The headteacher of the level III case-study school, for example, reported on the cluster plan and the adaptation of cluster policies to individual school situations:

> Well, we more or less fulfilled all the objectives that we had on that original cluster plan last year . . . But, yes the cluster is going from strength to strength. We did an Art policy, a Music policy . . . and then brought them back into our own schools and (adapted) them as a staff to fit our own schools. Some we altered, had to alter quite a bit, like the PE, because we haven't got a hall. Others were straightforward, and we virtually accepted them as they were. (Headteacher No. 33)

The curriculum coordinators were working together on joint plans and governor support for the cluster was evident: 'It's going to become a lifeline for us really, to be in the cluster.' A year later, another governor explained that the schools had coordinated the timing of their planned history topics so that they could share the costs by buying resources for one topic each. There was the flexibility to opt-out of a scheme, as for example a plan to buy sets of books for reading round the class:

> Now that's absolutely against my views. Now they do read around in groups, with activities that we do, things like prediction, you know . . . But I feel I get a lot more out of (that) than I would with class readers. The idea of it is just not me at all. So that, I didn't want to dip in to. But there are other schools who would be happy to. And so they can share. (Headteacher No. 33)

Once the cluster was established, this concern about the effects of cluster decisions on children's learning rather than on cluster conformity was more typical of cluster level IV. Gradually, greater cluster cohesion can permit diversity without fear of destabilization because the benefits of clustering are implicit in the minds of members, 'I feel quite certain, that if the money dried up, we'd still keep going. I'm sure we would, because we get such a lot out of it.' However, there remained just a slight reservation about total commitment evident in answer to a question about parental involvement in the cluster:

> ... there's nothing official. We haven't so far encouraged that. We're so close, geographically, that there is still an element of competition between us. It's really quite hard. We work well together as staff and improving what we offer to the children. But there is an element of, would the parents want to take the child down the road, if they went into school and saw it was better? I think that's the Government, who have done that to us ... if we're all honest, we all hold back just one little ace that makes our school different from the one down the road. I think we all do that. But it becomes less apparent as time goes on, because we're more interested in making sure that we all stay alive. (Headteacher No. 33)

By cluster level IV however, schools were confident enough about cluster benefits to involve fully parents and governors.

### *Cluster Level IV: Re-orientation*

Three of the case-study schools were in clusters in this category. The cluster sizes were of three, five and six schools. Their origins varied and the smallest was the result of a split in a larger cluster. All three had shared curriculum documents and cluster-development plans. Two clusters had moved to the point where cluster and school-development planning were an integrated process, with cluster planning giving a lead to school planning in some areas. This shift from a first cluster plan built up from the common ground in the individual school's plans to its successor in which cluster needs and schools' needs were at least partially fused demonstrates very clearly how the cluster now had an equally valuable but distinct identity, to those of the individual schools.

> You have an identity as a (cluster) school but we've still got an identity as (this) school so if I want to do something that's totally out of keeping with the others I will do it — for example at this moment we're piloting the healthy schools award. None of the others is doing it. (Headteacher No. 24)

**Cluster level IV**

| | |
|---|---|
| Governors | • regular involvement in own school activities |
| | • regular involvement in joint cluster activities |
| | • meetings with governors from other schools 6–12 times a year |
| Heads | • regular meetings with heads of other schools |
| Teachers | • joint INSET meetings 6–12 times a year |
| | • regular visits to other schools |
| | • lead INSET session |

|                | • work alongside teachers from other schools |
|                | • joint teachers' support meetings 6–12 times a year |
|                | • inter-school exchange of specialist curriculum areas |
| Coordination   | • cluster-development plan in use |
|                | • shared policy on most curriculum areas |
|                | • shared policy statements in use |
|                | • shared financial arrangements |
| Activities     | • very regular joint classroom-based activities |

At this level there were regular links between all groups including children, governors and parents, and these links were related by this stage to curricular issues such that parents were involved in mathematics or technology workshops, or were invited to sample the activities which would be part of the forthcoming cluster theme. Each of the three clusters collaborated closely on shared curriculum plans, but these were translated into action in different ways in the schools.

In the smallest cluster, there was close collaboration on curriculum planning, and frequent joint yeargroup activities. The schools were building up a cluster resource bank, but each school used its own topic programme because there were insufficient resources for the schools to do the same topics simultaneously. The second cluster had produced collaboratively a series of 'skeletal' cross-curricular cluster themes which identified relevant key questions, learning objectives and resources and could be adapted within each school according to whether the school used a topic-based or a subject-based approach. Resource sharing, joint activities and some teacher exchange took place but was organized between pairs of schools. The third cluster, however, preferred to work on the same curriculum topics at the same time, thus precluding resource sharing, but enabling the staff to enjoy mutual practical and moral support. During the case-study year, this cluster developed the

> . . . role of the *cluster curriculum coordinator*. We now have a maths, English and science curriculum coordinator, all of them have been paid for a year. It would pay them now the next step up on the pay spine so that's about £1,000 for the year and during the year they have several tasks that they have to accomplish and they have a job description and they're responsible to all six of the headteachers. (Headteacher No. 22)

One important feature of this scheme is the promotion opportunity and extended responsibility it offers teachers within small schools.

All the level IV clusters were committed to the view that the development of cluster expertise was achieved best through shared planning and cluster inset rather than by teacher exchange.

> We're still continuing with our theme planning, where subject coordinators — that have been identified within each school — help to plan the themes. And that is one way that I think subject coordinators can help to deliver a subject without having actually to teach it. (Headteacher No. 31)

Finally, at this cluster level, collaboration was now a force against competition in each of the clusters. The existence of common curricular and cluster-development plans was used to encourage parents to send their children to the local school.

We have a positive policy that we don't market against each other. We ring round if we've had someone from one of the other villages. What we try and emphasize is that we all work together and prospective parents soon find out that we know each other so well. You can't say, 'you can't go there' but we do positively discourage parents. We try and talk about the fact that they're in their own village, in their own environment and peer groups, so we don't market against each other at all . . . We know each other so well, if it did upset one of us we would say. (Headteacher No. 34)

Each cluster had a joint governors' committee or steering group which met at least termly. In each case, far from cluster issues being a matter of costs versus benefits, headteachers, teachers and governors spoke of the added value of clustering:

Staff in the cluster are now working as a cluster — now know the staff of the other schools almost as well as the staff in their own school. It's not now just a reduction of isolation but it's added to our personal lives, our self-esteem and motivation. (Headteacher No. 22)

The schools do a lot together — well it makes almost a small school like a large school with the cluster being able to do things like, have classes of thirty and two teachers, a man and a woman — one small school can't do this but it can through the cluster . . . (Governor No. 33)

One important aspect of this cluster level was that the cluster was able to focus on children's learning opportunities. This was evident in the level IV case-study schools in a number of ways. References to the review and evaluation of school and cluster activities and policies, with the dates of review and evaluation meetings were set in their year's programmes. In one cluster, practical ways to evaluate curricular activities were set out in the cluster policy documents. Despite the closeness of the clusters members, there were individual points on which they agreed to differ: essentially each school respected the others' individuality. A sense of team spirit existed within the schools and across the cluster. Headteachers' were concerned about the complexity of curriculum implementation and the process of teaching. Contrary to our initial hypothesis, we found that headteachers and teachers in the lower-cluster levels were more likely to express complete personal confidence of their individual ability to cope with the National Curriculum. What we seemed to be seeing in the level IV clusters was that cycles of curriculum planning, implementation and review were further on leading to a more critical awareness of the implications of teaching the National Curriculum.

The cluster development phases outlined above show a series of steps from confident independence, through a period of convergence and eventually to common-plus-individual identities. Fullan (1993, p. 34) vividly captures the extreme points of each position however, starting with professional isolation, 'which limits access to new ideas . . . , drives stress inward to fester and accumulate, . . . it allows . . . conservatism and resistance to innovation in teaching'. Collaboration, on the other hand, could lead to . . . 'Groupthink — uncritical conformity to the group, unthinking acceptance of the latest solution and suppression of individual dissent'. He concludes, however, that whilst complex change needs the insights of many people working together on the solution, equal attention should be given to individual and collective contributions.

The parallels with cluster development are easy to see both between teachers and the staff team within each school and then at cluster level, between each school and the cluster as a whole. It may be that a period of relative 'groupthink' is a prerequisite for a cluster state which can cope with individuality.

### Factors which Affect Collaboration

The combined findings of the research described above have suggested several factors which contribute to successful and effective collaboration. Two main points evident from both the SCENE and the INCSS projects are that certain factors are likely to be more effective at different times in the life of a cluster and that no one factor is sufficient alone. Further, different combinations will be appropriate for different clusters according to local conditions and attitudes. Some general points can be made.

- A cluster size of three to six small schools was optimal. Membership of very large clusters, cross-phase clusters, and/or several cooperative groups made communication more difficult and appeared to militate against active commitment to any one group.
- Cluster geography was important although geographical proximity alone was insufficient to engender successful collaboration, especially where it cut across existing links. Obstacles such as a major road bisecting a cluster represented a physical and a psychological barrier.
- Teacher exchanges or joint children's activities took place most satisfactorily between pairs of schools, often including the smallest, within five or six school clusters, see also Coopers and Lybrand, 1993. Paradoxically, the most commonly asserted benefits of collaboration, namely to enlarge peer groups, to facilitate teacher exchange and for the joint purchase of resources were most difficult to sustain when attempted prematurely across whole clusters.
- The greatest whole cluster benefits were for teachers to share the workloads of planning, preparing and collectively reviewing shared documents.
- LEA encouragement helped through modest funding combined with practical

support including: an inspector with an interest in small schools; regular meetings for cluster coordinators; constructive, but not prescriptive, advice on cluster development planning; a group of headteachers to work on ways to help introduce governors to clustering; and the availability of the inspector when invited to meet and talk to governors about clustering.

- Once established, a cluster-funded appointment such as cluster coordinator given cluster-funded time to deal with administrative issues was useful. This role also extended the opportunities for headteachers to extend their management expertise within small schools.
- The appointment of cluster curriculum coordinators, in an advanced cluster also provided further professional experience and promotion prospects for teachers in a cluster which would not be available in a single small school (see Atkins and Rivers, 1994).
- Full cluster cohesion demanded the involvement and support of governors but any expectation that a joint cluster governing committee can be formed any more instantly than inter-school collaboration can be forged is unrealistic, despite the optimism apparent in the DFE's leaflet on grant-maintained clusters (DFE, 1994).
- Finally, one LEA inspector suggested that cluster development usually 'boiled down to the work of one strong headteacher'. Application of this theory to cohesive clusters in both the SCENE and the INCSS studies suggested that although one 'strong headteacher' might be an essential ingredient, he or she was not enough. Indeed the headteachers of the schools in level I were 'strong'. Several like-minded headteachers, the cooperation of staff, and governor support and involvement are all important factors in effective and cohesive clustering.

### Collaboration: A Condition of Survival?

Our investigations indicated clearly that collaboration contributed much more than survival to the lives and work of teachers and children in established clusters. Members of these clusters were unable to suggest any limitations or disadvantages of clustering when asked but spoke of its advantages for all concerned. The achievement of this state was a long process, however.

We did find small schools which were confident of their ability to survive the demands of the National Curriculum without special commitment to a cluster although the headteachers' own expertise was crucial here. None of these schools was facing competition from neighbouring schools or lack of resources however. Webb (1994) depicts similar, evidently unclustered, small schools where 'the burden of producing policy and planning documents fell almost entirely on the . . . teaching heads' (p. 57). In contrast, our studies of small schools which were committed cluster members show them to be more advanced in whole school and whole cluster curriculum planning and review than the 'independent' small schools in our sample, and than many large primary schools (see Burgess *et al.*, 1994). Our findings show that collaboration among small schools can go well beyond being a mere condition for survival to offer models of teamwork and advanced curriculum development in the primary phase. Collaboration in these schools had become a strong force to combat competition.

### Acknowledgment

I wish to acknowledge the contribution of Chris Comber to this chapter as Research Associate to the INCSS project.

### References

ATKINS, V. and RIVERS, M. (1994) 'Clustering — what's in it for us?' *Management in Education*, 8, 1, pp. 16–21.

AUDIT COMMISSION (1991) *Rationalising Primary School Provision*, London, HMSO.

BELL, A. and SIGSWORTH, A. (1987) *The Small Rural Primary School: A Matter of Quality*, Lewes, Falmer Press.

BENNETT, N., WRAGG, E.C., CARRÉ, C.G. and CARTER, D.S.G. (1992) 'A longitudinal study of primary teachers perceived competence in, and concerns about National Curriculum implementation', *Research Papers in Education*, 7, 1, pp. 53–78.

BURGESS, H., SOUTHWORTH, G. and WEBB, R. (1994) 'Whole school planning in the primary school', in POLLARD, A. (Ed) *Look Before You Leap? Research Evidence for the Curriculum at Key Stage Two*, London, The Tufnell Press.

COOPERS and LYBRAND (1993) *Good Management in Small Schools*, London, Department for Education.

CURRICULUM COUNCIL FOR WALES (1989) *A Framework for the Whole Curriculum 5–16 in Wales*, Cardiff, Curriculum Council for Wales.

DEEKS, G. (1991) 'Managing change in a small school consortium', *Education Review*, 5, 1, pp. 24–30.

DEPARTMENT FOR EDUCATION (1994) *Going Grant-maintained with Other Schools: GM Clusters*, London, Department for Education.

FULLAN, M. (1993) *Change Forces: Probing the Depths of Educational Reform*, London, Falmer Press.

GALTON, M. (1993) *Managing Education in Small Primary Schools*, London, ASPE/Trentham Books.

GALTON, M., FOGELMAN, K., HARGREAVES, L. and CAVENDISH, S. (1991) *The Rural Schools' Curriculum Enhancement National Evaluation (SCENE) Project: Final Report*, London, DES.

HOPKINS, D. and ELLIS, P.D. (1991) 'The effective small primary school: Some significant factors', *School Organisation*, 11, 1, pp. 115–21.

KEAST, D. (Ed) (1987) *Small Schools (Primary) Perspectives 30*, Exeter, School of Education, University of Exeter.

WEBB, R. (1994) *After the Deluge: Changing Roles and Responsibilities in the Primary School*, Final report of research commissioned by the Association of Teachers and Lecturers, London, ATL publications.

WRAGG, E.C., BENNETT, N. and CARRÉ, C.G. (1989) 'Primary teachers and the National Curriculum', *Research Papers in Education*, 4, pp. 17–37.

# Chapter 4

# Collaboration, Competition and Cross-phase Liaison: The North Lowestoft Schools Network

*Mike Harbour*

### The Context

Lowestoft (population 56,500) is the major town in the North of Suffolk. It is divided by Lake Lothing and Oulton Broad into two parts. The north of the town, with its outlying villages, is served by two comprehensive 13–18 high schools, three 9–13 middle schools, ten primary schools and a special school. The buildings range from purpose-built and modern to Victorian and are located in both rural and urban communities. With some schools oversubscribed and others less popular in the educational market place, there is the potential for intense competition.

In March 1980 a working group of headteachers, officers and advisers was established in Suffolk, 'to review existing liaison practice, to consider transfer reports and to make recommendations on good liaison practices'.

The report observed:

> The working group were, however, concerned at the frequent absence of liaison to ensure reasonable curriculum continuity. Comparatively few Heads offered any evidence that such liaison was being given any real priority. The apparent lack of recording of liaison staff meetings was also noted by members, and there appeared to be some dissatisfaction with existing approaches to transfer documentation. (Suffolk Education Department, 1981)

The report made a range of recommendations to do with curriculum liaison, transfer of documentation between schools and the need to establish regular contacts between phases. They amount to a summary of good practice, and several of them, under the then County Education Officer Duncan Graham, became LEA (Local Education Authority) policy.

In the event implementation was patchy. By 1987 in North Lowestoft the situation could be summarized as follows:

- Early efforts had been made to develop liaison. The momentum had been lost partly because of the industrial action of the mid 1980s.
- Headteachers of pyramid middle and high schools met termly as did deputy heads and department heads/curriculum coordinators. There were no formal meetings of primary heads.
- Liaison meetings were perceived as being 'top–down'.
- The culture of the 'autonomous professional' persisted in some schools.
- Middle schools were preoccupied with establishing an identity which was different from the primaries and highs.
- There was professional distrust between phases. Could middle schools be relied on to deliver a rigorous curriculum? Were high schools concerned for the whole child?
- There was little liaison between schools in the same phase, although TVEI (Technical and Vocational Education Initiative) funding had enabled the high schools in the town and the college of further education to develop joint programmes for 14–16 year olds.
- Liaison tended to be confined to the transmission of a range of non-standardized information at points of pupil transfer. Whilst there were examples of subject teams working across phases to achieve continuity, these were the exception rather than the rule.
- Attempts had been made to use INSET days for liaison within pyramids but, as elsewhere, they had proved difficult to use effectively.

### Factors in Establishing the Collaborative Climate

The provision of schools in North Lowestoft was reviewed in 1986–7. As a result, children transferred to middle schools at 9 plus as opposed to 10 plus, from September 1988. Simultaneously, two junior schools were closed and 5–9 first schools were created, one of which was new. The consequent redeployment was managed by joint interview panels of LEA officers, headteachers and governors and was an early example of effective collaboration. As teachers moved to posts in different schools so they carried their sympathies and good practice with them. The LEA sought opportunities, throughout this period, to appoint governors to more than one local school. These factors were all helpful in establishing a cooperative climate.

Open enrolment had blurred catchment areas to the extent that the two high-school pyramids were no longer distinct. This, together with the introduction of the National Curriculum with Key Stages which did not match the ages of transfer, added impetus to the liaison process. Teachers and LEA advisers were acutely aware of the potential for criticism of the three-tier system on the grounds of curriculum discontinuity.

The teachers of the small village primary schools at Somerleyton, Corton and Blundeston (affectionately known as SCaB!) quickly realized that they each lacked the range of expertise necessary to deliver the National Curriculum. They established a structure of regular meetings and professional interchange which was to serve them well throughout this stormy period and their experience was to predispose them to further collaboration in the wider North Lowestoft network.

In the high schools the collaborative work 14–16, aided by TVEI, had led the heads to create the Lowestoft Sixth Form Consortium. Virtually all post-16 courses in the Lowestoft high schools were jointly funded, staffed and delivered with the support of the college of further education. Whilst this is another story, it demonstrates the level of cooperation within the educational community of the town. This experience cemented relationships between the high schools. It was difficult to compete for children at intake whilst developing close links for post-16 education. Although funding was an issue, and under LMS (Local Management of Schools) money follows students, the heads fought shy of marketing their schools competitively. Instead they concentrated on promoting their joint sixth form and identified the increase in post-16 participation rates as a target. (Historically low numbers of students remained in the Lowestoft Sixth Forms, 21–9 per cent of Year 11 throughout the late 1980s.) Key governors and LEA officials were keen to support this development which was the precursor of consortium developments elsewhere in the county.

Across the three phases there was a growing concern about educational aspirations and achievement in the town. It was recognized that educational standards needed to be raised and that this was best attempted jointly. Within the space of a year three of the five headships of the middle and high schools became vacant. The LEA used its influence on interview panels to appoint headteachers who were supportive of collaboration.

Following the review of provision in North Lowestoft in 1986–7, consideration was given to the need for an additional middle school. From the outset, the LEA adopted a consultative approach to this venture and the early discussions between officers, headteachers and governors in 1990 helped to build the trust which was to be so important as the network developed.

### The Middle- and High-school Initiative: One Step Forward and Two Steps Back?

A key series of meetings was held early in 1990 between the middle and high-school headteachers with the aim of developing effective liaison across the 'double-headed' pyramid. The discussions were informed by some of the developments cited above and by the NAHT (National Association of Headteachers) *National Curriculum Helpline Guidance* Note 8: Liaison Between Phases, in particular by Section 3, Managing Liaison:

3.1 Schools which are identifiably part of a common transfer 'cluster' will need to establish a management structure for liaison. This should have a policy group normally made up of the Headteacher of each school or a designated representative . . .

3.5 It is important to agree from the outset the aims and purpose of liaison. An agreement of aims is needed in order to:

— justify the time and commitment;
— inform the efforts of those involved;
— provide the basis for review and evaluation.
(NAHT, 1990)

The result of these discussions was the following draft policy document.

---

### North Lowestoft Pyramid Liaison: Draft Policy Document

*Introduction*

Traditionally pyramid liaison has concentrated upon an exchange of information between colleagues. Recent developments, both nationally and locally, demand a wider involvement in, and understanding of, the liaison process, since education is, in essence, a partnership between pupils, teachers, parents, governors, the LEA and the wider community.

It is accepted and acknowledged that there is already much good practice to draw upon throughout the pyramid, which will form a basis for further development.

We now need to review and extend the liaison process to enable us to meet the challenges created by the introduction of recent educational initiatives. Whilst accepting responsibility for designing this draft policy document we recognize that liaison within the pyramid will only be successful if colleagues have ownership of, and responsibility for, the total process (5–19).

Liaison is a joint venture involving all colleagues throughout the pyramid and is *not* the prerogative of any one group.

*Aims of Liaison*

1  To establish staff ownership of the liaison process and to share responsibility for its continued development.
2  To ensure continuity and progression of learning for pupils 5–19.
3  To support pupils throughout the process by facilitating transfer between phases.
4  To encourage and support staff at each stage to develop an appreciation of the total learning experience within the pyramid.
5  To involve governors, parents and the wider community in understanding and supporting pupils' learning as a continuous process (5–19).
6  To increase public confidence in the educational process (5–19).
7  To utilize the total resources available to the pyramid to facilitate liaison.

*Objectives (Numbers refer to Aims)*

1  To devise an appropriate structure to enable Aim 1 to be achieved.
2  • To review existing practice within the pyramid;

- To establish and sustain appropriate curriculum liaison throughout the pyramid for National Curriculum subjects, cross-curricular issues and religious education;
- To identify key curricular elements for development:
  a   to prioritize these developments, set targets and appropriate tasks;
  b   to establish criteria for success;
  c   to monitor progress and evaluate results.

3   • To establish appropriate support mechanisms to facilitate continuity;
- To create common formats for documentation;
- To exchange and share documentation e.g., policy statements, schemes of work;
- To introduce cross-phase curricular projects.

4   To establish a staff-development programme which may consider such strategies as:
  a   Staff exchanges within and across phases;
  b   Using experience within the pyramid to address specific issues e.g., pupil assessment by classroom observation;
  c   Sharing good practice;
  d   Joint meetings of pyramid staff.

5   • To encourage business–education and community links with the view to involving these agencies in the delivery of the curriculum;
- To encourage greater parental participation in the transfer process;
- To raise awareness among governors and parents of the continuity of the educational process (5–19).

6   • To establish appropriate forums for publicizing educational issues within the pyramid;
- To emphasize good liaison and continuity through improved public relations and marketing;

7   • To create one North Lowestoft INSET (In-Service Education and Training) fund for pyramid liaison;
- To consider financial-support mechanisms for the pyramid e.g., redistribution of INSET funds; seeking sponsorship from industry;
- To consider flexible deployment of human and material resources across the pyramid.

Throughout the process it was recognized that primary schools would need to contribute to the final policy. It was felt that, by producing a draft, the middle and high school heads would save their primary colleagues time and effort. This was an astonishingly patronizing view which, from the primary perspective, appeared to confirm the 'top–down' approach to liaison.

Primary schools were presented with this proposal at a time of considerable external pressure. The National Curriculum, teacher appraisal and LMS were making huge demands on colleagues who had little time or administrative support. They were not about to accept another external demand from the middle and high schools. In any event, there was good practical liaison taking place to *deliver* the curriculum in, for example, the Somerleyton, Corton and Blundeston (SCaB) group. So how dare these middle and high school grand-children teach their primary school grand-mothers to suck eggs!

When the policy was tabled at a joint heads' meeting in the summer term of 1990 it was therefore received with suspicion and not a little anger by primary heads! The pyramid had seemingly taken one step forward and two steps back.

Tuckman suggests that teams go through clear stages as they become more effective. They are: **Forming** (roles uncertain, anxiety, ambiguity), **Storming** (value of task questioned, principles and methods debated, conflict, opinions polarized), **Norming** (planning starts, roles clear, communication of feelings, mutual support, sense of team identity) and **Performing** (solutions emerge, decisions are translated into action, high levels of trust and interdependence, roles are flexible) (Tuckman, 1985).

Hitherto the occasional meetings of the heads of the whole double pyramid had operated at the forming level of group development and were suddenly at the storming stage. Perhaps the presentation of the policy had served to progress the development of the group.

It was to take a year before the policy document was fully accepted, during which an audit of liaison practice was carried out by a deputies' group; real efforts were made to understand each other's concerns and views; consensus was reached over a range of issues. It was recognized that, in order to achieve effective liaison, the schools needed:

- a management structure with clearly defined line responsibilities;
- a means of ensuring curriculum continuity and progression;
- a coordinated approach to cross-phase curriculum projects;
- the coordination of assessment, recording and reporting procedures;
- a common format for transfer documents;
- a higher profile for educational achievement in North Lowestoft;
- a means of identifying, financing and delivering in-service training for the joint pyramid;
- a method of monitoring and reviewing progress.

### The Development of Management and Support Structures

The deputies' review group had focused attention on the objectives of liaison as well as on organizational matters. They recommended that a joint in-service committee be formed to implement cross-phase training; that an assessment group be established to develop a pyramid-assessment policy; that primary-school representatives be invited to the middle/high school deputies' meeting; that a common primary–middle transfer document be developed. Discussions between headteachers led to regular meetings and by March 1992 a marketing group was established in order to raise the profile of education in the area.

The heads recognized that time and money were necessary to achieve liaison objectives and that primary schools were least advantaged and high schools most advantaged in terms of resources. Several support mechanisms were therefore put in place:

- the high schools provided secretarial support for pyramid heads' meetings;
- initially, supply cover was paid by the high and middle schools to allow the heads of the small primary schools to attend meetings;
- a pyramid GEST (Grant for Educational Support Training) fund was later created by viring 10 per cent of the INSET budget from high and middle schools and 5 per cent from primary schools into a central fund which was to be distributed to the advantage of primary schools and managed by a high school bursar;
- transport costs for intake familiarization days were paid by the schools receiving pupils;
- the marketing budget was managed by a high school and was created by a formula which generated 26 per cent of income from the primary sector, 34 per cent from middle schools and 40 per cent from the highs.

These comparatively modest efforts at the redistribution of resources were nevertheless effective in enabling the liaison process to develop as well as being practical tokens of goodwill.

By the end of the academic year 1991–2, headteachers were working in a new climate of frankness and honesty. They had entered the norming phase of their relationship. Significantly, the double pyramid had been renamed the North Lowestoft Schools Network.

A particular issue, a confusion over in-service arrangements, focused the heads on the roles of the various liaison groups and whether the implementation of pyramid policy was happening at an appropriate level. A working group of heads and deputies from all three phases, supported by an LEA Adviser, met from September to December 1992 to examine the management and organization of the network. It recommended the following structure which was adopted:

### Network Management Structure

Network Management Group will be responsible to the heads' group for the implementation of the long-term Network Development Plan.

It will have an overview of:

- curriculum key stages 1–4;
- assessment, record-keeping and reporting;
- Network INSET;
- the use of network financial resources;
- the work of task groups.

It will be responsible for:

- effective communication within the network;
- operational decisions;
- setting up task groups with clear criteria;
- evaluation of the effectiveness of delegated functions;
- the nomination of a 'primary pyramid contact person'.

The Key Stage 1–2 and 3–4 Management Groups rôle and function will be:

- ensuring that subject and pastoral teams meet regularly;
- monitoring the work of the two groups;
- receiving recommendations from these groups;
- allocating funds for specific key stage activities;
- keeping the Network Management Group informed of activities within their key stage;
- recommending to the Network Management Group whole network funded projects;
- setting tasks for key stage working groups;
- being responsible to the Network Management Group for the management of funds;
- nominating members to the Network Management Group.

This structure may appear bureaucratic, as if all the tasks are dictated by strict definitions of roles and jobs. In Handy's terms it appears to be the product of a role culture. And there is some truth in this perspective. It was complex and unwieldy and did not always empower people to get on with the job. Its real significance in terms of the development of the Network, however, is that the headteachers were prepared to accept and trust *representatives* to act for them and, in the case of Key Stages 3–4 management, they *delegated* responsibility to others. Moreover, significant work was done by task groups, for example the Network marketing group and the assessment group. They demonstrated the 'task' culture at work. Like bees in a hive, they grouped and regrouped in order to utilize the expertise available and to complete tasks quickly (Handy, 1984).

### The Role of the Governors

The liaison-policy document was shared with governors at an early stage. As the management of the network became formalized in the new structure, liaison became a regular item on the agendas of governors' meetings. The LEA introduced a half-termly bulletin 'News from North Lowestoft Schools', the content of which was provided by the schools. This often provided a focus for governors' discussions. Some governing bodies designated liaison governors. They attended events at other network schools and often contributed to parents' meetings at the point of transfer between phases. Joint governor-training sessions were provided and network governors' meetings established. They dealt with such issues as the launch of the network and meetings were held over the proposal to build a fourth middle school in North Lowestoft. These strategies developed and sustained a commitment to the network by governors. Thus when headships became vacant during this critical period governors actively sought candidates who were committed to collaboration.

## The Network in Practice: SCaB: Primary School Liaison

Somerleyton, Corton and Blundeston, the three most northerly villages in Suffolk, have a total primary-school population of approximately 200 children. The schools have a highly developed set of arrangements for the joint management, planning and delivery of the curriculum.

They work as a single entity in the network management groups with one representative acting for all three schools. One teacher has a responsibility for each National Curriculum subject and will liaise with middle schools, keep abreast of developments and disseminate good practice to colleagues.

The headteachers, staff and key stage coordinators meet regularly for planning and staff development. They have one or two school-development planning priorities in common (assessment and behaviour management for 1994–5) and write joint policies. They have created a four-year topic plan, which addresses the National Curriculum attainment targets. (For example, 'Where we live', a project which compares village life with urban living in the county town of Ipswich, delivers history and geography key stage objectives.) The schools operate joint activities such as an art week which took as its theme the rain forests. At the end of the week children and teachers from all three schools came together to share and celebrate their work.

Resources are shared between the schools. Videos, artefacts and books are bought for the group, specialist facilities are shared, teachers are exchanged and trips arranged jointly in order to cut costs. In-service priorities are determined by the group of headteachers after discussion in each school. GEST funds are then shared and colleagues will often attend courses on behalf of the group.

A common format is used for the school prospectus and a preschool book is provided for all parents. (This cleverly helps to assess preschool learning and suggests activities which parents could provide for their children.)

In addition to these structured arrangements, the teachers constantly use each other as a resource and a support network. As one head observed, 'Such things couldn't develop without working together. . . . I don't think that a small school such as this could operate efficiently on its own.'

### The Network in Practice: Science Liaison: Key Stage 3

As National Curriculum science came on stream at Key Stage 3 in 1989, the high-school heads of department and middle-school coordinators of science took common cause in arguing with headteachers about the allocation of time and resources for the subject in middle schools. An audit had revealed considerable discrepancies in provision which caused them real concern. This issue effectively helped to bond them as a team.

They quickly agreed the need to develop a North Lowestoft scheme of work for the delivery of science at Key Stage 3. Initially the curriculum was divided between the phases by levels but this was reviewed and an 'areas of knowledge' approach adopted. Within the scheme middle schools were to teach some areas to level 7, others were to be dealt with entirely in the high schools and some were to be revisited at this stage. Topics were then distributed between members of the group who developed the schemes of work individually and sought agreement of the others. Common middle-school tests were created and 'Science One' investigations were developed jointly as well as a common approach to them. Methodology was identified as a sensitive issue which was not tackled methodically elsewhere in the development of the scheme, although there was a sharing of approaches to teaching and learning through classroom observation across the phases.

The group developed one of the most collaborative approaches to curriculum continuity and progression in the network despite the change in mid-stream from seventeen attainment targets to four.

Several factors contributed to their success. One colleague observed that the key personnel were all reasonable people who were prepared to compromise and utilize each other's expertise. They were fortunate that the three middle-school science coordinators had different specialisms. They received significant support from the LEA advisory team. A two-day residential conference was held at the start which focused on attainment target statements and the allocation of curriculum content between phases and later advisors developed exemplar materials for investigations. Skilful intervention at school level was also critical. A departmental inspection provided the evidence to persuade one school to adhere to the agreed schemes of work and the science adviser acted as honest broker over the question of resources and time allocation. Finally, time out of the classroom to develop the scheme was paid for by the Network INSET fund.

### Marketing the North Lowestoft Network

In March 1992 a working group of heads and deputies from the three phases, supported by an LEA officer, was set up by the North Lowestoft headteachers to develop a marketing strategy. This initiative resulted from a shared concern about the profile of education in the area, the need to celebrate the considerable good practice and success of local schools and a desire to combat the negative messages about education which were coming from central government and some elements in the media.

In consultation with colleagues, the group identified the key messages which should be communicated to parents and the wider community and a range of methods to be employed. These included regular press releases, information leaflets, posters, and exhibitions and displays in local libraries and supermarkets. It became obvious that the double pyramid needed a clear identity in the eyes of the community and thus the title 'North Lowestoft Schools Network' was created with its motto 'Schools working together to provide a quality education for all'. A local marketing company was employed to design the logo and headed notepaper for the schools and to prepare for the network's official launch. In April 1993 the logo was unveiled in the presence of invited guests and the press with an exhibition of work across the three phases on display.

The work of this group was significant in the development of collaboration because it forced the headteachers to articulate their beliefs and goals and to seek common ground. It was part of the process of determining what the network stood for and thus helped to forge its identity. The celebration of educational success in the town raised morale. Moreover, in order to promote the network, it was necessary to set parameters for dealing with the press. This led to an agreement to avoid the negative marketing of partner schools which resulted in a greater sense of trust between colleagues.

### The New Middle School: A Test of Collaboration

The building of a fourth middle school in North Lowestoft was put on hold in 1990 after preliminary consultations but by January 1992 it was back on the agenda for commencement towards the end of the financial year 1993–4.

It had the potential to blow apart the newly formed network for several reasons:

- The middle school was to be built on a high-school campus and this arrangement could be seen to offer an unfair advantage in the liaison process.
- The location of the new middle school in the leafy suburbs and the interesting building design offered advantages that the existing middle schools did not possess.
- The redrawing of catchment areas would mean that the existing middle schools would lose children, and thus staff, in the short-term. Moreover, it was difficult to see how the catchment area of the new school could be created without adversely affecting the socio-economic balance within the existing middle schools. It quickly became apparent that there could be a knock-on effect to primary and high schools.

By coincidence, a twenty-four hour conference of middle- and high-school headteachers and deputies was held at the time when these issues were under discussion. It was significant because the conference resolved that the schools would act together for the benefit of the children in the area. Whilst support was given to the new middle school, concern was expressed about the lack of parity that could result from its creation. An early meeting with the LEA was requested to discuss the issues. The headteachers were beginning to utilize their collective voice in bargaining.

From the outset it was recognized that the LEA was not able to take the role it had played in the review of 1986–7. It no longer had the ability to redeploy staff. The temporary governing body would have the power of recruitment and appointment. Nor would it have as much flexibility over admissions given that the 1988 Education Act had tied admission limits to the standard number. Nevertheless, the LEA which was itself undergoing a cultural change, willingly embraced a partnership approach. In 1992–3 it embarked on a wide-ranging consultation called 'Setting new directions'. It argued for a new partnership, for the collective strength of schools and the LEA working together for the good of the community. Clearly this approach required an openness about its own policy and direction and the ability on the part of officers and advisers to act as facilitators and consultants as well as decision makers and the instruments of policy.

The building of the fourth North Lowestoft Middle School was to be an early test of the new partnership. A headteachers' and officers' steering group was established to plan the catchment areas, phasing arrangements and public meetings. Representation was from across all sectors. Individuals worked on different tasks according to their strengths. A colleague presented the catchment areas at a public meeting, supported by others, and another produced a curriculum model against which to test the effectiveness of the building. The steering group was displaying performing levels of trust, flexibility and inter-dependence. The LEA serviced the meetings, provided a constant stream of data and channelled communication to and from the education committee. Existing network structures were used to keep colleagues and governors fully informed.

Inevitably mistakes were made. The LEA misread the extent to which the headteachers were working collectively and approached them individually over their accommodation needs. This was seen as running contrary to the openness of the partnership. A proposal to align Somerleyton, Corton and Blundeston primary schools with different middle schools was met with resistance and, at a later stage, an LEA proposal to start the new middle school with two year groups rather than one, was similarly received.

Despite these setbacks, the consultative approach won through. The views of the SCaB group were accepted and a compromise was reached for the phased opening of the new school. The headteachers had been able to take a broad view of the needs of North Lowestoft; colleagues had represented each other over such fundamentals as catchment areas; collective pressure had been brought to bear to safeguard the interests of individual schools; the LEA had applied its philosophy of working in partnership to a highly sensitive issue.

## Conclusion

A range of local factors had prepared the ground in North Lowestoft for the growth of collaboration. Impetus had been given to it by the demands of the National

Curriculum and the growing concern about educational aspirations in the town. The liaison policy, despite the manner of its development, led to the formulation of shared goals and key tasks. Increasingly the headteachers saw that they had a collective power to influence events in a local authority which was moving towards greater collaboration and partnership with its schools.

Management structures were developed which significantly relied on representation and delegation and thus engendered a sense of ownership. This study concludes, however, that this was not the crucial factor in achieving network objectives. The task groups which were successful, and the curriculum areas which developed the best liaison practice, had become effective teams. They had reached the performing stage of their development and had a clear task focus. They contained individuals with a variety of skills and personality types who had gelled. Ironically these colleagues had not been *selected* to create balanced teams. As Belbin observes:

> Management teams are commonly made up of members holding particular appointments. They are there by virtue of the offices or responsibilities they represent. No overall sense of design governs the composition of the group. (Belbin, 1981, p. 132)

It is clearly essential to establish the right climate in which teams can operate and to try to achieve the right balance of qualities within them. Successful collaboration is a delicate thing. It relies on key individuals and the interaction between them in effective teams.

> Designing a team rests on a limited number of principles and concepts and involves various methods and techniques. But what turns team-building into an art is that the bricks, like legendary men, are made of different types of clay and not wholly predictable after firing. (Belbin, 1981, p. 142)

Team-building may indeed be an art, but this does not mean that the composition of teams should be left to chance. Attention should be paid to how individuals interact and to what extent they are able to fill complementary rôles in the team. If this is true for effective teams in separate institutions, the experience of the North Lowestoft network has shown that it is even more important in the building of teams across schools where issues of perceived status distrust, institutional jealousies and extreme pressure are potent threats.

### References

BELBIN, R.M. (1981) *Management Teams: Why they Succeed or Fail*, Oxford, Heinemann.
HANDY, C. (1984) *Taken for Granted? Understanding Schools as Organisations*, Harlow, Longman.
NAHT (1990) *National Curriculum Helpline Guidance*, Note 8: Liaison Between Phases.
SUFFOLK EDUCATION DEPARTMENT (1981) *Report of the Working Party on Liaison*.
TUCKMAN, B.W. (1985) 'Development Sequence in Small Groups', *Psychological Bulletin*, 63.

*Chapter 5*

# The Rationale and Experience of a 'Schools Association': The Ivel Schools' Association

*Ron Wallace*

## The Favourable Background

The Ivel is a small river running through south-east Bedfordshire, and a suitably neutral name to be adopted by a group of schools which have location as their common factor.

The Ivel Schools' Association (ISA) was founded in the Spring of 1994 by nineteen schools. The common ground was a desire that the schools should remain LEA-maintained (including voluntary-aided and controlled schools), that they should work more closely together in opposition to the prevailing mood of competition, and that they should make more formal and effective the curriculum liaison which already existed.

The schools were already a loose pyramid of fifteen lower schools, three middle schools and one upper school. The majority of the children in the area pass naturally up the pyramid. There is some seepage of pupils across the LEA boundary to an 11–18 school, but that is reducing and in any case is due to the breakdown of an earlier LEA agreement rather than to any parental view on the qualities of the schools. Similarly there is some seepage of pupils into one of the middle schools from a lower school outside the area. On the whole, however, pupils begin in one of the lower schools and end their formal education at the upper school.

There are a nursery school and nursery units, and an adult and youth-education service based at the upper school. There is much cross-over of responsibilities such as parents and teachers in one school being governors in another. The group of ISA schools are, therefore, in many ways self-contained in providing the state education service to the community.

In addition the schools are largely free from competition either between themselves or from outside. It sounds like an educator's dream, with nothing to distract from the task of education. Why then form an association and give up significant funds to pay for it?

### Motives: Why Collaborate?

Initial motives were varied. There was much idealism — a belief that collaboration between schools would be more effective than competition in improving education — and some political and financial aspects. An ephemeral factor, now almost forgotten, was the belief after the 1992 Conservative election victory, that all secondary schools would have to acquire grant-maintained status (GMS). This would have formally separated the middle and upper schools from the more numerous lower schools. Existing cooperation might have been lost. Participating in this anxiety, LEA officers were enthusiastic about seeking new ways of working with what were about to become schools with no obligation to maintain any links at all with the LEA. The LEA therefore provided resources, in the form of a Coopers and Lybrand study and officer time, to develop a prospectus for the new association. In the event, none of the schools sought grant-maintained status. The Gaderene tendency was resisted, as some observers, including the present writer, had predicted it could and would be. However, the LEA was committed. The act of planning had created its own momentum. The Coopers and Lybrand study was completed. It set the framework for the establishment of an association, with a set of aims, a draft constitution and a provisional budget. The Ivel Schools' Association was launched at a formal gathering attended by headteachers and chairs of governors of all schools, and by the Chief Education Officer.

There were other reasons, even in the early days, for a more formal association. The LEA had been one of the slowest of the shire counties to delegate resources for the local management of schools, particularly in comparison with its neighbours. At a county meeting for headteachers, the case for quickly and substantially increasing the level of delegation, in order to put much larger sums within the control of schools, was argued by the Deputy County Education Officer. Some heads, particularly of lower schools, wanted an association in order to advise on the use of this previously unimagined wealth. This was a serious and legitimate desire, for the view from schools in areas with a very high level of delegation is that it is the transfer of the last 5–10 per cent which provides management flexibility as a result of financial savings. The first 80 per cent or so is largely committed to inescapable staffing and premises costs. The movement of the last 5–10 per cent is often the belated transfer of funds to cover the responsibilities which have already been transferred by statute from the LEA to the schools. It is only when the costs of LEA central services are devolved that the money begins to follow the responsibilities which have passed from LEAs to schools as a result of legislation since the 1988 Act. There was both enthusiasm about greater control and nervousness in a few (but not all) of the smaller village schools, about how to deploy this new wealth. Heads and governors wanted to look collaboratively at what was now needed and how the newly delegated funds could be redirected to provide support for pupils' learning instead of increasingly irrelevant County Hall administration.

A fundamental aim from the outset was to promote curriculum development, in order to consolidate curriculum continuity in its broadest sense throughout the pyramid of schools. The aim was to use staff expertise in the schools for the benefit of the wider teaching community and to promote curricular initiatives. Within the first six months of the association's life, several activities had been planned. There was already a good base. There was considerable curriculum liaison, stronger in some subjects than others, and not always spread across the pyramid. There was a tendency for middle schools separately to hold liaison meetings with their feeder lower school. Similarly the three middle schools met upper-school representatives. There were few curriculum liaison activities covering the entire 5–18 age range and community education. Some subjects had no liaison at all. Another difference was that lower schools were often represented by their headteachers, whereas middle schools and the upper school were usually represented by subject heads of departments.

The new code of practice to identify and support pupils with special educational needs was introduced at a fortuitous time for a group of schools wishing to work on liaison across all of the schools. It had several advantages from the ISA point of view. The code itself favoured the clustering of schools. There was considerable expertise amongst teachers in the schools. It was *par excellence* an aspect of the curriculum where continuity was essential. There were practical things to be done. Every school had to respond to the code; it was not an optional development. There was national funding available from GEST (Grants for Educational Support and Training), which the LEA was required to delegate to schools.

A planning group was set up. It was the first such group, worked successfully and set a pattern of working for other groups. It consisted of key teachers from the three tiers. It concentrated on the practical needs of schools — drafting individual education plans (IEPs), the transfer of information between schools, and the assessment of pupils for the five stages in the code. The LEA's county-wide approach was quite different. It organized training separately by tiers of schools, so that lower schools fifty miles apart came together for training, when they had no reason to be working together. Similarly the middle and upper schools were kept separate. Almost every LEA agency which had an interest in the matter produced its own formats for individual education plans, so that the principal merit of having an LEA — the ability to plan and work economically for all schools, was squandered. By contrast, teachers in the ISA schools, working with a county advisor whose services they bought, saw that they could produce results, using their own expertise and experience.

Procurement of services and supplies was another initial task for ISA to undertake. This became much more important than originally intended. The start of ISA coincided with the delegation of a further 2 per cent of the schools' budget, not the 8–10 per cent which schools had expected; that is a theme for later. It quickly became clear to all schools that the LEA had made few preparations for further delegation. The exception was the advisory service, which had prepared options for schools to consider. Other services expected schools simply to send the money back and to continue to receive the 'free' service. Delegation like this would have been a wholly paper, and wholly pointless exercise. However, most schools outside the ISA did exactly as expected. The ISA schools became something of a maverick. It became clear that the County Hall had not expected schools to use the money as they wished. ISA schools were the leaders in exploiting what they recognized as their new authority. When one department at County Hall combined in one package two services, one of which schools could not do without and the other one which most schools did not want, ISA schools had no hesitation in rejecting the approach, whereas most other schools in the County accepted the offer.

Part of the LEA argument was that the additional money was not really delegated but devolved. The difference was that with devolution the Chief Education Officer was officially still in control of the money, even though he would allow schools to use it, by virement between services, as they wished. The aim was to deny GM schools the benefit which would otherwise be given to them by a shamelessly political device, which would increase their income at the expense of LEA schools and at no cost to the Treasury. The government method of increasing GM school income was to calculate it on the basis of last year's retained budget and this year's delegated budget, so that in any year when the LEA increased the amount of delegation, the GM school received the difference twice. All LEA schools willingly cooperated in this scheme to counteract such a device. ISA schools went further and used their power to choose.

The biggest shock to the LEA was when a highly regarded music service was put under the spotlight. Quality was not the question. It was widely regarded as a good service, but one with its own objectives not wholly aligned with those of the schools. ISA schools asked questions and demanded change. Why were only orchestral instruments taught (no keyboard and no guitar)? Was it that prestigious orchestras were seen as incompatible with broader aspects of instrumental education? Why were instrumental teachers, who were on annual teachers' contracts and in some cases on higher grades, being paid for by schools when the teachers guaranteed only thirty-three weeks of tuition to very small classes? ISA schools were discovering that, once they ceased to be patronized as a 'user group' to be consulted about how the service could improve its quality, and became the negotiators for the spending of money which was their own, the relationship changed. There were suggestions that ISA schools were being aggressive and spoiling a hitherto pleasant relationship. In reality the schools were never less than courteous. What was happening was that County personnel were experiencing the pain of losing control.

### Tensions

Some of the problems and tensions of change have already emerged in this discussion of the ISA's aims. There were others. The most important was the state of the LEA itself. It was politically divided and under threat from local government review. None of the three political parties had overall control. They did not, even within themselves, hold consistent views. At extremes there were some Labour councillors who had a civic view of their role — they were the providers of the service. Some did not favour LMS at all. At the other extreme there were some Conservative councillors who took the view that, if schools wanted more control, they should seek GMS and have entire control over their budgets. The

Ivel Schools' Association consisted of schools which wanted both to remain LEA-maintained and to have more delegation of budgets.

The difficulty was acute. It meant that enormous amounts of time had to be spent on negotiations and lobbying, distracting from the association's main purposes. When the money did not flow, the role of the ISA changed. It became the negotiating body for schools to extract more money, to question whether all LEA activities were necessary, and to unlock previously mysterious arrangements. Obtaining the money became for a time the preoccupation, since there was no point in planning its use until its arrival was sure.

The LEA had seen ISA as a means of keeping schools in the LEA family if they became GM. The reaction of LEA officers to this changed role for the ISA, in which it had become a negotiator for the schools against the LEA, can be imagined and does not need to be described. More interesting was the response of a few schools. It became clear that, for some, managerial responsibility was a burden. The patronizing argument from officers, that heads really preferred 'to teach rather than to manage', did not fall on wholly deaf ears. Much work was needed by fellow heads to convince some heads that they had always been managers as well as heads, and that LMS was about liberation and ending dependency. It was also necessary for some heads to take a 'political' view, which had not been their custom and which was unwelcome to them. They had to grasp that legislation had given them and their governors no choice, since most responsibility was now located at school level.

There was an element of the incarcerated who no longer wanted freedom. This was not in any way surprising. A decade of turmoil — a national curriculum introduced and changed radically before it had run its course, tests introduced and abandoned, GMS, etc. — had created a general mood of 'enough is enough'. If this turmoil coincided with the last quarter of a head's career, it is not difficult to understand why yet another apparent increase in decisions to be taken at school level was not always welcome. For a time there was a potential alliance between LEA officers who did not wish to change long-established procedures and a few heads who did not immediately see that they already had the responsibility, but not the money.

Another major problem was a temporary loss of trust between officers of the LEA and the more active heads and governors in the ISA. This came about because heads had been given the prospect of greatly increased delegation of budgets to schools, and this did not happen. Summoned to a meeting with a very senior education officer, they had heard about the merits of greater delegation. One of their former headteacher colleagues, now a head in a neighbouring LEA with a high level of delegation, spoke of massive savings on LEA services, which had enabled him to spend many thousands of pounds on more direct support for pupils' learning. The heads naturally assumed that there was a purpose to this presentation. When funds started to arrive in schools the following year, the meal on the plate was altogether more modest than the tempting feast which had whet the appetites of specially assembled headteachers. Reputations tumbled. Difficult meetings ensued. Trust took a hammering. Senior LEA officers tried diversions, hinting that

ISA was aggressive or unreasonable, although the feeling of broken trust was widespread among secondary heads in all parts of the county. Attempts were made to separate the lower schools from the secondary schools. It was not a pleasant period. Steadfastness amongst the more active headteachers was needed and it was there. The chairman, a leading County councillor, was solid, imaginative, relentless and inventive. Trust was restored, because the association did not wilt.

Another source of tension was uncertainty about the continued existence of the LEA itself. The local government review proposed the division of the LEA into three unitary authorities. There was little local support for this proposal. It contrasted with the recommendation for two neighbouring councils that a two-tier local government should continue, with the LEAs unaltered. Petitions were signed. Meetings were held. The ISA was more vociferous than most. Yet there was at least a guilty undertone that the LEA was proving unresponsive to the schools' desire for a new relationship, and that many of the problems created by it for ISA would disappear if it were to cease. Intelligence was brought from other areas where very small unitary authorities with responsibility for education were proposed on the basis of an existing borough council. There, heads and governors were talking to the chief executive, and advising that, with maximum delegation under LMS, and with advisers and inspectors acting as freelance agents and finding more than enough work if they were of quality, there was no need to create the full panoply of an LEA. Although little heard aloud, the view was whispered that the demise of the existing LEA would enable schools which wanted to keep their joint approach and their local accountabilities, to achieve this goal more easily and not need to have to consider the grant-maintained route.

One of the potentially divisive movements with which the ISA had to contend was a countywide organization, with some superficial similarities to the ISA, but limited to primary schools. Schools could not afford to belong to two groups. Primary schools in the ISA area had to choose between a countywide primary-school organization and a more local organization embracing all schools. From the ISA perspective the other organization had the fundamental flaw that it was limited to one phase. Sympathy with the argument that primary education needed a lobby was balanced with a recognition that primary schools outside the ISA had as a *genus* quickly succumbed to the LEA officer line that the LEA could relieve small schools of the burden of administration and allow them to devote their energies to teaching. The preposterous nature of this argument, when the greatest burden on small schools was the LEA requirement that they carry out all aspects of LMS finances through County Hall, thus turning LMS into a burden not a release, was not clear to many small school heads. Some of the smallest school heads were very active members, indeed the founding members, of the ISA. They saw through the argument, but many heads elsewhere in the county proved less sophisticated in their understanding. For some ISA heads, the pull of their primary sector county colleagues was a serious factor. There was the possibility of a split in the ISA between the middle, upper and some lower schools on the one hand, and a few lower schools on the other.

Tension of another kind arose between the LEA and ISA. It was not so much a lack of trust, as has already been noted, but ISA exasperation with the LEA reluctance to provide information. The sensitivities of officers, whose jobs were threatened by so many forces (local government review and LMS in particular), were appreciated. Exasperation arose for two reasons. First, many schools had themselves been through many difficulties involving job insecurity during the periods of falling rolls in the 1980s. There was at least a hope that officers who had organized some of those events might have gained an appreciation of the uncertainties created by threats to posts. Second, the perceived reluctance to share management information was justified by arguments that such information was 'commercially sensitive' even though there was an apparent reluctance on the part of services to expose themselves to commercial competition.

Perhaps the greatest difficulty in the first few months was in undertaking activities involving classroom teachers. The 'political' and financial dimensions consumed too much energy at the expense of curricular developments. It was probable in any case that it would take two years before sufficient curricular activities would be in place to touch enough class teachers to enable them to enjoy the benefits of the association. There was much concern amongst the active governors and headteachers that they could see benefits which it would take some time for other governors and teachers to see. Sharing the vision before there is much activity is always a problem for new organizations.

These then were some of the pressures which an association, born of idealism and a desire by schools to take greater control of their destinies on the basis of cooperation and local accountability, confronted. Whether it has survived the height of these pressures will be known when this book is published. It is not known as this chapter is written. If the Ivel Schools' Association has survived, it will be, not only because the vision was sound, but because those who had the vision were clear-minded and tough.

## The Vision

The vision of the founders is already being turned into reality. A register of curriculum and other educational expertise within the nineteen schools has been established. Various curricular projects have been started. The first training organized by the association and led by teachers from the schools has been held and has been regarded by participants as a great success. Negotiations have wrung better prices and better services from council departments. Outward-looking activities, such as support for Albania, have been started. A start has been made on a quality-assurance programme, in which schools are developing their skills at evaluating the quality of learning received by pupils. A register of good local builders and other trades people, based on the experience of the schools themselves, has been established. This is not only useful in practical terms, but is also an example of net-working amongst the schools for their mutual benefit. The promotion of the arts through festivals is planned. The possibility of a schools-funded local bursarial and personnel service is being explored, with the schools being in control.

The hallmark of all these activities is that they arise from schools' expressed needs, that they are started only if they are needed (not because they have always existed and inertia keeps them going), and that the schools control them. Although some schools participate in some activities and not in others, all activities have the characteristic that they are undertaken cooperatively. Not all districts lend themselves so readily to such cooperation, but not all groups of schools have had to fight so hard for greater control of their budgets. The founders of the Ivel Schools' Association had a fine vision which, whether or not it is realized quickly or at all in South East Bedfordshire, has validity for the future. It should appeal to groups of schools which reject division and low-grade competition between schools as the spur to improvement, and which believe that rigorous and unsentimental cooperation between self-governing schools can release and focus energies and enhance the quality of education.

# Chapter 6

# Education 2000: Collaboration and Cooperation as a Model of Change Management

*Lynne Monck and Chris Husbands*

### Introduction

Over the last decade and a half, national policy in education has emphasized competition between schools. The long-run consequences of encouraging the individualized development of schools as autonomous institutions with responsibility only to their governing bodies and parents are potentially far-reaching for the national education system. In particular, as each school in a locality makes individual planning decisions to maximize success, educational quality across the whole community is most likely to become unevenly spread. There can be no genuine local involvement between a community and its educational life — only individual deals for short-term, opportunistic gain. The philosophy of Education 2000 since its inception has been quite different: far from seeing the enhancement of educational quality as a responsibility of individual schools, Education 2000 has considered the regeneration of schooling and its reshaping for the demands of an increasingly competitive world a responsibility of the whole community.

Education 2000 was established as a charitable trust in 1982, and grew out of both professional and industrial unease about the education system. It had what Brian Knight has described as a 'powerful underlying rationale: that in a changing world better educated and more capable young adults are a resource so valuable that the local community and industry can be led to see that investment in education is both logical and necessary' (Knight, 1991, p. 36). Education 2000 argued that it was in the interests of the whole community, not least of industry, that schools should avoid the 'emergence of two societies — one with work to do and all the advantages and advances of new technologies; and the other without work, knowledge or hope' (CUP, 1983). From this perspective, the Education 2000 Trust sought to bring about fundamental changes in schooling, in ways working and in the relationship between teachers and students. It sought to move the emphasis of schools away from teaching and towards learning, to vitalize schools and to help them develop in young people the capacity for learning throughout their adult lives. The key to releasing the potential of schools and schooling lay in two crucial elements: widening the conception of the 'educative community' and tapping the resources of information technology in order to transform teaching and learning. Whilst the long-run ambitions of the trustees were far-reaching, there was a commitment to developing the ideas of Education 2000 in a pilot project in one community, and from 1985 onwards the Hertfordshire Project was established in the north Hertfordshire town of Letchworth (Cook and Dalton, 1989).

The heads of the six Letchworth secondary schools who came together to form the pilot Education 2000 Project shared this vision of a wider community commitment to supporting and managing educational change. In retrospect, it can be seen that Letchworth was particularly fecund soil for the messages of Education 2000: Letchworth, with a population of some 25,000, had been established in the early years of the twentieth century as the first 'Garden City' as a communitarian response to the strains of nineteenth-century industrial urbanism, and the Garden City Corporation retained a strong commitment to the early ideals. More generally, rapid economic change in north Hertfordshire in the 1980s produced a commercial and industrial base increasingly characterized by dependence on high technology and high skill, so that by the middle 1980s employers in the region were acutely aware of their own demand for highly competent and flexible employees themselves committed to continuous learning and development. There were already powerful links between Letchworth schools. Throughout the 1970s and 1980s, there was a strong tradition of cross-town cooperation between the four state comprehensive schools, and a shared sense of identity within the overall framework of Hertfordshire LEA. Given the traditions of the town, it is perhaps not surprising that relationships between the comprehensive schools and the two independent schools in the two were extremely good. Thus, the six Letchworth schools were able to adopt the common objectives for the Education 2000 Project articulated by the project's education consultant, Ray Dalton:

- to build a wide community dialogue to establish a consensus of opinion on the objectives for education and to provide for this within an educative community;
- to effect a permanent shift towards effective learning strategies giving empowerment to the individual, supported by exploitation of the full potential of information technology, libraries and access to a full range of learning resources and techniques; and
- to establish a shared model for the continuing professional development of teachers.

The model of educational change adopted by Education 2000 depended on a commitment to collaborative working. Schools were to advance together on a broadly parallel basis by sharing expertise and approaches, with pairs or groups of schools exploring methodologies for the benefit of all on the basis of collaborative work involving staff and other members of the community. The opportunities and challenges presented by these objectives had enormous cross-curricular and cross-school implications in the commitment of resources and in establishing mechanisms for facilitating contacts as well as for building and supporting networks between schools.

At its inception, the Letchworth Project identified four components to achieve these objectives:

- the educative community;
- curriculum development;
- information technology; and
- the needs of the young people.

All of these potentially could involve close cooperation between the schools and were initially financed jointly by the schools and by both local and national industry (£1.5 million). This chapter will examine each of these components in relation to the theme of cooperation and collaboration.

## The Educative Community

From 1985, a group of six deputy heads led by a headteacher of one of the six schools seconded for a term (in rotation) met regularly to discuss the nature of the local community and attempt to identify individuals and interest groups who might represent differing opinions and view points about the community's expectations of its young people.

Meetings and visits were arranged with individual community representatives. These meetings ostensibly served the dual purpose of informing the community about the project and seeking its views and support. However the work of this group, made up of important policy makers from each school served another important purpose. The process of articulating their beliefs and ideas about education to a wider and occasionally hostile audience clarified their own joint understanding of the educational philosophy underlying the project and, in the longer run, gave them a sense of their own shared joint purpose.

Central to the work of the project throughout its ten-year life have been the regular monthly meetings of headteachers. Their continuing work has ensured both that the project has not become marginalized in any of the schools — a critical issue given the extent to which all of the schools have simultaneously been responding to an unprecedented volume and pace of externally imposed change — and that the purpose of the project has been continually redefined in the light of rapidly changing circumstances. In the latter context, the gradually closer involvement of Mike Fischer, managing director of Research Machines the life of the Letchworth project has been critical. As external changes, such as Local Management of Schools, the National Curriculum and national assessment impinged on schools more closely, it would have been possible for the Letchworth schools to focus on the management of change in individual schools with less and less explicit concern with collaborative working. Fischer and the Letchworth heads took a different approach. Fischer asked Jim Knight of School Management South to work with senior management teams in the schools on a project supporting management of change in project schools. This involved the senior teams of five of the schools (one was now going through the process of closure and therefore was only peripherally involved). It gave senior teams the opportunity to review how they worked together as well as how they could cooperate across institutions. One result of this was the 'Peer assisted investigation', where each school used three members of the SMT. Each one joined with colleagues from two other schools to investigate an aspect of the curriculum or the management of the schools. In each school there was a home-based member of the team plus two visitors from different schools. Peter Cook, the Deputy Headteacher at Fearnhill briefed staff as follows:

> The 'Peer assisted investigation' involves other colleagues coming into the school and helping with the gathering and interpretation of information . . . They will act as unbiased but critical friends, fellow professionals who understand the problems we face and have a genuine desire to help us further the best interests of the school.

As those involved subsequently explained, the opportunity to work in this way was felt to be exceptionally valuable. One deputy head commented that 'We have a lot to learn from the way other institutions tackle their tasks', whilst another observed that this was 'a chance to see another senior team in natural surroundings at work. It gave me a chance to reflect on ours.'

The commitment to an educative community went far wider than the Letchworth schools. The issues of links with wider community groups, focusing outside schools were addressed by a number of study groups involving among others the Letchworth churches, the Letchworth Rotary Club, business community members and various voluntary organizations. A number of initiatives arose from this — the production of a local-community voluntary-service newsletter, a local directory of youth activities (jointly with the youth and community service). Work placements for teachers flourished and about fifty teachers took the opportunity to visit various businesses in the two years 1987–9. Sixth-form conferences became a regular occurance covering moral, industrial, and political themes. External observers have commented that sixth-form students across Letchworth move between institutions with great confidence and assurance and instanced by the creation of a joint 'young enterprise' company from the private girls' Catholic school (St Francis) and a state comprehensive (Fearnhill) who successfully reached the regional finals of the competition — to the surprise of judges and fellow competitors alike.

However the wider-community involvement and vision of the educative community has not been sustainable over the years since the project's community coordinator returned to his school after a two-year secondment (1989). Community links, community service, work placements and industrial links flourish and continue as they do in many schools, but the lesson appears to be that relationships with wider-community groups depend on continuing hard work. Whilst the participating schools continue to share the commitment to collaborative work, as a part of which they routinely inform each other of what they are doing and disseminate good practice regularly, the pioneering sense of a commitment to the broadest conception of community involvement has proved more difficult to sustain.

By 1990, external funding for the local project had all but ceased. Despite the commitment of the schools, the afterglow of involvement in a stimulating enterprise was rapidly fading. The arrival of Mike Fischer as director of the local project was a turning point. His own enabling and facilitating management style as well as his interest in, and very tangible financial support, not only for, Information Technology — which derived from the long-standing commitment of Research Machines to the project — but also in projects such as the partnership with Cambridge University in initial teacher training and the recent numeracy and literacy project gave the Letchworth heads renewed confidence in long-term health of the project.

Under the guidance of Mike Fischer, the Letchworth heads undertook a brain-storming session which in some respects refocused the concept of the educative community, and highlighted the significance to heads and their schools of a reshaped focus on aims for achievement across the participating schools, defined as:

the achievement of the empowered pupil;
the achievement of the valued and effective teacher; and
the achievement of the satisfied parent.

Thereafter, the heads' group, together with Fischer, translated these over-arching aims into a series of specific targets to be achieved by schools working within the framework of the Letchworth Project:

- halving the number of students leaving school functionally illiterate and innumerate;
- testing parent and student attitudes by means of a statistically valid questionnaire (the Keele model has been chosen);
- expanding the community involvement of students; and
- working on achieving 'Investors in People Standard' for the schools (one school has achieved it already). This is considered an excellent vehicle to help achieve effective and valued staff, both teaching staff and support staff.

Such a set of concerns for the concept of an 'educative community' may be a long way from the project's original vision but the schools have travelled the road together and have overcome great tensions. In the later 1980s, during a stressful LEA review of educational provision in Letchworth, at one time or other over a two-year period three out of the four state schools were earmarked for closure before eventually one of the four was closed. Over- and under-subscription occurred as parental preference moved from school to school inside and outside the Letchworth community. The publication of examination results was another threat to cooperative relationships between the schools. Nonetheless, the original commitment of the project to change through collaboration was important in planting a concept of commitment to joint working where schools have learnt together that cooperation is both cost-effective and good for the public perception of education.

**Information Technology**

Perhaps the most obvious visible consequence of the Letchworth schools' involvement in Education 2000 is the extensive investment of the funds made available from the industrial sponsors in computers. In 1985, the project chose Research Machines as its preferred option not only because it offered excellent hardware and commercial standard software but also it offered an *educational* vision of the future provided by Mike Fischer and the promise, later fulfilled, of high-quality technical support. Collaborative working made development of Information Technology-led curriculum work less painful and innovation less risky than would otherwise have been the case.

The project has provided the six participating schools with a large quantity of hardware and software, large networks that rarely, if ever, crash, trained teaching and support staff, support services and overall cooperation across the schools. These achievements are not simply the result of industrial largesse. They have depended crucially on several features. Of great significance was the appointment of a shared IT coordinator, Nick Peace, who works across all schools and is funded pro-rata according to school size. He has helped with school-development planning in relation to IT, and has supported network managers as well as giving up-to-date guidance and advice to the IT coordinators. Equally important has been a shared first-line repair system which arose when the LEA stopped funding a service. Two schools employ trained technicians who are given time to repair machines for all five schools. A different, but highly significant development has been an enormous expansion in the use of libraries across the schools after two libraries (St Christopher and Fearnhills) volunteered to pilot different computer-management systems. The enthusiasm generated by these systems soon spread and other librarians in the project became involved. In all of this the complexities and politics of managing budgets across private and state schools were not simple, but the end product was gratifyingly consensual.

A non-simultaneous conferencing facility was donated by Digital (called Ebenezer, after Ebenezer Howard the founder of Letchworth) and provided such an effective communication system between schools that a flourishing sixth-form dating service was soon in operation! However its curriculum potential was appreciated by staff working in areas of the curriculum where communication skills are at a premium. Business studies students welcomed the opportunity it gave students between schools to practise union–employer negotiating skills. On one day, all Letchworth sixth-form students became involved in a simulation activity based on a political crisis in an imaginary South American state. Groups taking parts as diverse as multinational companies, left-wing terrorists, right-wing dictators and the Catholic Church attempted to resolve issues unfolding across the network throughout an intensive day. Much of this curriculum work was not sustainable within an increasingly constrained national curriculum and mainly academic sixth form. However the lessons learned may be valuable if a planned Ebenezer 2 — an Internet system — comes into the project schools. The post-Dearing liberation of the 11–16 curriculum together with new GNVQ courses may provide the impetus for Ebenezer 2 to make a more sustained impact on the school curriculum.

If Information Technology has produced the most obviously physical effect on the schools, it has also demonstrated most clearly both the benefits of the project's collaborative approach and its limitations. Early on, the project team grasped that the potential of Information Technology to enhance and develop learning was far from being a straightforwardly technical issue and in the later 1980s there was substantial investment in the in-service training of teachers in Information Technology. Across all six schools, such investment produced a highly computer-literate staff, able and enthusiastic about the integration of Information Technology into teaching. At the same time, the twin pressures of technological change — which inevitably produce a continuous need to update and consolidate Information Technology skills — and externally imposed curriculum change both mean that the victories won in terms of developing the potential of Information Technology can appear transitory. In this respect, the experience of Ebenezer has been instructive for all involved: it was, in its early days, deployed in the schools without a clear curriculum rationale; it was used by sixth formers and others for purposes which cannot be described as wholly educational; it has been used patchily across different curriculum areas. Increasingly, however, in some areas, its potential has been grasped and is, five years on, being exploited to enhance and develop learning. Perhaps its most significant contribution in Letchworth has been, and will continue to be, that it provides a simple and easily used method of sustaining the communication on which the concept of the educative community depends.

## Curriculum Development

From the outset, Education 2000 had a central concern with the development and renewal of the curriculum. The project grew out of a critique with what one observer called the 'over blown, over academic' school curriculum which was seen as being increasingly irrelevant to the 'real needs' of learners and of the wider community, and a real stumbling block to the development of effective teaching and learning styles. Yet the project's early concern with curriculum development grew out of a different set of educational circumstances. It evolved when examinations at 16+ were still separately conducted by GCE and CSE examination boards and well before the National Curriculum had been conceived. Thus the period since 1988 has been exceptionally unsympathetic to the original conception of curriculum development as articulated in Education 2000. Whilst some developments — the introduction of GCSE coursework, the extension of TVEI and the implementation of Records of Achievement — provided contexts in which to extend the principles of Education 2000, it would be idle to pretend that circumstances have been propitious.

In the later 1980s, during the earlier phases of the project, cross-school curriculum development groups were given time by staff enhancement or by the provision of supply cover. Their brief, broadly conceived was to consider the impact of new technology on their subject, to share good practice in teaching, learning and assessment, and, particularly, to look at new material available to deliver their subject. The groups that evolved were wide-ranging, from CDT to RE and from modern languages to Special Needs. Given the changes in national policy which increasingly impinged on curriculum and school policy from the later 1980s, it is difficult to be clear about either the impact such groups had or the ways in which their work should be evaluated. At one level, they were clearly a success: for those involved in the groups, their participation created for them a network of (usually) like-minded colleagues in other schools with whom they could explore ideas and test out new approaches. In the longer run, and viewed from the impact such groups had on curriculum development in the six schools, it is much more difficult to be positive about their achievements. The constraints of time in an era of multiple and discontinuous change led many of the groups to cease meeting. Groups such as these need to see an agenda relevant to their continuing day-to-day professional work and a purpose behind spending time on meetings. Nonetheless, whilst some groups did fall by the wayside, others have continued to meet. Those which continue to exist include the craft, design and technology, special needs, IT and librarian groups. All of these have clear agendas which include the need for cross school collaboration. The continued work of the IT group and the librarian group in particular suggest a commitment to the other components of the project.

### Needs of the Young People

Education 2000 began with the intention of using the community and technology 'to satisfy the needs of young people as the end'. It is difficult, if not impossible to define what this component will achieve on its own; many teachers at the time said that they found it insulting and superfluous: 'Surely,' they say, 'our purpose as teachers and schools *is* to meet the needs of young people.' However there were a number of initiatives identified under this heading. The personal and social education programmes in place in the project schools were examined and extended where necessary to include further study skills, self-evaluation, self-organization and time management. Study groups of students were set up with members from across the schools ranging in ages from 14–19. Such groups provided a forum for some young people to express their views on a range of issues including community provision and education. As with the curriculum-development groups, these groups proved difficult to sustain and difficult to relate to the agendas emerging from the other components of the project. Perhaps, in this context, the key issue is to note that, in its own words, 'the project asserts that the future success of young people will depend on their social skills as much as it will on their intellectual skills'.

### Conclusion

From the perspective of 1995, has Education 2000 succeeded? This, as in so many other studies of educational change and innovation is a tauntingly difficult question to answer. Even in areas where there might arguably be measurable outcomes of the project, we do not have the data we could use to measure our success — we did not measure parent or student or teacher satisfaction and if we did would it be a measure of progress or of the change in political climate over the last ten years? Where there *are* figures, they frequently refer to the processes which the project has used in order to advance its objectives: the numbers of teachers engaged in in-service training supported by the project; the number of computers installed in the Letchworth schools.

There is a different way of evaluating the project. It represents a commitment to the successful management of educational change based on school and community renewal drawing on as wide a net of community resources as possible. Those involved in the project in the Letchworth schools have maintained a commitment to these principles through some of the most destabilizing years the education service has seen. The project — particularly through the involvement of Mike Fischer has both shown the need to respond to the pressures created by those changes and the capacity to respond to them within the overall framework of commitments and principles which sustained its early work. The four components of the project have all acted as both a spur to schools to cooperate, and a demonstration that collaborative approaches to the implementation and management of change are powerful ones for those involved in change. The open question, which we find difficult to judge, remains just how far the results of this cooperation enriched the experiences of staff and students. At least schools do not feel that they are competing against each other in the town. They see education as a national and local imperative creating a culture of cooperation to gain the best deal for all our youngsters, using the talents and skills of the community in the widest sense. There is no way in which schools try to hive off resources for one group at the expense of another. It is with this strength that the educational community can feel safe in charting a course for our children without feeling we are alone on a raft at the mercy of whatever directive happens to blow.

### Acknowledgment

We would like to thank Nigel Coulthard and John Abbott for contributions on which this chapter is based: neither is responsible for the views we express about Education 2000.

### References

CAMBRIDGE UNIVERSITY PRESS (CUP) (1983) *A Consultative Document on Hypotheses for Education in the year 2000*, Cambridge, CUP.

COOK, P. and DALTON, R. (1989) 'Schools and communities: The Hertfordshire Education 2000 project', in SAYER, J. and WILLIAMS, V. (Eds) *Schools and External Relations: Managing the New Relationships*, London, Cassell, pp. 116–28.

KNIGHT, B. (1991) 'Seeds of achievement', *Education Magazine*, 11 January 1991, p. 36.

*Chapter 7*

# A Consortium Approach to Staff Development

*Peter Upton and Phil Cozens*

Not everything that counts can be counted and not everything that can be counted counts. *Albert Einstein* (quoted in Herman, 1992, p. v)

The past is never dead, it's not even past. *William Faulkner* (*Requiem for a Nun*, 1953, Act 1, Scene 3)

## Introduction

This chapter examines the structure, effectiveness and micro-politics of a consortium approach towards staff development. In particular, it seeks to highlight the attitudinal tensions that emerged as schools sought to rationalize the benefits of collaboration in a local context of increased competition. It examines the challenges which emerged including a questioning of existing management systems, of hierarchical perceptions, of the effectiveness of staff development as well as issues relating to the nature of the development-planning process in schools. What individual staff wanted, needed or even hoped for was not being systematically provided for and nor were whole-school issues being resolved through training. Staff development was in danger of believing its own mythology of individual development, yet despite some failures and limitations, what did emerge from the process of consortium working was a structure for progress and a means by which entitlement to training became a system of liberation. The work of Rudduck (1992) suggests similar tensions between universities and schools seeking to establish partnership programmes and the fault line that is common to both is the unwillingness to translate philosophy and principle into daily practice. This chapter also gives further strength to the analysis of Fullan (1991) in his critique of staff development. Fullan was concerned by the often hierarchical nature of staff development, in its use as a form of power brokering within organizations and the strictly limited relationship and impact upon the learning needs of staff and pupils. The experience of the Confederation confirms the fears of Fullan that the gap between rhetoric and reality of staff development or collaboration is still too wide.

**The Context**

The North East Coastal Confederation of Secondary Schools was launched by Professor Tim Brighouse in 1990. It consists of a partnership of five NE Essex secondary schools situated within the Tendring Peninsula. The schools in this partnership are; Clacton County, Colbayns, Harwich, Tendring and Colne School. All are 11–18 mixed comprehensives and all are now grant-maintained. The schools have an average pupil population of 1,300 with over 200 in each sixth form. The catchment of the consortium provides a distinct range of pupils from across all socio-economic backgrounds. Harwich, Clacton and Colbayns are all schools with a focused urban catchment whilst Colne and Tendring draw pupils from a semi-rural area. Tendring District has been awarded 'assisted-area status' in response to the problems of unemployment and the school communities have been pressed into responding to a range of social issues such as the prevention of substance abuse, anti-bullying programmes and sexual-health matters. The Tendring Peninsula is an isolated geographical area and this has impacted upon local economic, social and educational opportunities. More importantly it has had a particular impact upon the attitudes of headteachers as well as those colleagues involved in leadership decisions more generally. All five heads were male at the time of the launch of the Confederation and the leadership groupings of senior staff in all five schools were, and remain, predictably dominated by men. The issue of gender balance was to remain an unresolved tension within the culture of the Confederation. One that was to percolate through a range of issues including the management of staff development. In 1990 three of the heads had been in post for a protracted period of time although two were new to the Confederation. Taken together with a stable and consequently ageing staff structure, all these factors exacerbated the sense of isolation and unease in the management of new ideas. An established staff does not have to be innately conservative, however, it is easier for a static mind set to become rooted in such an environment, especially when aided by the widespread staff perception of remoteness from the mainstream of educational culture. This was clearly illustrated when the Confederation, which sought to champion the notion of collaboration and the culture of collegiality, refused to allow another school to join their partnership because it would dilute their effectiveness, or so it was claimed. One observer was more acerbic suggesting that it was more concerned with the maintenance of privilege and an all-male leadership model than any concern over quality. What the rejection of an extended partnership did reveal was the unstated exclusivity of the grouping. The school that sought to join the partnership was 11–16 and based in Colchester. Its catchment area was depressed and the female headteacher was seeking to develop a network of partners for cooperation. The rejection was based on geography (Tendring vs Colchester), perceived school status (11–16 vs 11–18) and more importantly school effectiveness (Confederation schools were successful and perhaps . . . ). Collaboration was to be explicitly limited within the strict parameters of the Confederation, interestingly it was a manifestation of the same practice which the Confederation has so bitterly criticized Essex LEA for displaying.

The Confederation evolved as a loose alliance between the five schools. Initially this was for reasons of mutual protection, as a response to frustrations with Essex LEA and as a means by which the cancer of local competition could be resisted. Each of the schools had distinct management systems that ranged from a highly centralized directive mode to a flexible devolved model of accountability. These variations in management style reflected fundamental differences in attitudes and expectations that touched all aspects of school life from curriculum planning to external relationships. The Confederation was not united by deep-rooted principle or philosophy but by the climate of educational uncertainty and an abiding belief that collaboration was superior to competition. Support for collaboration, both as a value system and as a guiding principle, was in practice to transcend the differences between the schools leading towards a collegiate culture. Currently, many headteachers view collaboration, whether between organizations or within their own school communities, as a means by which predetermined outcomes can be realized through a veneer of consultation. In its most sophisticated form, collaboration can enable a sharing of ideas, an openness of debate and a critical reflection by those who hold power. This can develop a culture of collegiality which celebrates the sharing of professional values and not the imposition of an educational culture determined solely by those who hold authority within a school. Nevertheless, considerable confusion exists between the notions of *collaboration* and *collegiality*.

Collaboration is a structural response which seeks, in its most positive form, to generate a partnership of understanding and an environment of tolerance to ideas and practice. Collegiality is concerned with the culture of professionalism, with the creation of an ethos that shares power, generates serious professional dialogue and abandons the arbitrary notions of hierarchy. It is not to be equated with the absence of professional educational management but rather its logical outcome is in the liberation of the skills of professionals within our educational communities. This is the true task of educational leaders and managers. Many decision makers within the Confederation; headteachers, faculty managers and heads of year, believed that any form of collaboration would immediately, almost magically, create a collegiate atmosphere of mutual respect, dissipating the tensions and frustrations surrounding many schools and their communities. Such could not be the case, for collegiality is not a quality like loyalty that is, in essence unthinking. Collegiality demands a positive, non posturing approach to problem-solving from all those who have power and influence in school communities. Moreover, it requires a willingness to be open to the ideas of others especially those who have no power. The language of collegiality is easy but the practice is demanding. What headteachers and others in the Confederation wanted was the culture of collegiality but they framed their organizational thinking, their language and their structures around the principle of collaboration. As a group they understood collaboration in terms of harmonizing school structures, and agreeing the limits of collective responsibility and authority. It was, in essence, a mechanistic response to a mutuality of need which would lead, so they believed, to increased understanding between schools and, therefore, a collegiate culture.

### Schools and the LEA

There existed within all of these school communities a powerful belief that the LEA was unsympathetic to their needs, that their distance from the centre of power in Chelmsford meant that they were either ignored or marginalized. However, at a deeper level this attitude towards the LEA was somewhat inconsistent. It was entrenched in the dual notion that the LEA was simultaneously too interfering and too directive, yet lacking vision and leadership as well as not encouraging the Confederation to become a model for future LEA development with schools. Colleagues in the Confederation believed that they had pioneered an alternative structure for school development, one that should have been recognized in Chelmsford and supported with LEA funding. There was a clear sense of missed opportunity and envy, that once again an interesting and promising initiative was ignored because it was too far from the centre of LEA power, too remote from the mainstream. The Confederation could only have achieved the recognition it sought through a highly centralized and autocratic model of LEA leadership. The CEO for Essex was endeavouring to move towards a more dispersed and regional approach to management in response to concerns that the LEA was too remote. Both the Confederation and the LEA were victims of their own perceptions of recent experience. The 1991 debacle concerning the freezing of all staff-development budgets by the LEA, was an example of this. In January of that year, all school INSET budgets were frozen and staff development ceased. The Confederation schools viewed this episode as an example of LEA mismanagement especially when it was suggested that the budgetary problems were the fault of headteachers. The LEA was trapped with limited funding, increasing demands and an increasingly fractious relationship with heads. Both groups refused to acknowledge the national political dimension which had generated the preconditions for this conflict and they merely retreated to an exchange of abusive statements. There were also jealousies that schools in other parts of the County appeared to be more favoured and a widely articulated view that the schools in the Tendring District had not received their fair share of the resources. The reality of this claim is hard to assess and in many ways it is irrelevant, for the sense of dislocation from the centre was too strong and already too entrenched. When a consortium of schools in Billericay was given some LEA officer support, this was seen as a definitive testimony to the notion that the LEA did not value the work of the Confederation, even though it had already developed a living, working structure far more sophisticated than that which the LEA was supporting. The key point is that the Confederation did have a legitimate perception that the LEA system was failing them at the very moment of a national shift in the educational climate. In north-east Essex this perception was a springboard for GM status.

The sense of geographical isolation enabled the Confederation to promote its own particular responses to the issues which confronted them. The governing bodies of all the schools reflected this insularity with policies being discussed in narrow terms and the work of the LEA often caricatured as alien and irrelevant. In this context, the schools were ripe for the GM message of supposed independence from interfering LEAs or in this instance allegedly negligent ones. The appointment of two new headteachers to the Coastal Schools in 1991 challenged some of the existing traditions and practice, and in particular gave rise to a wide-ranging discussion about the effectiveness of staff development. This debate touched on questions surrounding staff competence but more importantly on the exercise of power within the school, on the willingness to engage in genuine collaboration and on the move towards a critical approach to school effectiveness through action research. Exposed in this debate was the need for a flexible approach to the Confederation and for the notion of collegiality to be actively developed rather than assumed as the natural product of collaboration. It laid bare many of the conflicts and contradictions that surrounded national issues.

The Confederation was, therefore, rooted in local networks, insular in its outlook and confronting a series of tensions within its own hinterland. It was within this context that the Training Agency emerged as a means by which orthodoxy was to be challenged.

### Power Structures and Staff Development Before the Training Agency

The management of the Confederation had been located within a headteachers' steering group. At half termly meetings, the five heads were supposed to have oversight of general policy and direction. The reality was that the group were reactive to issues as they arose and operated as a clearing house for the resolution of potential friction between schools. Through the sharing of information, through an appreciation of the factors affecting individual schools there would be less opportunity, it was believed, for an individual organization's response to be perceived as threatening to the Confederation. It was a tokenist approach but one that was essential for providing a platform of understanding and trust from which future developments could emerge. The main problem was that the Confederation had not articulated its overall strategy and had not agreed how to resolve points of conflict. Should tensions be resolved through a voting system and if so, how did this fit with the role and power of governors? In essence, the Confederation had already moved beyond its initial remit as a loose alliance and stood on the threshold of determining whether to move into a more dynamic and assertive form of partnership or to remain static. The problem was, of course, that genuine partnership requires a willingness to compromise, to see overall benefits rather than individual ones. In particular this would become sharply focused in the debate over the role and management of the Training Agency.

A common thread of discussion amongst the heads was the effectiveness of staff training. In particular, the deputies' groups currently managing training were not operating in harmony with the heads and appeared to have a misplaced understanding of their role. Whilst this confusion was understandable given the absence of clear planning and direction, there were wider concerns emerging. All five heads were interested in the concept of school improvement and two had raised the issue of creating genuine learning communities. This demanded a highly motivated, flexible and responsive teaching force. At the same time concerns over staff recruitment, the changing demands of the National Curriculum and the increased level of competition between schools focused the debate over staff development. All of the heads accepted that this, the challenge of creating a community of professional teachers encouraged to sustain critical reflection through staff development, was a fundamental strand. It could provide a living reality to the principle of collaboration. It could lead to the culture of collegiality and the only question was how to achieve it.

Prior to the establishment of a Training Agency, staff development had operated as a flexible network managed by five deputy heads, one from each of the Confederation schools. A one-day conference for all Confederation teachers was held annually and departments met on a termly basis in different schools. The basis of training was localized, subject-driven and had no relationship to whole-school issues or to inter-school challenges. There was no agreement concerning the allocation of time for differing activities or priorities. The annual conferences were popular with up to 400 staff attending a day's INSET on broad themes with option workshops. Nationally known speakers such as Tim Brighouse, professor of education at Keele and Bill Laar, the Chief Inspector for Westminster were heard but whilst the groupings provided a physical testament to the principle of collaboration the reality was different. It was, in essence, a reductionist approach to staff training based on the idea that familiarity with other colleagues would provide a catalyst to real collaboration. At best it was an illusory notion and at worst it was a cynical exercise of control. The label of collegiality and collaboration was branded to all activities but the veneer of language was soon eroded. Staff demands were not to be blunted by the propaganda of collegiality when the daily reality meant that teaching staff were being expected to deliver more. Some staff were claiming that consultation on development and training was more curtailed within the Confederation than when schools operated independently. The climate in which teachers were operating had become politicized and challenging now that the concept of school effectiveness, league tables and performance-related pay stood starkly on the horizon as another perceived threat. Collaboration sits uneasily with the fear of unemployment. For some, training and staff development was a release from the frustration of the classroom whilst for others it was a means for occupational mobility, it was a crucial element in the mind set of the majority of teachers in the Confederation. Evidence was to show that staff perceived that the allocation of training to be random, unrelated to developmental needs and more concerned with status levels within the differing schools.

Staff development was seen as the preserve of a core group of deputies who in turn viewed this role as a means by which their power and influence could be maintained and legitimized. It was a defining element of status in an uncertain world but moreover, if deputies determined the who, what and when of training and development it derived from their own concepts and not those of departments, nor those of individuals or schools. Whilst there were areas in which there was harmony between departmental needs and the provision made by the deputy's steering group, there were large areas of discord. Some of the deputies originally responsible for the management of staff development believed that they were exercising their authority in a reasoned and rational manner but there was unease amongst the headteachers group who felt that an alternative power system was beginning to emerge. The lack of effective management and direction for the Confederation was creating the conditions for misunderstanding and friction between heads and some deputies. This was a structural as well as a philosophical problem. The absence of debate about the role and remit of the deputies steering group, the poverty of information being exchanged between the heads and deputies group was unhelpful. Poor organization and strategy combined with a traditional series of values to frustrate progress. Some deputies felt that they were better informed about staff needs than the heads. They saw any intrusion into this area as a lack of trust and an unwillingness to delegate by heads, a characteristic which sat uneasily against a collegiate or collaborative approach. Whilst they may indeed have had a better perspective than the heads, their response was still based upon their own perceptions. No research, no audit of staff needs had been conducted nor was it considered necessary. Without a clear vision or direction, with the absence of any sense of corporate belief, the Deputies Steering Group was not operating to a negotiated agenda. It was not a matter of trust but rather one of principle, as to the very role and function of staff development. The Deputies Steering Group did not seek to challenge the individual power of the heads of schools but their actions did strike a counterpoint to the principle and reality of collaboration, particularly when they took to commenting critically on different schools and their management systems. This tension was further exposed when overt criticism was made of one school that was seeking to manage a growing element of competition through a more sophisticated marketing strategy. Rather than uniting and celebrating the success of one school as a reflection of collective strength it was viewed with hostility. What was emerging from this early practice was that a steering group managed and maintained by a small core of deputies without guiding principles, without an overall strategy and without an agreed pattern of leadership was incapable of providing staff development in a coherent manner. Some teaching colleagues perceived the situation as an abuse of power. Those deputies who controlled INSET were able to demonstrate their influence within school communities in a direct and daily manner. It was a system based upon grace and favour rather than on the needs of individual members of staff, departments or the overall strategic needs of each of the schools. It bore no connection with whole-school development planning and was purely reactive, as one teacher commented 'the future has been placed on hold'.

### The Establishment of the Training Agency

With the arrival of two new heads to the Confederation, the opportunity arose for a review of the practice and politics of partnership. A systematic audit of all aspects of the Confederation was undertaken. It was a moment when past practice could be assessed and future development planned. The problem for the heads was to determine what shape the Confederation should have, how it should respond to the pressure for GM and the apparent implosion of the LEA. A fundamental principle was being confronted, namely should the Confederation operate from the basis of being a loose mutually defensive alliance which would ensure that the five schools would not compete with each other and which would allow for staff development based upon a sharing of information or should it seek a more determined pathway. To do so would require a changed mind set, a willingness to think about partnership in new terms with a recognition that the reality would require a level of compromise previously uncalled for. It also demanded the recognition that the rhetoric of the Confederation fell far short in its daily reality for students, staff and parents. Such a leap of thinking is not to be underestimated for the willingness to yield power is the hallmark of partnership. The LEA was under pressure and in retreat as many of its flagship schools opted for GM, a seemingly attractive world of independence and autonomy was marketed under the GM brand name and the fear for the Confederation, was that any complex partnership might just re-invent the bureaucracy and attendant alienation of a mini LEA. All these were powerful ghosts at the debating table concerning the future direction of the Confederation. The safest option was a loose alliance but that posed the possibility of schools within the group forming new patterns of relationships elsewhere, it might not be strong enough to cement a working partnership. There was a clear recognition that the Confederation had to be concerned with partnership, and partnership was a positive not a defensive response, it demanded a living philosophy that could be seen and evaluated. The group was endeavouring to rationalize the twin strands of on the one hand insularity with its emphasis on loose federal relationships and on the other partnership with its emphasis upon sharing power, flexible structures of authority and most importantly, taking risks.

In the autumn of 1991 the Heads Steering Group began the process of systematic review. Discussions took place on the coordination of strategy towards GM and visits were arranged to Stantonbury Campus and other schools. A review of working practice with the LEA occurred and research was carried out into alternative patterns of relationship with the LEA and other providers of supports. A member of the management team of one of the schools was seconded for a term to investigate the possibility of all five schools becoming community colleges and a series of conferences were held by the heads to examine a range of policy options. A joint meeting of the chair and vice-chairs of governing bodies of the schools took place and throughout this period, the debate was focused sharply on the issue of power relationships between the schools. Each head undertook research into a key policy area and ultimately this led to fundamental decisions being made about future strategic direction. This process demanded a willingness to confront new possibilities and the debate was wide-ranging, tense yet ultimately constructive.

It was agreed that each head would oversee a key area of policy direction and these were determined as 'training', 'resources', 'curriculum', 'community' and 'management'. Each head would lead a mixed team of staff representing each of the schools to manage these responsibilities. What was being agreed was that a head from one school would lead and coordinate the work of the other schools in a targeted field such as staff development or resources. Partnership was being put into practice through a culture of common cause and compromise. The recognition that change is a means of growth had become rooted within the thinking of the heads group. At the heart of this was the desire to use the Confederation as a means of enhancing school effectiveness. Such a structure could, it was believed, provide the framework by which collectively and individually schools could embrace the principle and practice of a genuine learning community through collegiality. The development of quality schools demands a critical reflection, a willingness to challenge preconceived notions, the need to provide for a critical mass for staff development and this structure would, they believed, provide and promote the guidelines for this. This did not imply that there had to be a synchronization of the curriculum or that the five schools were seeking to achieve a uniformity of response. They sought to build upon common factors, whether at Key Stage 4 or in response to post-16 issues, or in the provision of agreed homework policies or in meeting students rights and responsibilities. The Confederation was seeking to provide an ethos of entitlement that spanned five schools.

The central problem remained power. This model of working practice demanded that some power was devolved to other leaders and managers. Would they operate with the same care and core concern for the interests of each school? Could they or would they be able to understand the unique blend of influences that affected the judgments made by heads rooted in their own culture? Who would pick up the debris for failure and who would be accountable? Would the opportunity to promote a fresh perspective, a new working pattern and new relationships generate the momentum for further development? The real question was whether this strategy would lead to any improvement in the quality of learning or whether it was a structural response to a fundamentally cultural issue and as such promote only the mirage and not the substance of change. The work of Fullan (1991), Smyth (1993) and Leithwood *et al.* (1994) offers ample evidence of structural responses to the problems of school culture. Furthermore, a collaborative strategy was in opposition to the current trend of celebrating the individuality and independence of power for schools, particularly heads and governing bodies. It also raised sensitive issues with regard to governors who whilst supporting the Confederation in principle might become concerned at the perceived loss of individual institutional independence. The heads group, however, agreed that in points of dispute a four-to-one majority would be needed to implement plans. That this agreement took place was testament to a shift in the cultural perception of the heads, for they were willing to accept the reality of supporting a programme which individually they may have wished to oppose. These principles were to be tested with the Training Agency as a clash over power, culture and conformity ensued.

### The Training Agency: Power, Progress and Success?

One of the decisions that emerged from the review was the establishment of Training Agency for Staff Development. From the outset it was characterized by a fundamentally different agenda to that which had gone before for it sought to articulate the real needs of staff, pupils and the school community. The areas of broad concern were identified as:

1  Staff development must reflect the strategic needs of the Confederation such as differentiation, national curriculum planning and special needs.
2  Staff development must respond to whole-school developments for individual partner schools.
3  Training must be provided for improved classroom performance.
4  Development must enable individual growth for teaching colleagues.
5  Access to training development must be 'transparent'.

This agenda was broadly agreed by the heads and then devolved to the lead school for this policy area. Staff development was to be available to all those who worked within the community of the schools, teaching and associate staff. A development plan was to be created that would highlight clearly defined strands of training. These strands identified four main themes for development: firstly, those issues which required training across the Confederation; secondly, those that were rooted in the individual needs of partner schools; thirdly, those that were a response to the needs of middle managers in individual departments and finally, those that were to enable individual growth and extension for all staff. The opportunity to build interweaving networks between these strands was clearly available. The agency would be able to commission courses, establish staff-development programmes and initiate action research. The opportunities seemed limitless with an 'internal market' of over 400 teachers and 100 associate staff and a combined staff-training budget of over £150,000 (after the transition to GM status this rose to a possible budget of £350,000). The problems that quickly arose were articulated in terms of relevance, evaluation, assessment and quality but they are more easily translated into a single reality, for it was at root a question of power relationships. Who controlled the resourcing and who made the decisions? Thus, the Training Agency was to be the testing ground for the principle and practice of partnership.

The appointment of one of the heads to lead the Training Agency ruffled the professional feathers of the Deputies Steering Group. The composition of this group had not changed and they persisted with the same attitudes claiming that now the leadership was devolved to one of the heads, it undermined their own competence and standing. The structure was to be different but the issue of how to change the culture remained. The early meetings of the group with the head were formal and restrained. It was agreed that the deputy from the newly appointed heads school would act as convener to the group and professional secretarial support would be provided. This approach touched a range of tensions, the deputy convening the group was the youngest colleague present and was met with some hostility from older counterparts. The secretarial support was seen as 'educational yuppyism', inappropriate to a professional group. The demand for a coherent staff-development plan that spanned the Confederation was regarded as both unwise and unnecessary. The belief that staff development had worked well previously persisted: as one of these colleagues pointed out at the meeting 'If it ain't broke don't fix it.' There was inevitable some tension when he was offered a variation on this theme; 'We used to say if it ain't broke don't fix it, well actually what we should be saying is fix it anyway because you just haven't seen what the problem is.'

Whilst the Training Agency steering group was coming to terms with a range of new demands, research was commissioned into the effectiveness and validity of staff development. An advisor from Essex LEA was asked to examine staff perceptions concerning the Confederation, the role of INSET and the availability of information on course opportunities. The adviser was familiar with all of the schools and proposed a detailed audit. She interviewed the deputy responsible for training in each school, enquiring about the organization, evaluation and information concerning development opportunities. She was particularly interested to determine how staff were able to gain access to training facilities and whether the Confederation was seen as an effective provider of such courses. This information was then tested by interviewing samples of teaching staff to assess their perspective on the issue. She sought to examine the relationship between the rhetoric as claims made for training with the reality. The results whilst not surprising were nevertheless disturbing and they mirrored the research by Fullan (1991, p. 316) who found that staff development failed for a complex matrix of reasons including lack of relevance, poor follow-up to training as well as an absence of response to individual concerns. Staff did not perceive the Confederation as important for training opportunities for the following:

1   Staff development was seen as a closed garden with staff unaware of training opportunities.
2   Some staff believed that training was allocated by individual whim and not school needs.
3   Some believed that it was a means by which senior staff could pursue their own career paths by organizing courses which they then led.
4   Training was not linked to development plans either for departments or whole-school issues.
5   Some staff bemoaned the absence of a professional and organized programme of personal development when they had been in post for a protracted period of time.
6   Some staff claimed that they were not being trained for the tasks they were asked to undertake.
7   Many staff claimed that training was random, lacked follow-up and was not relevant to their needs.
8   Some staff claimed there was an absence of genuine discussion about what staff development was needed.

The fabric of collegiality was threadbare. Whilst such perceptions are common to most educational communities and communications can always be improved, the difference here was the breadth and depth of opinion that suggested that staff development was not open, accessible, relevant or even effectively targeted. The research provided the evidence for the reform of staff training, legitimizing the quest for a changed culture of development which the heads were seeking. Staff were articulating the divergence between expectation and delivery, they were in essence demanding that the Confederation live up to its potential. Hopkins *et al.* (1994), Fullan (1991) and Leithwood *et al.* (1994) have all identified problems with the provision of staff development whether by school communities or external institutional providers. The problems within the Confederation, however, took on a new dimension for staff development was seen as the cornerstone of collaboration and had to be made to work. Whether the perception of staff was legitimate or not was not relevant. The perception had become the common currency of expectation and as such it had to be challenged and changed.

Thus, the evidence was available that training was at best random and at worst irrelevant to individual and group needs; that the main plank of success was a network approach between differing schools on a departmental level; and that progress must be achieved across a wider spectrum of training. This focused the problem directly onto the managers of staff training and how change was to be affected. The senior personnel in this group had not changed and yet they would be expected to bring about a fundamental shift in thinking, planning and delivery. The expectation was that those who were most resistant to change would be in the vanguard of new patterns of training. It was a delicate balance between professional trust and creating the opportunities for development.

The steering group overseeing staff training and development began work on a planned programme of development. It was important to consider how to meet the strands of training and how to resource them without falling into political snares or claims of spending without accountability. The research had shown that the networking approach had been widely supported although it had operated at an unsophisticated level. The evidence revealed that the network operated as a clearing house for information and ideas. Whilst useful in its existing pattern it also had the potential to act as a catalyst for a much wider debate. The steering group recognized the need to formalize the network of departmental meetings between schools. This would be supported through the allocation of funding, the provision of supply cover and was also given sharper focus by linking the meetings into issues that touched the whole Confederation. In essence, this was to become the fifth strand which unified the other four dimensions of training. Discussion and debate was not to be confined to local departmental interests, though this was still relevant. All departments were required to advise on homework policies, ethos, attitudes towards teaching and learning. The Confederation was thus generating a dialogue within departments and across schools about fundamental issues affecting classroom culture and the effectiveness of teaching. These groups became a means by which discussion into the quality of educational provision began to impact upon classroom thinking. It also enabled the Confederation to develop common approaches to issues such as testing and changes to the National Curriculum. Breaking down the insularity of individual departments through exposure to a challenging range of different perspectives was a means by which professional attitudes and expectations could be and were transformed. The extension of this network approach was important for it reflected the commonality of issues affecting the Confederation and yet was taking place within a safe and secure context. The problem was in the management of ideas, the channelling of debate and ensuring that agreement on issues did not operate from the lowest common denominator. This raised a host of related problems such as training for leadership, chairing and listening skills as well as how to absorb opinions from departments. This strand of training was developing its own inertia for it touched the professional core concerns of teachers. With over twelve differing departmental groups meeting on a half-termly basis, the networking of ideas was positive. The next logical step was to encourage teacher exchanges between schools and this took place with several colleagues working in different schools for a period of time. It also allowed new teachers to see the work of departments in other schools and created a sense of place, a sense that the Confederation was special.

The successful extension of the networking approach enabled critical debate to occur beyond an individual department; it was actively encouraging teachers to remain as reflective practitioners within an increasingly creative educational climate. The fact that the network was successful stemmed from the security of its departmental root and the extension into whole-school or Confederation issues was not confrontational or personally challenging. Departmental networking was never seen as a threatening development. The Training Agency steering group could see and accept the legitimacy and logic of such a role. They sought to manage this in a reasoned manner but this networking led to demands for training, for the provision of specialist courses and a more critical appraisal of staff development.

Whilst the expansion of departmental networking was taking place, an intense debate was being held within the steering group. What form should the development plan take? How could non-teaching staff be involved in training for professionals and anyway, where was the funding to come from? Who was to determine what were issues for the whole Confederation and who had mandated the funding for this? Debate intensified when the judgment was made that the development plan would include a statement of principles, an articulated value system, an outline of the differing strands of training and the means by which they were to be evaluated. The plan was to be made available to all staff for if partnership was to be real, all of those who had a stake in staff training needed to be able to comment upon it. Discussion on these features was powerful with questions raised on the following issues: if all staff had access to the plan it could it become a vehicle for criticism? Would it not lead to a climate of false expectation with staff anticipating training that they may not be entitled to? How could values be articulated for five schools and was this not a responsibility of governors? These were a selection of the issues raised in the discussions about the plan, it was, in fact, a debate about accountability and responsibility, about openness and the ability to reach out beyond current limitations.

Within a few meetings the Training Agency steering group was openly split with two distinct and conflicting views. One group supported the ideals surrounding the development plan and the shift towards a more professional service for staff training. The countervailing view was that the plan was misplaced and over ambitious, that it could not meet the needs it sought to address but moreover, it was forcing schools to yield a level of independence beyond the remit of heads to determine. This latent conflict was now made explicit and individuals sought to articulate their views and perspectives to their own heads. It was a defining moment for the Confederation and for the heads group. Would they bypass the conflict and seek to ameliorate the tension through some compromise? Would they support their nominated colleague and accept the risk of some alienated senior staff? The heads group was not surprised by the conflict, the shift in thinking about the principles of collaboration had been difficult for them and they expected others would find it as demanding. Their debate about the future of the Training Agency and its organization was thorough, systematic and thoughtful. They were committed to staff development as a means of generating school improvement, they were committed to an expansion of staff training but they were also aware that some deputies might lose status if plans continued. They agreed to maintain their original principles but determined to change some of the staff serving on the steering group of the agency. However, whilst upholding their original values they were also under pressure over funding. It was suggested to them that the tensions within the Training Agency were a reflection of the same issues of conflict that had driven them from the LEA. Was this not abrogating financial independence for training without direct control of the quality, structure and systems for delivery? Was it not moving the focus away from the needs of the schools, and thereby, the teachers, to a possibly remote Training Agency? Whilst much of this was extreme and unfounded it did strike a chord of concern especially with some colleagues whose recent memories of relationships with the LEA were less than cordial. The end result was that whilst the strands of training were supported and maintained, the pattern of funding was to be changed. A percentage of the training budget was to be allocated for each strand, although each school would retain control over its own funding. The agency would act as the vehicle for delivery of all training. It could still commission courses, organize conferences and determine the priorities but its position had been limited by its ability to find the consensus of need. This was a necessary compromise, illustrating collegiality and partnership in practice. The principles were sustained but the need for flexibility and the need to build upon successful relationships were recognized.

The Training Agency moved quickly beyond this point of conflict and a development plan was agreed. The pattern and nature of training provision underwent reform. The new structure ensured that all staff were made aware of new courses, guaranteed an entitlement to training for all and provided a critical evaluation of the quality of provision. Each year, key areas were identified that affected the Confederation and were made a priority for development. Staff were actively encouraged to seek out the training package that was most appropriate to them, departments were provided with closely tailored courses using a mixed economy of outside support and internal staff skills. The strategic areas for training were agreed between the heads and the Training Agency steering group and they included themes as diverse as staff rights and responsibilities to the provision of agreed strategies for sex education. Staff training had emerged from the secret garden and moved into the open fields of entitlement. Leadership and management training were provided across the Confederation and the needs of staff were being systematically assessed. Action research was emerging as a means by which further developmental work could be promoted. The need to ensure that female colleagues were actively supported and trained for promotion became a major element of concern as did the issues surrounding the management of student behaviour to eliminate bullying. Schools began to consider whether 'total quality management' should become the hallmark of their work. The Training Agency continued to reach out and provide a range of courses that met a complex pattern of needs. The quality and breadth of training has engendered much positive comment. Non-teaching staff were provided with their own course of development and wherever possible they were involved in the preparation and delivery of support programmes. Staff development was recognized by teaching colleagues as the means for professional enhancement and not a professional chore. There were, of course, failures, courses that did not succeed but instead of returning to school and making negative comments, the consistent expectation was to make specific recommendations so as to improve the core activity, to ensure quality. Staff training was portrayed as a collective responsibility where evaluation, preparation, content, delivery and attendance were all part of seamless cloak of partnership and collegiality. The Training Agency moved into the role of quality management, diversity of provision and a commitment to entitlement. It placed the concept of professional development and lifelong learning at the heart of all its work and the results were impressive. It was this that enabled the Confederation to work in partnership with Suffolk College, itself an associate college of the University of East Anglia to deliver a SCITT (School Centred Initial Teacher Training) programme in 1994. The success of the bid for SCITT was due to the generation of professional self-confidence amongst staff, to the successful networking between departments but most importantly to the changing culture within the Confederation that sought to embrace creative and innovative developments rather than reject them. The SCITT scheme was seen as opportunity to further enhance the professional development of colleagues through collaboration with Suffolk College and UEA but moreover, it reflected the willingness to meet the challenge of new partnerships.

There were key factors that enabled the Confederation to develop a model of partnership and these were:

1   Partnership was recognized as power sharing not posturing.
2   The Training Agency for staff development was concerned with the principle of entitlement.
3   Staff development was a collective responsibility that needed to be shared with and by all.
4   Structures need to be flexible and responsive to local needs.
5   Leadership from heads was crucial in creating the climate for success.
6   Critical reflection and evaluation are essential tools for legitimizing action and improving the service.
7   Collegiality was a culture that demanded a commitment to all staff from all colleagues.

8  Improvement in the effectiveness of teaching and learning could only be achieved through a commitment to continual staff renewal.

The successful pattern of collaboration which evolved within the Confederation was not a response to geography or pre-existing alliances, nor was it purely a response to a collapsing LEA and the unseemly yet powerful drive for GM status within Essex, these were all, in truth, handicaps to real partnership. Collaboration succeeded because it derived from the need to generate a quality learning community; from the recognition that quality schools are rooted in effective classroom practice and that demands quality of training. Collaboration was both an emotional and critical response to school development. It is capable of being translated to almost any educational environment, all it requires is a willingness to be open, to share power and to focus on the opportunities for collective success rather than individual prowess.

Each and every year all members of the teaching and support staff of all five schools are touched by the work of the Training Agency. The fact that it became successful, that it was able to meet the challenge of balancing individual and group needs was a living testament to the principle of collaboration. At heart, the success of the Confederation was based not only on the principle of collaboration but in the reality that partnership needed a defining expression and that this was to be through the medium of staff development. All five schools were able to avoid the insularity and introspection that has become a feature of much of the educational landscape. Through genuine collegiality rather than informal collaboration, they were able to remove the barriers to development. Collaboration and the culture of collegiality is neither easy nor comfortable if it is to be genuine, for it requires the courage to engage in compromise, to articulate values and to be willing to accept a wider responsibility than the narrowness of one's own horizon. Yet whether this can be sustained, whether the necessary inherent flexibility of thinking and structural responsiveness can be maintained against a background of competition and individuality has yet to be determined.

### References

BAYNE-JARDINE, C. and HOLLY, P. (1994) *Developing Quality Schools*, Lewes, Falmer Press.

FAULKNER, W. (1953) *Requiem for a Nun*, London, Chatto and Windus.

FULLAN, M. (1991) *The New Meaning of Educational Change*, London, Cassell.

FULLAN, M. (1993) *Change Forces*, London, Falmer Press.

HERMAN, J., ASCBACHER, R. and WINTERS, R. (1992) *A Practical Guide to Alternative Assessment*, University of California: The Association for Supervision and Curriculum Development.

HOPKINS, D., AINSCOW, M. and WEST, M. (1994) *School Improvement in an Era of Change*, London, Cassell.

LEITHWOOD, K., BEGLEY, P. and COUSINS, J. (1994) *Developing Expert Leadership for Future Schools*, London, Falmer Press.

RUDDUCK, J. (1992) 'Universities in partnership with schools', in FULLAN, M. and HARGREAVES, A. *Teacher Development And Educational Change*, Lewes, Falmer Press.

SMYTH, J. (1993) *A Socially Critical View of the Self Managing School*, London, Falmer Press.

# Chapter 8

# Collaboration and Competition in Education: Marriage not Divorce

*Sylvia West*

### A Question of Leadership

A county paper 'After the 1988 Act — The Role and Work of the LEA', circulated in January 1989, seemed to indicate a wish on the part of Cambridgeshire heads that the LEA should take a lead in formulating an educational vision and policy:

> The quality of professional leadership from the LEA in the sense of participating and promoting a positive statement of educational values is something which has come through strongly from headteachers as a critically important feature of the LEA role. One headteacher put it as seeking, above all, for 'a signal of an LEA determined to espouse a set of positive ideals about the nature of education and the values it seeks to promote in society at large'. (Cambridgeshire County Council 1989, p. 7)

However, by 1992 that call for leadership seemed no longer so relevant to a third of the county's schools which had sought, or were seeking, to opt out of local-authority control. The picture today is as follows:

| Secondary | Number of pupils | % of GM Schools |
|-----------|------------------|-----------------|
| LEA 28 | 25304 | |
| GM 16 | 15145 | 37.44 |

| Primary | | |
|---------|------------------|-----------------|
| LEA 258 | 54864 | |
| GM 6 | 1879 | 3.31 |

**Voted against by parents:**
Primary 3
Secondary 6

**Rejected by Secretary of State**
Primary 1
Secondary 1

This state of affairs took many of Cambridgeshire's actors and onlookers very much by surprise, for the county, with its history of innovative village colleges, had been leading the way again in the 1980s and 1990s in its support of the self-managing school. No county, it seemed, could have done more to minimize bureaucratic control of schools and to encourage their independence within a local-authority context. John Ferguson, director of Cambridgeshire LEA, reflected on the situation in his address to a group of educationalists, the All Souls Group, in Oxford thus:

> There is . . . [in] Cambridgeshire's story . . . the drive, almost zeal, for self-managing schools. That drive was not intended to challenge the educational framework and fabric of the LEA. The educational philosophy (though never formally articulated) was, and continues to be, about dynamic, powerful connection between self-managing schools, self-managing communities and self-managing individuals. The continuing essential infrastructure of the LEA, which enabled that to take place and develop, was not until recently, in question. Even a year or two ago this self-managing philosophy (which was never meant to be selfish or self-interested) was finding new expression in ideas about a new partnership with heads and governors deliberately being brought in to share in the management of the LEA . . . You might think, therefore, that Cambridgeshire heads and governors, especially those from the village colleges, would have resisted GMS. Initially they did, but they are not immune from resource problems (far from it, we are a county peculiarly badly hit by the curiosities of SSA calculations) and, perhaps more importantly, they have a sense of history moving on and now want to work out, collectively, how to apply enduring ideas of access and entitlement to comprehensive community education in the new world rather than the old. (Ferguson, 1992, paras. 5–7)

### A More Profound Crisis

There is no doubt that John Ferguson was right in identifying two crucial factors in the reasons for the secession: the low SSA (Standard Spending Assessment) and a sense of history hurrying on after the election of April 1992 very much coloured the mood of many of the county's schools in that year. However, at the root of the problem was a more profound social crisis, I would argue, and that was, and is, a crisis of culture in a world in which we can no longer assume common vocabularies and corporate ethical purposes. We have moved into an age in which traditional assumptions and authority are breaking down and we need new vocabularies to replace them. We have traded too long on what Nietzsche calls 'the inherited capital of morality which our forefathers accumulated, and which we squander instead of increasing' (Nietzsche, 1965, p. 11).

In order for any society to have common vocabularies and purposes, the members of that society need to share canons of belief and texts. As MacIntyre underlines in his essay 'The Idea of an Educated Public', there is a need for:

> some large degree . . . of background beliefs and attitudes, informed by the
> widespread reading of a common body of texts . . . accorded a canonical
> status within that particular community. (MacIntyre, 1987, p. 19)

However, for many people the external authorities for such canons no longer
remain: there is an increasing scepticism towards unexamined authority and abso-
lutes. Language has become unloosed from traditional verities in an interrogative
process which stretches from the High Middle Ages to the neo-pragmatism of
postmodernists like Rorty who argue that language is a human creation and does
not correspond to any higher reality or an objective reality 'out there' in the world
(Rorty, 1989). Yet, we still continue to act as if these 'metanarratives' (Lyotard,
1984) or philosophical stories about reality and goodness still underpin our values,
for, if they do not, where does authority lie? The utopian imperative is no longer
convincing:

> Today, these ideologies are exhausted. The events behind this important
> sociological change are complex and varied. Such calamities as the Mos-
> cow Trials, the Nazi-Soviet pact, the concentration camps, the suppression
> of Hungarian workers form one chain; . . . For the radical intelligentsia,
> the old ideologies have lost their 'truth' and their power to persuade. Few
> serious minds believe any longer that one can set down 'blue-prints' and
> through 'social engineering' bring about a new utopia of social harmony.
> At the same time, the older 'counter beliefs' have lost their intellectual
> force as well. (Bell, 1990, p. 293)

Thus, we find ourselves today caught by the loss of faith and ideologies which
in the past could do three things: 'simplify ideas, establish a claim to truth, and, in
the union of the two, demand a commitment to action' (ibid.). I would add on to
Bell's three functions of ideology a fourth: provide a basis for corporate identity,
for the emphasis on a rugged individualism leaves out the notion of collective
responsibilities.

### Third Person Grammar

In the absence of a common language of essential/foundational truths, we have
tended to fall back on a technocratic language and a pseudo-scientific 'third person'
grammar in which abstractions are reified and given status as virtual realities — a
sort of linguistic cyberspace. The ideas which once connected to a sense of human
destiny now attach to abstractions such as the bathetic notion of the market which
has become not only reified, but even deified, by the New Right as the 'new
religion/meta-narrative':

> The blind, unplanned, *uncoordinated wisdom* of the market . . . is
> overwhelmingly *superior* to the well researched, rational, systematic,

well-meaning, cooperative, science-based, forward-looking, statistically respectable plans of government . . . The market system is the greatest generator of national wealth known to mankind: coordinating and *fulfilling the diverse needs* of countless individuals in a way which no human mind or minds could ever comprehend, without coercion, without direction, without bureaucratic interference. (Joseph, 1976, quoted in Lawton, 1989, p. 50 emphasis added)

As a bastard child of the Enlightenment faith in science and reason, the new 'utopia' of the market is more prosaic than its parent: it is to be found in an identification with possessions rather than with great ideals. The ages of reason and progress have translated into the age of technocratic rationality in which consumption closes the circle on imagination and possibility:

We are . . . confronted with one of the most vexing aspects of advanced industrial civilization: the rational character of its irrationality. . . . The prevailing forms of social control are technological in a new sense . . . to the point where even individual protest is affected at its roots. The intellectual and emotional refusal 'to go along' appears neurotic and impotent . . . in a specific sense advanced industrial culture is *more* ideological than its predecessor, inasmuch as today the ideology is in the process of production itself. (Marcuse, 1964/1986, p. 9 and p. 11)

## A Reductive Rational Temper

This reductive rational temper has increasingly pervaded our social institutions, not least our educational institutions, where a managerialist language has almost wholly displaced that of educative and ethical possibilities. Individual and social values are submerged, masked by the 'logic' and imperatives of the virtual reality of the linguistic landscape which language constructs create. Human ends and values are assumed in constructs which focus on pure process and technique: performance takes the place of interrogation of process and/or technique and the 'why' of education shifts to the 'how'.

Greenfield has been perhaps one of the major critics of this abstract/performative focus, a trend in management since the 1950s. As he points out in 'The decline and fall of science in educational administration':

administrative science has devalued the study of human choice and rationality. It has insisted that decision-making be dealt with *as though it were* fully explainable in rational and logical terms. This has allowed administrative science to deal with values surreptitiously, behind a mask of objectivity and impartiality, while denying it is doing so. (Greenfield *et al.*, 1993, p. 152)

Certainly in this climate, the great texts of education have become squeezed out. Teacher training and the professional leadership of LEAs have been almost wholly usurped by a new culture of administration and managerialism. As one head, interviewed in a survey I conducted across seven local authorities for the National Educational Assessment Centre, Oxfordshire, in 1991, commented,

> [the LEA is] very much contemplating its navel, and moving from a philosophical basis to an almost too mechanistic administrative basis. [They] sharpened up and tidied up the administration, maybe at the expense of the esoteric. (quoted in West 1993, p. 47)

This contrasted with his initial experiences within that authority where the LEA had provided collegiality and inspiration:

> ... one came thinking one was entering something special, and indeed one was. ... you became part of a special 'club', a 'professional college', for want of a better phrase, whereby you were mixing fairly regularly with some very inspired people, inspired educators, and the pay-off there was that they were helping me in my development and I was contributing to the growth of the whole. (ibid, p. 48)

### A Culture of 'Exit'

Not only has the shift to the purely administrative silenced a language of professional and educational possibility over recent decades, but the market ideology has also increasingly justified a culture of silent 'exit' (Hirschman, 1970) within the logical imperatives of its competitive systems. Within a market paradigm of choice and diversity of product, individuals need not exchange meanings and views upon a 'product' but cast instead a silent judgment by voting with their feet. Advocates of the free market, like Milton Friedman, think this mechanism applied to schools will make them more efficient for parental 'voice', for example, can only be otherwise expressed through, 'cumbrous political channels' (Friedman, 1955, p. 129).

However, the fact is that whilst voicing one's views through democratic channels may be 'cumbersome', such channels are the only means within which any society professing to uphold democratic ideals can work:

> ... voice is just the opposite of exit. It is a far more 'messy' concept ... it implies articulation of one's critical opinions rather than a private 'secret' vote in the anonymity of the supermarket; ... Voice is political action par excellence ... [and is] what else is the political, and indeed the democratic, process than the digging, the use, and hopefully the slow improvement of these very channels. (Hirschman, 1970, pp. 16–17)

Silent relationships do not foster a political dialogue or interrogation of the status quo; they foster rather manipulative relationships and fragmentation as individuals pursue their own concerns, failing to see, perhaps, in their enjoyment of an apparent autonomy and self-interested freedom, the responsibilities which are the other side of freedom rights in a democracy. Nor does a purely silent and manipulative culture foster the critical discernment and interrogation of 'truth effects' which modern societies need. As our certainties about essential and authoritative Truth in today's plural conditions cede ground to contingence, we need to be able to unpack with discernment the truth effects which a play of language and image in a technological age can create. Indeed, as Bell above underlines, the ideologies and myths of powerful states/movements in this century have shown us how dangerous the suppression of such critical faculties can be.

However, the problem today goes even beyond the manipulations of states or fundamentalist individuals and movements. Global communication systems have decentred such 'authority' in a radical way:

> Global networks remove from the State its unique access to totalising power. A multinational business with incomes greater than the national incomes of some smaller countries of the world can have devastating effects on nations and regions within even first world countries. Individuals, as part of a network, like the butterfly in chaos theory which can be the cause of a hurricane, can subvert the operations of major enterprises and even nations. (Schostak, 1993, p. 3)

> What might seem to be definitively moral or authoritative might simply be perspectival, emanating from systems and networks which have no obvious centre, but rather many changing, competing, conflicting or cooperating centres that endure for a period to be replaced by others . . . Where historically a totalised system has located itself territorially in real space, global networks are virtual. Global systems dance over real territories, the contest is symbolic but the power and the victims are real. As a virtual system globalisation commands the gaze, constructing worlds for the gaze and the desire. It is not concerned with translating the experience of others but rather with producing truth effects that have real consequences for desire. (ibid, pp. 3–4)

Indeed, it is possibly the realization that politics is not sufficiently addressing the needs of today's world which has led to a disillusionment with politics which could prove both an opportunity or a threat to democratic possibilities. I cite Will Hutton (*The Guardian* 21st/22nd January 1995):

> Britain's national affairs are reaching explosive levels of stress. The individualistic, *laissez-faire* values which imbue the economic and political elite have been found wanting — but with the decline of socialism, there seems to be no coherent alternative . . . what binds together the disorders of the British system is a fundamental amorality . . . — to consume now, to pay as little to the commonwealth as possible, to satisfy desires

instantaneously — [which now] must be accompanied by responsibilities
. . . To break out of this cycle of decline and to build cooperative institutions,
Britain must complete the unfinished business of the 17th century and equip
itself with a constitution that permits a new form of economic, social and
political citizenship . . . (Hutton, 1995, p. 21)

### Cambridgeshire and the Self-managing School

Cambridgeshire's fragmentation into GM and LEA schools reflects in a considerable degree the tensions of today's culture and language as I have very briefly
outlined them. In connotations of liberal and anti-bureaucratic language, Cambridgeshire, prior to the GM secession of a third of its schools, doubtlessly believed itself
to be offering a democratic freedom to schools, and in many respects it was. However, what was overlooked in such vocabulary in the 1980s and early 1990s, I
believe, was the narrowness and abstraction of the self-managing vocabulary. Within
its own terms of reference, such language has an internal logic which does not
necessarily relate to social, ethical and political contexts. Such narratives are masked
by a pseudo-scientific third-person grammar such as that evident in a Peat, Marwick
and McLintock consultancy document commissioned by the county in 1990.
Human and communal questions are wholly lost in the mechanistic as the county,
subject to the logic of shrinking services and the imperatives to be efficient within
the market, relates itself as a service provider to the schools as customers:

> We have used the term 'buyer' extensively in compiling the principles
> underpinning the provision of support services. We define 'buyer' as the
> manager of the service which needs to use support services to effect ser-
> vice delivery. A headteacher is a buyer of the support services necessary
> to run a school as a self-managing institution; the support services will
> include (for example) financial, legal and personnel services as well as a
> range of services currently provided from within the Education Department.
> (Cambridgeshire County Council, 1990, pp. 7–8, 3.3).

Clearly such language promotes the notions of people as functions rather than
individuals and of transactional ties rather than ones based on collectively interrog-
ated values: these are assumed. It thus allows for decisions within its abstract terms
of reference which are divorced from narrative in the amoral sense that Hutton
suggests above. When such rationality coincided with the straits that Cambridgeshire schools have found themselves in, the amoral logic became difficult to resist.
Given the removed quality of this language from the narrative of schools and communities, it is hardly surprising, either, that in a county with established community-
college traditions the allegiance of those communities might centre increasingly on
the immediately local. Here, relationships are still likely to be characterized by
first- and second-person vocabularies, by traditions of 'interpretative understanding' and by commonly experienced/contextualized 'canons of belief'. However, in
such a withdrawal, the commitment and mechanisms to establish relations with the

wider and other communities may also be weakened. In other words, if the traditional centre cannot hold, parochialism and self-interest compound the disintegration.

## Self-management Does not Interrogate the Political Context

Self-management has no answer to such problems despite its apparently liberal and anti-bureaucratic language, for its frame of reference does not take account of the political context in which its assumptions are exercised. This lack of awareness is very clearly apparent in the new industry of advice on the self-managing school where the closed frame of reference within which self-management is very often working is missed: it is not individuals who are empowered but the school as a reproductive organ of the performance and efficiency ethic. Lawrence Angus sees a naivety in this respect in texts such as Caldwell's and Spinks' *The Self-Managing School* (1988) or Hargreaves' and Hopkins' *The Empowered School* (1991). What so much of this literature lacks, he argues, is any critique of the broader context in which the self-managed school is operating:

> In essence, Caldwell and Spinks's approach seems devoid of any theoretical or political analysis of educational policy — indeed, it seems to eschew politics . . . For instance, Caldwell and Spinks accept without reservation the notion that 'decentralisation is administrative rather than political, with decisions at the local level being made within a framework of local, state or national policies and guidelines'. (Angus, 1993, p. 20)

Cambridgeshire schools and LEA, slipped into this reductiveness despite its history of inspired educators, such as Henry Morris, the Secretary of Education in Cambridgeshire in the 1920s, 1930s and post-war period and founder of the village college. Morris set his vision into a political/governance context:

> [t]he whole welfare of communities and the vigour and prosperity of their intellectual and social life depend on the extent to which centres of unfettered initiative can be developed within them. In the state, frankly organizing itself as an educational institution, freedom and richness will be secured by the development within the state of large numbers of adult autonomous societies. (Morris, 1926, p. 41)

The focus of Cambridgeshire, as elsewhere, has shifted increasingly to the 'how' of systems and performance rather than the 'why'.

There have, of course, been statements of mission and values, (the Chief Officer's published Mission Statement of 1989, for example). There has been an effort, too, to communicate a quality of education to parents and the community at large. This new openness needed to go further and indeed. Cambridgeshire appeared to be moving towards a more consultative style if one compares the more descriptive and promotional aspect of 'Learning Now' 1988 (an account of the work of school) with 'Shared Values' 1992 (a discussion document on the work and values of community education). In the event, however, even the latter seems to have been increasingly overtaken by a contract culture which requires of the colleges not that they provide 'unfettered initiative' but that they deliver a contract which allows the county to demonstrate 'value for money' against certain criteria. Thus, though a greater window has been provided on the various parts of the service and their aims and objectives, the involvement of local communities in the shaping and the political context of the service has become increasingly limited by performative/efficiency concerns. Without the promotion of collective vocabularies and political owner-ship, self-management remains a limited means of civic participation. It remains ineffective, too, in combating the de-integrative possibilities of the market.

### A Question of High Moral Ground

By the Cambridgeshire's heads' conference of 1992, the divisiveness of the mar-ket's a-, or im-, morality had wrought its effects. One group of heads, for example, indignant at the perceived selfishness of certain schools in the market place, some of which were going GM and thus taking resources away from the LEA, sought to force the issue by asking those present to clarify their moral commitment to certain collective issues. In what was described as a 'litmus test' of this commitment, heads were asked by a show of hands to indicate the real quality of their moral position on certain issues, such as the admission of children with special needs and so on. This assumption by the challenging lobby of the high moral ground, how-ever, still demonstrated a failure on their part to understand the real crisis: this was, and is, the difficulty in today's conditions of answering the question, how do we assert any morally authoritative position? Who or what is the authoritative 'we' in our society?

The question should not have been 'This is right. Who does or does not comply?' but 'Upon what, if anything, do we agree?' or 'What do we feel schools should be trying to achieve and stand for?' Neither the tradition of assumption nor the manipulative silence of the market encourages educational thinking from such a starting point. In the competitive market heads/schools are rather locked into questions like: 'How do we ensure that we are performing efficiently within the market place?' More fundamental thinking is emerging, however, through crisis. However 'messy' the starting point, the 1992 conference marked the rupture of assumption and politeness and registered a *malaise* that something was deeply wrong. The question for the Cambridgeshire heads and the LEA was to consider whether there was any way back to more collective purposes and values, or whether the 'exit' culture was to prevail?

### A Potential Divorce

The answer in the first instance did not appear to be encouraging, for the 1992 con-ference marked a split of the county into two camps: LEASH — LEA Secondary

Heads and GMSHA — Grant Maintained Secondary Heads. Divorce looked inevitable. In the wake of this split, however, a group of GM and LEA heads got together to discuss the need for a 'professional college' which would focus on what might unite schools rather than what might drive them apart. The result was the founding of the Cambridgeshire Secondary Educational Trust — CSET — which represents an experimental dialogic forum in which Heads can take stock and look forward outside traditional structures, habits and assumptions. The membership of CSET recognizes that heads need time to examine educational issues and to be able to relate as a body to whatever groups and events have a bearing on educational policy and resourcing. At its inaugural meeting at the George Hotel, Huntingdon, 18 February 1993, it received the support of thirty-three out of forty-six secondary heads from both GM and LEA sectors. Its inaugural charter includes the following statements:

1   CSET is a new independent professional college which seeks to be constituted as a charitable trust. The Trust is a forum for educational leadership at local and national level. This entails an inspirational and visionary outlook on educational values and issues.
2   The Trust aims to improve understanding of matters of educational quality through a programme of professional development, foresight, advocacy and lobbying. The Trust recognizes the key partnership with students, teachers, parents and governors and builds on shared concerns, not least the learning of individuals throughout their lives.
3   The Trust undertakes to develop effective and coherent networks with other organizations.
4   Membership is open to the heads of Cambridgeshire state-maintained secondary schools and colleges, including special schools and sixth-form colleges.

Not all the wounds of the 1992 conference can be healed by CSET. Some heads will perhaps remain unforgiving of the GM flirtations and adultery and/or the competitive manoeuvres of some neighbouring schools which might have affected their own establishments adversely. It could be said, too, that there is a tacit agreement amongst members not to talk about the causes of the 'marital' difficulties or ruptures of the past but rather to concentrate on what unites schools and challenges them in the present and for the future. There seems to have been almost a tacit agreement not to dwell on financial disparities between GM and LEA schools in order to allow collegiality to re-emerge.

### First Person Grammar

This re-emergent collegiality has been characterized and encouraged by a move away from 'third-person' grammar to that of a 'first-and-second' person grammar. For example, there has been a concentration on heads' biographies and openness about their values and dilemmas, facilitated by a researcher Rob McBride, University of East Anglia, who has interviewed volunteer heads who have subsequently shared those interviews with colleagues. A shared vulnerability and humour have surfaced: indeed at one seminar, one head remarked, that it had been a long time since she had heard so much laughter at heads' meetings.

Whilst it is important that heads regain some professional perspective, the need to extend that perspective to educated and active communities is also paramount. The crises that heads have experienced are now being registered more widely, for example. Given the deepening budgetry crises of counties like Cambridgeshire, there is no doubt that the silenced political tensions are likely to surface acutely in the late 1990s. Already in 1995 and 1996, all Cambridgeshire schools are facing swingeing cuts. A cushion of 4 million from the LEA's balances will not be repeated in 1996/7 and, given that in 1995/6 that this cushion is still not enough to cover teachers' salaries and other inescapables, several further de-integrative imperatives might test the CSET harmonies. On the other hand, the new collegiality and a weariness with 'exit' and competition may well unite all the heads to a greater extent than before. As cuts deepen, the possibility of escape through grant-maintained status is not likely to compensate schools adequately for the reductions in the service. Nor will the use of the 'exit' model for schools or parents (i.e., opting out of LEA control or switching from one school to another) necessarily guarantee an escape from stringencies. There will be few safe havens.

Certainly heads need to feel united, for their contribution will be needed in working with a variety of partners in establishing dialogue and dialectic about the service. 'Reconstructing the state and the economy cannot be the preserve of any one political party' (Hutton, *Guardian*, 21st January, 1995 p. 21); nor can it be the preserve of professionals alone. In the 'silence' and confusion of today, professionals need space to explore what is happening to them and their schools if they are to be effective leaders and partners in the tensions and confusions of today's culture. The questions facing professionals also face parents, governors and the wider community, and, as I have maintained in *Educational Values for School Leadership* (West, 1993), the problems of modern society can only be resolved by the fostering of new civic partnerships: the involvement of education's stakeholders. The political voice and skills of governing bodies and local communities are important elements in this: the only elements at present perhaps that can lift schools out of the sterile concentration of administration and technique: there is in other words a need for the concept of self-management to extend to that of self-governance and co-governance, for without political voice and participation, at the local level the skills of government could so easily be replaced by a tier of technocrats — the accessories of hegemony. We have to begin again in building the democratic process and in unearthing civic awareness from traditional assumptions, paternalism and market silences. I cite again John Ferguson:

> People will realise that securing quality, securing sufficient school places
> in sensible systems of school organisation and securing fair and equal
> access . . . will, in the end have to be dealt with not by market forces . . . but

by some system of *government* where the accountability is discharged and operated locally. . . . One confusion has been to muddle public service with government . . . The prime and prior job of an LEA should really be to decide things, not necessarily to provide things . . . to many people this has all felt fudged and has often smacked of self-interest . . . I think it might be wise to design the next version of local government in education in different bits . . . deciding about school organisation, admission arrangements. . . . securing access . . . The third part would be about securing added value services . . . All the while this new version of local government . . . is coming into existence, the schools themselves will . . . be working out what kind of groupings are best suited to their various purposes . . . most heads think they can only hold for some time . . . Much will depend on how quickly public opinion comes to realise that something must be done. . . . It need not have been like that. But it looks as if it's got to be. I suspect the truth is that we have so neglected participation and understanding of *government* as a nation, that we have got to start virtually all over again. (Ferguson, 1992, paras. 18, 22, 25, 26, 27 and 29, my emphasis)

## References

ANGUS, L. (1993) 'Democratic participation or efficient site management: The social and political location of the self-managing school,' in SMYTH, J. (Ed) *A Socially Critical View of the Self-Managing School*, London, Falmer Press, pp. 11–33.

BELL, D. (1990) 'The end of ideology in the West', in ALEXANDER, J.C. and SEIDMAN, S. (Eds) *Culture and Society*, Cambridge, Cambridge University Press, pp. 290–7.

CALDWELL, B.J. and SPINKS, J.M. (1988) *The Self-Managing School*, Lewes, Falmer Press.

CAMBRIDGESHIRE COUNTY COUNCIL (1988) *Learning Now*, Cambridge, Cambridgeshire Education Department.

CAMBRIDGESHIRE COUNTY COUNCIL (1989) 'After the 1988 Education Act — The Role and Work of the LEA', A Report to the Education Committee, January 1989 from the Chief Education Officer and Head of Corporate Planning.

CAMBRIDGESHIRE COUNTY COUNCIL (1990) *Support Services Review*, Final Report, Vol. 1, prepared by KPMG Peat Marwick McLintock, October.

CAMBRIDGESHIRE COUNTY COUNCIL (1992) *Sharing Values*, Coventry, Community Education Development Centre.

FERGUSON, J. (1992) 'What's left to be governed?', A paper for the 'All Souls' Group', Oxford, October.

FRIEDMAN, M. (1955) 'The role of government in education', in SOLO, R.A. (Ed) *'Economics and the Public Interest'*, Rutgers, New Jersey, University Press.

GREENFIELD, T.B. and RIBBINS, P. (1993) *Greenfield on Educational Administration: Towards a Humane Science*, London, Routledge.

HARGREAVES, D.H. and HOPKINS, D. (1991) *The Empowered School*, London, Cassell.

HIRSCHMAN, A.O. (1970) *Exit, Voice, And Loyalty — Responses to Decline in Firms, Organizations and States*, Harvard University Press.

HUTTON, W. (1995) 'Wrench this place apart', in *The Guardian*, January 21, 22, p. 21.

LAWTON, D. (1989) *Education, Culture and the National Curriculum*, London, Hodder and Stoughton.

LYOTARD, J.-F. (1984) *The Postmodern Condition: A Report on Knowledge*, Manchester, Manchester University Press.

MACINTYRE, A. (1987) 'The idea of an educated public', in HAYDON, G. (Ed) *Education and Values*, London, Institute of Education, London University, pp. 15–36.

MARCUSE, H. (1964/1986) *One Dimensional Man*, London, Routledge and Kegan Paul.

MORRIS, H. (1926) 'Institutionalism and freedom in education', in REE, H. (Ed) (1984) *The Henry Morris Collection*, Cambridge, Cambridge University Press.

NIETZSCHE, F. (1965) *Schopenhauer as Educator*, Indiana, Regnery/Gateway Inc.

RORTY, R. (1989) *Contingency, Irony and Solidarity*, Cambridge, Cambridge University Press.

SCHOSTAK, J. (1993) 'Ways of connecting individual lives with public knowledge', Unrevised working paper given at Ontario University, October.

WEST, S. (1993) *Educational Values for School Leadership*, London, Kogan Page.

# Chapter 9

# Collaboration for School Improvement: The Power of Partnership

*Michael Johnson and Michael Barber*

## Introduction

The 1970s and 1980s have seen a steady decline in the fortunes of the British economy which has led to considerable change in the country's educational needs and priorities. The closure of long-standing heavy industries and the weakening of the manufacturing base has meant that the security of limitless unskilled and semi-skilled employment is no longer an option. Education and training have become a prerequisite for employment and those without education and training face an uncertain future.

Nowhere is the need for change more acute than in the inner-cities where there has been no tradition of continuity in education beyond the statutory leaving age. The educational potential of the pupil population has not changed but the structural stability of the communities and families from which the schools draw their populations has weakened. There are diminishing employment prospects. Young people who would have left school in the past to take jobs in local industries and business find that such jobs have disappeared and they need to understand the changes taking place in their communities and be aware of the need to acquire the appropriate skills for contributing to the society in which they will live in the twenty-first century.

Underachievement and low expectation have long been endemic to the inner-cities. Some local education authorities became increasingly conscious of the need to raise both expectations and the skill level of the workforce. In Stoke-on-Trent in 1989 the question occupying Philip Hunter, Staffordshire's Chief Education Officer, was how the problem could best be addressed. Was it within the capability of the education system to do something about the fact that in some schools less than 20 per cent of the population stayed on in school beyond 16 and less than 3 per cent went on into higher education? At the same time, Tim Brighouse, the newly appointed professor of education at Keele University, was contemplating how the most recent research in school effectiveness and school improvement could be put to best use for the benefit of young people in the local context.

It is hard to remember that until late in the 1970s most people, in the United Kingdom at least, accepted the given wisdom that schools could not much change life chances and that 'heredity' or the influences of 'society' would be the predominant determinant of children's behaviour, aspirations and attainment. With the publication of Michael Rutter's *Fifteen Thousand Hours* in 1979, however, views began to change. The research findings of Rutter and his colleagues not only indicated that schools do make a difference to pupils' attainment but also pointed to particular strategies by means of which schools could improve.

> Schools do indeed have an important impact on children's development and it does matter which school a child attends. Moreover, the results provide strong indications of what are the particular features of school organisation and functioning which make for success. (Rutter, 1979)

Rutter's findings ushered in a decade of research into school effectiveness and school improvement. A series of studies in this country and North America have built on the work of Rutter to reach broad areas of agreement about ways in which school can materially change the achievement and attainment of their pupils.

Discussions began between Tim Brighouse and Philip Hunter, the CEO of Staffordshire, towards the end of 1989 and explored the possibility of a collaborative initiative in secondary education in the northern part of Stoke-on-Trent. The intention was to bring together an education partnership comprising the Local Education Authority (LEA), local universities and colleges, the Careers Service, the local business community and the Training and Enterprise Council (TEC) to support a pilot project which would seek to promote, in three secondary schools, the processes identified in the research findings as important for raising achievement. Funding for the project was sought successfully from the Staffordshire and The Paul Hamlyn Foundation.

The research identifies a number of characteristics which are associated with successful schools. The achievement of quality in teaching and learning is about purposeful leadership at all levels within the school and the creation of a school climate and environment conducive to learning. It involves extending and enriching the school curriculum. It demands teacher commitment, good pupil–teacher relationships and raising the level of expectation the teacher has of the pupil. It requires a school to review and reflect on its own performance and recreate itself as a community where teaching and learning are seen by all the pupils as legitimate activities and the principal purpose of the school. It means involving parents as partners in their children's education. In *The Quality of Schooling: Frameworks for Judgement* (1990), John Gray suggests that 'As a rule schools which do the kinds of things the research suggests make a difference, tend to get better results (however the measures are assessed).' Tim Brighouse cautions us in *The Potteries: Continuity and Change in a Staffordshire Conurbation* (1993), that, 'Research on school effectiveness tells everyone all the characteristics evident in successful schools. What research does not reveal as obviously is how a school can become a place where those characteristics appear.' It was to apply these theories that the Two Towns project was born.

### Origins of the Two Towns Project

The purpose of The Two Towns Project was, therefore, to raise ambitions, expectations and achievement in Burslem and Tunstall, two of the constituent towns of Stoke-on-Trent. The discussions initiated in late 1989 by Tim Brighouse continued through the spring of 1990 and the project was officially launched at a meeting at Haywood High School in September of that year.

Tim Brighouse and Philip Hunter believed that a collaborative school-based initiative would affect for the better the educational culture of the whole community. The three county high schools, Brownhills, Haywood and James Brindley, which serve the towns of Burslem and Tunstall were at the heart of the project. The idea was to implement an initial five-year programme of measures to bring educational success to these city schools. This would be followed by a period of redefinition of goals and the dissemination of practice throughout the county. The goal for teachers was, 'to ensure that their pupils do not adopt fixed views of their own abilities but, rather, come to realise that they have considerable potential which, given motivation and good teaching in an effective school, can be realised' (Mortimore *et al.*, 1988). The strategy was to harness the energies of teachers, pupils and parents of the three schools to improving attitudes and performance and for their efforts to be supported by the LEA, post-16 colleges, the careers service and local universities with funding from The Paul Hamlyn Foundation and the Staffordshire Training and Enterprise Council.

Coordination of the project was and continues to be provided by a steering group chaired by Philip Hunter. This group includes representatives of all participants with administration provided by the project coordinator at Keele. Its role is to determine policy and monitor the progress of the project. A second tier of management, the project-group, also serviced by the coordinator at Keele University, includes representatives of schools, colleges, careers service, universities and the Staffordshire TEC, and is responsible for implementing the decisions of the steering group.

Against a background of comparative failure, where, in 1988, no more than 19 per cent of the school population stayed on in education beyond 16 and less than 5 per cent reached higher education, the steering group set targets for the project to meet. These were as follows:

1    To improve participation rates post-16 by 50 per cent over the first five years of the programme.
2    To improve GCSE examination results by raising the pupil average score for each pupil by 1 point over the same period (using the GCSE grades point system where Grade A = 7 and Grade G = 1).
3    To increase attendance rates by 5 per cent over the whole programme.

Above and beyond these indicators, however, was a much broader and more ambitious agenda, including a strategy, more difficult to monitor and evaluate, which sought to win hearts and minds, to instil the belief that it is possible to promote an achievement philosophy and to improve the education progress and academic success of all pupils in the urban context. The aim was to create a climate where commitment and achievement are celebrated and in which it becomes possible for teachers, pupils and parents to enjoy success, initially in the three high schools and ultimately in the community as a whole.

From the outset there was a drive toward quality in each of the schools. School processes and values have been reviewed and revised and translated into appropriate systems to deliver the desired outcomes. Internal management has been restructured to support the project through, for example, the appointment of project coordinators and identified staff responsible for linking with partner institutions.

The three schools have taken note of the research findings at Keele and elsewhere of characteristics evident in successful schools and have engaged in systematic collective review of their practices with cross-school and cross-phase in-service training. Staff have worked together with enormous commitment to develop an ethos of high expectation which will create lasting, long-term benefit to the regional community by contributing to the adaptable, multi-skilled workforce necessary to move away from the traditional dependence on the mining and pottery industries and provide the kind of educated workforce to drive the more varied economy of the future.

Records of Achievement have been used for each individual pupil with a consistent policy of rewards for good attendance, effort and progress at all levels. The schools have taken imaginative and ambitious initiatives to improve the quality of teaching and learning. They have made fundamental changes in organization, introducing extra posts of responsibility to oversee the project and to create a school climate conducive to pupil achievement and positive behaviour patterns. Every opportunity has been sought to involve parents in the schools and as joint educators of the children. From the outset, there has been a determination to move forward simultaneously with the interests of all three groups involved in raising standards — not only teacher but also pupils and parents.

Major initiatives taken so far include:

- providing opportunities for volunteers to take extra lessons for extension or compensation outside the normal curriculum.
- extended school library hours with staff available to provide facilities for pupils wishing to stay on and work after school.
- arrangements to keep schools open with volunteer staffing during holiday periods, particularly at Easter, to enable pupils wishing to do so to continue to study for examination success.
- personal tutoring schemes where staff accept responsibility for small groups of Year 11 pupils and give ongoing help and advice with study skills, examination preparation, revision technique, coursework presentation, Records of Achievement etc.
- the development — with the help and experience of the post-16 colleges — of flexible learning packages to facilitate supported self-study for the pupils.
- individual action planning — provided in cooperation with the County

Careers Service — to ensure that the pupil is given guidance in seeking out career opportunities, is aware of the qualification implications, and has a set of achievable short-term targets.

- taster courses and college experience made available in the post-16 colleges to allow pupils to sample the next step in the educational process.
- residential experiences provided in collaboration with Keele and Staffordshire Universities to give Year 11 pupils in the three schools a taste of university life and teaching at first hand.

It is crucial to the Two Towns Project that the parents and the school work together and share the same aims and aspirations for the children. The schools have consequently attempted to keep parents constantly informed of developments in the life and work of the school. The number of opportunities for the parents to visit the schools has been increased and creche facilities provided to encourage those with small children to attend. Systems have been introduced to monitor the numbers of parents accepting such invitations. Termly newsletters are sent out to keep parents in touch. Each school has developed a 'day book' which monitors progress in every aspect of the children's school life and which is regularly taken home for the parents to read and comment on. It is a measure of the quality of processes in the school and the shared commitment among staff that the day books have been consistently maintained and play a central part in ensuring that parents and teachers have a shared understanding of what is expected of the pupils. Courses have been run in collaboration with the colleges and universities to advise parents on strategies for dealing with their children during their school years.

The Two Towns Project is a partnership not only between the pupils, parents and staff of the three high schools but also between them and the Careers Service, the post-16 institutions, the post-18 institutions, the local primary schools and the business and industrial community. The three high schools are highly dependent upon the work done in the primary schools particularly in respect of literacy and numeracy and they have actively sought to forge links with their primary partners to focus on achievement, concentrating on work in these areas. With hindsight many of the participants in the project now believe that the primary schools should have been integrally involved at the outset.

At the other end of the age range there have been growing links with colleges and universities whose commitment and support for the work of the schools has been a significant factor in the success of the project. Keele and Staffordshire Universities have shown, by their public expression of interest in the schools' activities, by their presence at school functions, by their endorsement of the schools Records of Achievement, the importance of encouragement, enthusiasm, and empathy from external agencies for raising the self-esteem of pupils, parents and staff.

### Outcomes of the Project in the Schools

In terms of the agreed performance indicators for the schools, the project targets had already been met by the halfway point of the initial programme.

1    Participation rates in full-time post-16 education rose from 22 per cent in 1989 to more than 52 per cent in 1992 — a rise of 136 per cent and by 1993 the participation rates were well over 50 per cent.
2    The numbers of pupils achieving five or more GCSE grades A–C rose from 10 per cent in 1989 to 23 per cent in 1992 — a rise of almost 121 per cent. By 1993 the figure had risen to 22 per cent.
3    Attendance has improved beyond the target 5 per cent in all schools.

It can be seen, therefore, that targets that seemed in 1990 to be over-ambitious, proved ultimately to err on the side of caution.

### Case Study: Brownhills High School: An Improving School

The systematic use of rewards as an integral part of a behavioural management strategy or in the context of an 'assertive disciple' scheme is a comparatively new innovation in many schools. At Brownhills High School in Stoke-on-Trent staff have been carefully developing a rewards system for more than four years. 'Praise postcards' are distributed when a pupil has done a piece of work that demonstrates improvement or quality. A teacher fills in the details on a card which the head signs and posts to the parent at home. The praise postcards are symbolic of the efforts at Brownhills to shift the culture of low aspirations which formerly dominated the school and the community. Through awards evenings, displays of work and constant insistence on high expectations across the staff, the culture is indeed changing dramatically. There is the hard evidence of success. In 1988, 4 per cent of the cohort gained five GCSEs at grades A–C. Four years later 13 per cent did so. In 1994 it was 22 per cent.

Some observers have commented to the headteacher, that 22 per cent is probably the sort of level to be satisfied with, in a school in a disadvantaged urban area with high unemployment and a tradition of expecting little from education. She dismisses such complacency, 'You can't look at cohort as so-called bad years, you have to think about your knowledge of the group: what are the barriers to their success and how can they be removed?' Her sights are set on continuous improvement through to the end of the century. If by then her success rate has doubled, she would still be demonstrating her quiet but firm commitment to improvement. Nor does any year get described as a particularly good year by the head; that can cause complacency, she suggests. The job of school management is never to panic — whatever the pressures — and always to aim very high.

It is clear from talking to staff that her commitment and steadfastness has communicated itself to staff. A senior member of staff, a maths teacher with management responsibilities, says that the staff are constantly stumbling across new ideas. The climate in the school means they have the courage to implement them. For example, he has recently implemented a voluntary system of additional tutorials for small groups of pupils where twelve staff volunteered to give extra attention to the needs of sixty pupils. The demand came from the pupils. The staff responded, and the evidence suggests that the pupils involved performed noticeably better at GCSE than peers of similar ability.

The English department has involved artists-in-residence in their literacy strategy. Pupils are constantly encouraged to read and review books. In technology, participation of pupils in a science and technology week at the local college raises aspirations and encourages staying on. Another member of staff, meanwhile runs a community education project from the school which, among other things, teaches parents how to support their children's education. Here they learn what the demands of coursework on young people will be and how they can be encouraged to read and to study. 'It is all part of changing aspirations in the community', he said. A few years ago a pupil told him she wanted to be an estate agent. 'Why not become a chartered surveyor?' he said. She had never heard of one of those then, but recently he heard that she had become just that. In Brownhills like other successful urban schools the real meaning of high expectations is in details like that.

Pupils are the first to acknowledge that the peer-group culture has changed. They say they are proud to attend Brownshills and that the atmosphere in the classroom has changed dramatically over five years. The head places great emphasis on discipline. 'If that's wrong', she says, 'you can never get the classroom experience right.' Rather than a system of punishing offenders, they tackled the aspects of school which seemed to create the opportunities for trouble. The rewards system — praise postcards included — was overhauled. Lunchtime caused problems and provided opportunities for some pupils to skip the afternoon, so the school moved to a continuous day. There are always lessons in progress now. Each year group in turn has a forty-minute break during which they must stay on the premises. School finishes early — at 3.05 — but is followed by 90 minutes of additional voluntary extension activities including an oversubscribed homework club.

The head recognizes that the school's success depends on the quality and commitment of her staff. The improvement strategy consciously involved all of them from the beginning. 'They have to give a lot', she comments, 'but the growing evidence of success provides its own rewards'. She acknowledges too that participation in the Two Towns Project with other local schools, the LEA and nearby universities was crucial. It provided a source of ideas and the encouragement to take risks. 'It enabled us to do in three years what might otherwise have taken ten', she suggests. The increasing attention the school's success is bringing provides further encouragement. She particularly appreciated the phone call from the CEO when this year's GCSE results were published.

The popular image of school improvement is one of a charismatic head wielding authority and driving staff and pupils on. The Brownhills' experience belies such a picture. School improvement is to do with absolute commitment to high expectations, an openness about performance data, a pragmatic 'what works' approach in which taking risks is encouraged and in attending constantly to the details, like the praise postcards.

### Evaluation of the Two Towns Project

At school level the project has been subjected to evaluation on three occasions since its inception in 1990. An early report to point the way for the project was carried out in 1991 by W.S. Walton, formerly the Chief Education Officer of Sheffield. An interim evaluation was carried out in 1992 by Quality Learning Services, Staffordshire and Gordon Hainsworth, formerly the Chief Executive for Manchester. A final evaluation was conducted in 1993 by a Keele University team, including a headteacher and two teachers from the Haggerston School in Hackney to ensure external validation.

### *The Contribution of the Partner Institutions*

The Two Towns Project has derived great strength from the fact that is has func-tioned as a loose network, led by and focused on the three high schools. But substantial contributions have been made by the local education authority, the local universities and colleges and Staffordshire Careers Service. The nature of the con-tribution of each of these is summarized below.

- The active participation of the Chief Education Officer of Staffordshire and his part in the initiation of the project has given it status and credibility within the schools and the local community. The availability of the officers of the authority throughout the project has been a valuable support in getting things 'delivered'.
- The influence and moral authority of the LEA, rather than its statutory powers, have drawn together the partnership network.
- The collaboration of the LEA with the Staffordshire TEC has resulted in substantial funding for the project.
- The expertise of universities and colleges in, and knowledge of, the pro-cess of educational change and development was central to the underlying philosophy of the project.
- Keele University's first material contribution to the project was to negoti-ate funding by entering into agreement with The Paul Hamlyn Foundation. The foundation has provided the salary for a project coordinator who has been based at Keele and provided with accommodation and support ser-vices there. The foundation funded residential experiences which have been organized and delivered at the university.
- One of the lessons of the Two Towns has been the need for universities to have particular criteria for local students who traditionally would not be expected to enter university. Keele and Staffordshire Universities' response has been a review of admissions procedures and the implementation of a guaranteed entry to local youngsters who can demonstrate that they are of serious intent and committed to study. Students admitted by this route — the Staffordshire Access Scheme — since October 1993 have been closely

monitored and the evidence suggests that they are succeeding in higher education.

- One of the early lessons learned from the Two Towns Project was that a residential experience at an institute of higher education might raise significantly the aspirations of the pupils who attend. Each September since 1991 the universities have hosted a three-day residential experience, funded by The Paul Hamlyn Foundation, for 150 Year 11 pupils. This event is supported by all the members of the partnership. The young people attend workshops and seminars with staff and students from the post-16 institutions and the universities, the careers service and with management teams from local and national industry. They visit university departments, live in student accommodation and enjoy the social life of the campus.

- A student-tutoring programme has been piloted in local schools since October 1992. It has been funded by a small grant from British Petroleum and community-service volunteers. Student volunteers from universities and colleges have worked alongside teachers to act as role models for pupils at secondary level or to support the development of reading and speaking skills in the primary schools, particularly with children from ethnic-minority groups. As from October 1994 additional money from the Staffordshire TEC will facilitate the expansion of the tutoring scheme into all the Two Towns high schools and three of their primary feeder schools. The benefits from the scheme for the school children is already becoming apparent as are a variety of spin-off benefits for the universities and colleges.

- A function of the Two Towns coordinator at Keele has been to monitor the project's performance indicators and undertake the research which informs the debate on school-improvement measures in the schools and colleges. The research profile of the education department at Keele has been significantly influenced by this work and a 'centre for successful schools' has been developed around the project. The centre has undertaken work related directly to the project, identifying ways, for example, in which a failing school can reverse the downward spiral and become a place where characteristics evident in successful schools appear. Surveys were carried out, by questionnaire and interview techniques, on the attitudes held by all students in their last year of compulsory schooling, seeking, in particular, to establish their attitude to staying on in education post-16. Similar surveys have been conducted to research the attitudes to education of parents from the three schools. Adapted versions of these surveys are now in widespread use.

- University involvement in community projects is normally perceived as a contribution by the university to the community. The benefit for the university tends to be measured in public-relations terms. In the case of the Two Towns Project much more significant gains have been made from the university's point of view. There has been an influence on the teaching and the quality of experience gained by associate teachers on the university Post-Graduate Certificate of Education Course. Even more significant has been the direction it has given to the university's educational research. A variety of developments have resulted from, or been inspired by, the university's involvement in the Two Towns Project.

- The Staffordshire Careers Service has shown a consistently strong commitment to the project. Representatives have been provided for the steering and project groups and there has been a careers presence at every Two Towns function. Its most important contribution has been to ensure that each Year 10 and Year 11 pupil in the three schools has been provided with an opportunity to work on an Individual Action Plan to record career aspirations and the steps to be taken, in terms of personal development and obtaining qualifications, for these ambitions to be realized. The plan involves individual support in setting short- and long-term targets.

*Lessons Learned from the Two Towns Project*

1  There is a great deal of research evidence about the characteristics of effective schools. It would seem from the Two Towns Project that urban schools which target their resources and energy on strategies for developing these characteristics are more likely to raise children's aspirations and achievement.
2  Loose collaboration rather than formal structures has successfully provided the pattern for the organization of The Two Towns Project.
3  Management structures succeeded because they reflected the loose nature of collaboration and placed the initiative firmly with the schools involved.
4  Clear measurable targets were essential.
5  Relatively small amounts of additional funding, spent well, made a huge difference.

In the case of the Two Towns Project the following features appeared to be important:

- the planning of expenditure integrally involved the schools themselves;
- outside consultants, with high credibility, provided insight and analysis and gave the initiative status;
- significant numbers of teachers in the schools were involved in planning and consultation;
- there was limited but significant expenditure on symbolic change (such as establishing high-quality displays of pupil work and other achievements in entrance halls);
- there were focused attempts to change pupil (peer group) attitudes and staff attitudes and expectations;
- provision was made for professional-development opportunities related to the goals of the project;

- the additional expenditure became an integral part of a school's development strategy.

Beyond this, we would argue that there are, indeed some generalizable lessons to be learned from the Two Towns Project.

Participation in an initiative is not an alternative to getting the in-school factors right. As we have suggested above, the initiatives with the greatest chance of bringing about sustainable improvement are those that assist schools in creating the conditions for improvement from within. It should be emphasized that participating in an initiative is not an alternative to a school taking responsibility for its own improvement. Instead it is a means of assisting it improve and may act as a catalyst in helping it change and improve more quickly.

Cooperating agencies as well as schools can benefit from urban school-improvement initiatives. While the focus of the Two Towns Project is clearly school improvement, or some aspects of it, it is clear that the collaboration can provide benefits to other participating agencies. For example, a university can accumulate data and experience which will contribute to its research and publication profile. TECs, for example, can gain through understanding better the links between schools, FE and employers. LEAs can learn lessons applicable to all their schools and gain in terms of their public profile.

These wider benefits ought to be taken into account by those at local level who are considering investing in urban education initiatives. The investment may reap benefits far beyond those immediately specified in the project goals. Furthermore given the potential for mutual benefit schools should see their role in such projects as being active partners, rather than passive beneficiaries.

*The Next Steps*

The achievements of the Two Towns Project to date underline the need for the partners to reaffirm their commitment to present policies: to maintaining and improving standards of examination performance and school attendance; to curriculum extension; to ever closer links with primary and post-16 partners; to providing individual counselling and career advice; to enhanced and enriched learning experiences, and to the increasing involvement of parents. Targets for the next phase of the project should include the following: a preschool programme building on the lessons of the 'Headstart' programme in the USA, (it is hoped that the preschool agencies will be better coordinated), closer involvement of the primary sector, and enhancement of the status of pupils who do not necessarily 'stay on' in full-time education but who, nevertheless, pursue interests which have structured learning post-16 as an integral ingredient.

Consideration will be given to which aspects of the project are replicable elsewhere. What are the implications for the rest of the education system? Staffordshire LEA will make use of the Two Towns experience in its strategy for education across the county to improve schools and encourage a gradual turnround in peer group and parental pressure in favour of a climate of achievement. The involvement of the universities with the LEA and the TEC in support of local schools has proved a powerful influence and there is a need to establish how this influence might be spread more widely.

## References

BARBER, M.B., COLLARBONE, P., CULLEN, E. and OWEN, D. (1994) *Raising Expectation and Achievement in City Schools: The Two Towns School Improvement Project*, London, OFSTED.

BRIGHOUSE, T.R.P. (1993) 'Education in Stoke-on-Trent: The two towns project', in *The Potteries: Continuity and Change in a Staffordshire Conurbation* PHILLIPS, A.D.M. (Ed), Butler and Tanner.

FULLAN, M. (1991) *The New Meaning of Educational Change*, Cassell, London.

GODDARD, D., HAINSWORTH, G. and LOVE, R. (1993) *The Two Towns Evaluation Report*, Stafford, Staffordshire County Council.

GRAY, J. (1990) 'The quality of schooling: Frameworks for judgement', in *British Journal of Education Studies*, 38, 3, August.

JOHNSON, M. (1994) *The Two Towns Project — Raising Expectation and Achievement in City Schools*, Keele, Keele University.

RUTTER, M., MAUGHAN, B., MORTIMORE, P. and OUSTON, J. (1979) *Fifteen Thousand Hours*, Somerset Open Books.

*Part 2*

*Issues in the Development of Collaborative Networks*

*Chapter 10*

# Consortium Collaboration: The Experience of TVEI

*Ann Bridgwood*

## Introduction

From the outset consortium collaboration under the auspices of the Technical and Vocational Educational Initiative (TVEI) differed from other types of inter-institutional cooperation. Unlike link courses, CPVE or A level consortia (Dean *et al.*, 1979; FEU, 1985; ACFHE/APTI, 1979), the initial impetus for most TVEI consortia arose not from local initiatives by practitioners, but from a national programme funded by the Employment Department. This was made explicit at the extension phase of TVEI, when the criteria laid down for extension programmes specified that 'each authority's extension plan . . . should normally include the arrangements for grouping of schools/colleges in ways appropriate to each area'.

This chapter is based on examinations of consortium working during the pilot (Bridgwood, 1989) and early extension phases of TVEI (Saunders *et al.*, 1991). It does not go into detail about the most recent stages of consortium development, but draws on evidence from two extensive pieces of research whose findings had much in common. At the pilot stage, a broad-brush view of consortium working was provided by a suite of six management questionnaires completed by managers and TVEI practitioners in approximately seventy further education (FE) colleges and 200 schools. Semi-structured interviews with a range of TVEI practitioners in six pilot projects provided more detailed information about the day-to-day functioning of consortia. In-depth case studies were conducted in six local education authorities (LEAs) during the early extension phase.

TVEI was an Employment Department initiative which aimed to equip 14 to 18 year-olds for 'the demands of working life in a changing society'. The first pilot projects were established in six LEAs in 1983–4, followed by further pilot schemes in subsequent academic years. The Secretary of State for Employment announced in 1987 that the initiative would be extended on a phased basis to all LEAs. Although the organization of individual projects varied, they were usually managed by a project coordinator, reporting to a steering group. TVEI coordinators were nominated in each of the participating schools and colleges. Some projects established a TVEI centre, which ranged from little more than an office for the project coordinator and his (very few of the early coordinators were women) secretary, to fully equipped centres providing a base for a team of centrally funded advisory teachers, classrooms and workshops for the use of students and teachers.

## Types of Collaboration

During the pilot phase of TVEI, two-thirds of schemes had only one consortium, which meant that the consortium was often identical to the project, making it difficult to distinguish clearly between changes and developments due to the establishment of the TVEI project and those resulting from consortium working. The majority of pilot consortia consisted of one college and three to six schools. Despite the similarity of membership, consortia differed in the depth of involvement by and the nature of the links between the participating institutions. A 'shallow' college-centred consortium, for example, might consist solely of the provision of link or taster courses for 14–16-year-olds by an FE college. At the other end of the spectrum were networking consortia, characterized by interlocking and overlapping links and exchanges between all the member institutions, an active set of curriculum working parties, jointly developed courses and the exchange of students and sometimes of staff. This latter type of consortium sometimes had no obvious centre, but a stronger sense of ownership by practitioners, a theme to which I will return later.

The stated aim of most consortia was to improve provision for students by promoting curriculum development and provision. More specifically, this was to be achieved through the provision of entitlement or core curricula, curriculum pathways, enhancement programmes, joint Business and Technician Education Council (BTEC) and Certificate of Pre-Vocational Education (CPVE) courses or taster courses. An important aim of this new curricular provision was to improve progression and continuity between the 14–16 and post-16 phases of TVEI. Integral to the overall aim was the joint organization of staff development, in part to try and effect a shift towards more student-centred learning, and the deployment of resources in the form of staff, equipment and money. Consortia in the extension phase of TVEI took on additional roles, such as acting as a lever for whole-institution change and as a facilitator of self-evaluation (Saunders *et al.*, 1991).

During the pilot phase, most consortia had four levels of management, which in most cases were also the management structures of the TVEI project. The highest level was the steering group, a formal body which set broad policy and often had little involvement in the day-to-day running of the project. Below this was the management group, comprising the project coordinator, school heads and college principals — seen as the real decision makers in most projects. The coordinators' committee, as the name suggests, consisted of the school and college TVEI coordinators; the role was formally to implement the policy developed by the steering and management groups, although in practice it often developed *ad hoc* policy during the process of running TVEI. Curriculum working groups were established to undertake specific subject or task-based development projects, such as developing the curriculum pathways, entitlement curricula or taster courses which formed the kernel of consortium collaboration. During the early extension phase, a fifth level of management, consisting of consortium managers, was introduced (Saunders *et al.*, 1991).

### Aids and Hindrances to Collaboration

The remainder of the chapter examines some of the factors which have helped or hindered inter-institutional collaboration under the auspices of TVEI. It concentrates on consortium working in 1988–90 and does not examine in detail the contexts for collaboration following more recent legislation changes. Nevertheless, many of the issues raised may be relevant to the rather different circumstances in which consortia presently operate. My starting point is the question of effectiveness; that is, the extent to which factors external and internal to consortia enabled or prevented them from achieving their stated aims. In formulating the discussion, I have found Giddens' (1989) concept of 'structuration' helpful. An examination of formal management structures can give one type of picture of how consortia operate, but the picture would be incomplete without some account of the social processes which create and maintain consortia over time. TVEI consortia were unusual because, being introduced largely as the result of an external initiative, they afforded an opportunity to observe and evaluate the process of structuration, by which key players generated, reproduced, sustained (or undermined) and adapted the formal structures in response to the development of TVEI.

The factors which facilitated or prevented effective cooperation were both external and internal to consortia and their member institutions. Although some extended existing links, the impetus for the initial establishment of most TVEI consortia was external — a push towards collaboration from the Employment Department, especially when extension funding was explicitly tied to the development of consortia. Other external factors were, at the time of the pilot evaluation, falling rolls and changes permitted by the 1988 Education Reform Act such as open enrolment up to 1979 levels. The introduction of the local management of schools and grant-maintained status, which allowed schools to opt out of local authority control, also shaped the context in which consortia operated. In 1993, FE colleges were also removed from local authority control under incorporation. All of these carried the potential for competition for students between schools and colleges, particularly for the post-16 age group. Other priorities, such as the need to maintain a sixth form in the face of possible tertiary reorganization meant that A level consortia were sometimes given precedence over the TVEI consortium. The introduction of a contractual obligation for school teachers to work an annual total of 1265 hours directed time focused attention on activities which took them out of school during any of that directed time.

In addition to these and other external factors, internal factors such as geography, the organization and culture of member institutions and the attitudes of key players also shaped the effectiveness of consortia. Practical issues like the coordination of timetables by several institutions or arranging student transport, although potentially straightforward to resolve, could absorb a lot of time and creative energy — not always to good purpose. While it would be a mistake to ignore these issues — it is often over nitty-gritty details that an initiative flourishes or flounders, such technical issues will not be discussed here except in passing. Focusing on the example of curriculum working groups, I will explore three themes, whilst recognizing that they do not exhaust the discussion. These are the appropriateness of formal management structures for achieving the aims of consortia; the effectiveness of channels of communication and dissemination; and the depth of involvement and degree of articulation with the consortium by practitioners, with consequent implications for their sense of ownership.

### Effective Structures: The Example of Curriculum Working Parties

The aims of curriculum working parties, as mentioned, were primarily to develop the curriculum pathways, entitlement curricula or joint courses which would form the core of TVEI provision. As consortia developed, they took on further roles, such as developing records of achievement or negotiating with examination boards for recognition of new curricula such as General Certificate of Secondary Education (GCSE) integrated science courses. From the outset, they also satisfied more informal and unstated needs, such as providing opportunities for career and personal development for their members. They often functioned as a support network for practitioners, some of whom felt isolated when trying to introduce new courses or modify teaching and learning styles in their home institutions.

In the early stages of consortium development, curriculum working parties provided a framework within which groups of individuals with specialist knowledge could work together, pooling their expertise to generate new modules, courses and curriculum pathways. These usually needed to be in place within a very short time of TVEI getting off the ground, so the process of development was often a very intense one. The groups were usually task-based, with clear goals to work towards, and small enough for everyone to make a meaningful contribution. They often operated relatively autonomously, within the broad policy framework laid down by the steering group and the management group. The structure was appropriate for the early days of TVEI, when a very specific job had to be done very quickly.

Structures can become fossilized and inappropriate if they do not respond to changing circumstances. TVEI consortia, like other organizations, were not static entities, but passed through discernible development cycles. In the pilot phase, these were characterized as orientation, separate development, consolidation and extension (Bridgwood, 1989). In the early extension phase of TVEI, the cycle was characterized as mobilization, implementation, institutionalization and self-sustaining community (Saunders *et al.*, 1991). Curriculum working parties therefore needed to be flexible in order to adapt to the changing aims of the consortium in these different phases. Once the new courses or curriculum pathways had been developed, the emphasis needed to shift towards, for example, dissemination, seeking recognition from examination boards or curriculum development geared towards meeting the requirements of the (then) recently introduced National Curriculum. At the time of the pilot evaluation some groups, having achieved their initial aims, had lost focus and clearly outlived their usefulness. Where this had happened, the sense of being involved in new developments was not as evident as complaints about the amount of time which curriculum working parties took up. At this stage, practitioners argued that unless a new function could be found for the groups, they should be disbanded.

What was the impact of curriculum working parties on existing educational structures? TVEI as an initiative had already bypassed existing structures to some extent by developing new channels for funding and by establishing inter-institutional structures and roles which were independent of internal school and college hierarchies. The school and college TVEI coordinators, for example, were charged with implementing an externally generated and funded initiative in their own school or college, which could have implications for existing curriculum provision and for the allocation of resources within the institution. Coordinators were situated within two lines of reporting — to the head of their home institution and to the TVEI project coordinator — and sometimes faced conflicting demands. In effect, the local education authority (LEA), the TVEI project and the member institutions had become participants in a matrix management structure, without this being explicitly spelled out. Some heads who took part in the evaluation felt that their authority was being undermined and that their school was losing a degree of autonomy. At an institutional level, participation in the curriculum working parties by teachers and lecturers had both positive and negative outcomes for individual schools and colleges. On the positive side, the developments being generated by the groups were realized in the form of new courses and changed classroom practice, with a shift towards more student-centred learning. They could strengthen the hand of practitioners like curriculum deputies who were already pushing in their own institution for the kind of change promoted by TVEI.

On the negative side, it was acknowledged by heads and by some practitioners themselves that developments were sometimes being achieved at the expense of ongoing work. Attendance at curriculum working-party meetings, for example, meant that an innovative and forward-looking member of staff was absent from school or college, which could cause difficulties in arranging cover — particularly in shortage subjects. In some instances, the difficulty of replacing specialist staff meant that cover could amount to little more than 'baby-sitting', which was not in the students' best interests. Interestingly, feedback from students indicated that the benefits of consortium working were not always immediately apparent to them; some complained about the long teaching periods necessitated by joint timetabling and the exchange of staff and students, or about the amount of time spent travelling between school and college. Some felt lonely or unable to use the sixth-form common room when away from their home institution, which could lead to a preference for maintaining existing structures rather than developing new forms of collaboration.

### Communication and Dissemination

The location of the curriculum working parties within the four-level management structure clearly showed the need for effective two-way vertical channels of communication. To achieve the stated aims of the consortium, the groups had to operate within the broad policy framework set by the steering group and the management group and to ensure that their approach was compatible with the implementation of that policy by the TVEI coordinators. They therefore needed to be kept informed of the decisions reached by policy makers. Equally, it was necessary for the managers and coordinators to be aware of developments generated by the groups if these were to inform further policy development. While formal channels of horizontal communication between members of the steering group or members of the coordinators' committee usually operated effectively, vertical-communication channels between the different levels of the management structure were often less developed. Some consortia had well-developed formal channels of communication for feeding policy decisions taken by the steering group and the management group down to coordinators and curriculum working parties. In others, an *ad hoc* and therefore more haphazard system of communication existed by virtue of overlapping membership of different committees. Communication between the four levels of management structure was most effective when the formal structures were supported by informal networks between practitioners.

An important role of the curriculum working parties, particularly as the pilot projects moved into the extension, was to disseminate their developments in pilot and non-TVEI schools and colleges. Some consortia had well-developed channels of dissemination in place, asking members of curriculum working parties to, for example, take a formal role in disseminating developments in a particular non-TVEI school which was scheduled to join the extension phase of the initiative, or inviting potential extension schools to join the working parties. In other cases, dissemination was more informal and thus less systematic, amounting, in the words of one practitioner, to little more than 'dissemination by gossip'.

### Commitment, Ownership and Effectiveness

Giddens' (1989) concept of structuration highlights the need to examine the social processes which create, maintain and sustain structures. Within TVEI, there was a complex interplay between commitment, effectiveness and ownership, which shaped the day-to-day functioning of consortia, and which had concomitant implications for formal management structures. Commitment was essential if consortium aims were to be achieved. Cooperation required a lot of time, energy and hard work from practitioners who already had heavy responsibilities and who were not always fully supported by colleagues in their home institutions. Yet, as Silverman (1970) has shown, individuals come to organizations with their own agendas and this was as true of TVEI as of any other form of collaborative working. Some key players were fully committed to consortium ideals from the outset; other views ranged from paying lip service, through fighting for the needs of individual institutions at the expense of the consortium as a whole, to intentions to undermine.

Some participants had a definite preference for a 'weak' rather than a 'strong' model of the consortium. After the introduction of teacher conditions of service specifying an annual commitment 1265 hours, one of the ways in which this could be demonstrated was over whether or not the time spent at curriculum working-party meetings should count as directed time. A decision that it should could act as a marker of the degree of commitment to the consortium by a school manager; equally, the recognition that the curriculum working parties were considered worthy of official time could increase members' commitment to them. A refusal to allocate directed time, which amounted to telling teachers that they had to attend in their own time, sent a powerful message about the low priority accorded to the consortium.

Commitment could clearly enhance effectiveness; blocks and barriers often dissolved when key individuals resolved to overcome them. Organizational and cultural differences between schools and FE, for example, became less important 'once faces were known'. Evidence of effective consortium working could itself generate further commitment, thus establishing a positive feedback loop. A sense of commitment and involvement in the day-to-day working of the consortium often resulted in the generation of informal networks and structures.

Informal structures can work both ways; they can either strengthen and compensate for gaps in formal management structures or they can undermine them. An informal caucus or well-organized cabal is able to sabotage initiatives just as surely as outright opposition in formal meetings. As Lukes (1974) has shown, the ability to control an agenda and determine which subjects are publicly aired can be as effective an exercise of power as the ability to prevail in decision-making. More importantly, the social and cultural context in which debates about the allocation of resources — Lukes' 'three-dimensional' view of power — ensures that debates do not always take place on a level playing field. Legislation, inequalities of power or prevailing attitudes can load the dice in favour of one of the protagonists. Local management of schools (and the incorporation of FE colleges), open enrolment up to 1989 levels and the possibility of opting out of LEA control gave individual institutions a greater structural autonomy. The withdrawal of TVEI funding will shift the balance even more in their favour as they will exercise greater control over the allocation of resources than the consortium. Against this background, the decision to mobilize informal networks for or against a consortium will be made on pragmatic or instrumental grounds — on the basis of 'what's in it for us?'. If the answer is 'little or nothing', then there will seem to be little point in participating in consortia.

A challenge for consortium managers was how to generate commitment in the face of these countervailing tendencies. A key factor, both at an individual and institutional level, was the degree of ownership which practitioners and institutions felt that they had over consortium developments. A sense of ownership was particularly noticeable among members of curriculum working parties during the pilot phase of TVEI, when developments were often bottom–up and teacher-led. The extent to which individuals were committed to consortium aims also depended on whether they had been involved in generating them. Practitioners who had contributed to their initial formulation were often more committed than those who had had the aims — and TVEI in general — imposed upon them. Working against the tide is hard, but it is easier when it involves new and exciting developments and when practitioners can feel that they are generating real change.

The extent to which consortia met practitioners' own needs and the needs of member institutions was another important factor. It was easier for individuals to feel more committed to the consortium if it offered opportunities for personal development, or the chance to exercise management skills or enhance career prospects. Once consortia moved into the consolidation or institutionalization phases, it could be more difficult to feel the same degree of commitment and personal reward; the task became one of implementation rather than of developing something new, and a well-established initiative sometimes offered fewer opportunities for personal advancement or development. Similarly, heads and principals were more likely to be committed to consortia if they were seen to offer clear advantages for their own school or college. In the early stages of TVEI, a number of managers felt that consortia undermined their autonomy and that the management structures of TVEI cut across those of the school or college. Some initial sceptics were, sometimes to their surprise, converted to the consortium ideal once it could be demonstrated that there were tangible benefits for their school or college. In the context of the local management of schools, once TVEI funding ceases and heads and principals are required to commit their own resources, consortia will have to offer clear instrumental advantages if they are to flourish. In the case of the curriculum working parties, these are likely to take the form of courses and modules which meet the changing requirements of the National Curriculum or of new initiatives such as General National Vocational Qualifications (GNVQs) and vocational courses for 14–16-year-olds, as these can be more effectively developed on a collective than on an institution-by-institution basis. Curriculum working parties may also be well-placed to provide staff development or consultancy which schools and colleges can buy in from the consortium.

Stoney (1986) has demonstrated that a strong sense of ownership over developments was generally associated with devolved management structures in the early pilot phase of TVEI. This was borne out by the evaluation of pilot consortia; curriculum working parties functioned relatively autonomously — perhaps too much so in some cases — and their members generally felt a strong sense of ownership over developments. Achieving the right balance between devolution and ownership is, however, not straightforward. Whilst a strongly centralized management structure can make members feel disenfranchised, devolving management responsibility in the absence of a clear focus and sense of direction can result in initiatives becoming diffused. Devolution in a potentially competitive environment can also result in the needs of member institutions being given priority at the expense of the consortium as a whole. Ideally, a balance has to be struck between maintaining a clear focus and aims for the consortium on the one hand, and encouraging devolution to generate ownership and commitment on the other. Whether this can be achieved will depend on convincing members that cooperation can serve the ends of both the consortium and the member institutions.

## Conclusion

The preceding discussion has focused on the role of curriculum working parties in TVEI consortia. In this final section of the chapter, I would like to draw out some of the general points which can be applied to other forms of consortium collaboration. Firstly, the example of TVEI shows that, if consortia are to operate effectively, their formal management structures need to be appropriate for achieving their stated aims and flexible enough to adapt to changing environments and circumstances. Committees and working parties which no longer serve any useful function need either to take on new tasks or to disband to avoid the risk of degenerating into 'talking shops'. Secondly, where several levels of management structure exist within a consortium, clear channels of vertical as well as horizontal communication need to be in place. These work most effectively when supported by informal links, but it is dangerous to rely solely on informal networks.

The attitudes of key participants are central to the process of successfully maintaining and reproducing structures. The informal links and networks which they generate can be crucial in increasing commitment and enhancing effectiveness and can be a powerful constructive force if successfully mobilized. Conversely, ignoring the needs and individual agendas of practitioners can lead to unforeseen and negative consequences and undermine or weaken consortia. Management structures which allow for the acknowledgment of the power of informal networks and which facilitate the mobilization of practitioner commitment to furthering the aims of consortia are likely to be more effective than those which emphasize the role of formal hierarchies and insist on following rigid procedures. This suggests that consortium structures need to be of a loose networking type, flexible and adaptable to changing circumstances. They need to provide a coordinating framework within which practitioners and institutions have sufficient scope for acting autonomously to generate a sense of ownership, while keeping the overall aims of the consortium in view. This should help them to work towards achieving the aims of the consortium, and not solely towards meeting their own needs and agendas.

## References

ASSOCIATION OF COLLEGES OF FURTHER AND HIGHER EDUCATION/ASSOCIATION OF PRINCIPALS IN TECHNICAL INSTITUTIONS (1979) 'After 16: The case for the tertiary college', London, ACFHE/APTI.

BRIDGWOOD, A. (1989) 'Working together: consortium links in TVEI', Sheffield, Training Agency.

DEAN, J., BRADLEY, K., CHOPPIN, B. and VINCENT, D. (1979) *The Sixth Form and its Alternatives*, Windsor, NFER.

FURTHER EDUCATION UNIT (1985) *CPVE in Action*, London, FEU.

GIDDENS, A. (1989) *Sociology*, Cambridge, Polity Press.

LUKES, S. (1974) *Power: A Radical View*, London, MacMillan.

SAUNDERS, L., STRADLING, B., MORRIS, M. and MURRAY, K. (1991) 'Clusters and consortia: Co-ordinating educational change in the 1990s', Sheffield, Employment Department.

SILVERMAN, D. (1970) *The Theory of Organisations*, London, Heinemann.

STONEY, S.M. (1986) 'Implementing TVEI: Some project and school perspectives', in STONEY, S.M., POLE, C.J. and SIMS, D. *The Management of TVEI*, Sheffield, Manpower Services Commission, pp. 3–25.

# Chapter 11

# Consortium Collaboration in Teacher Education: The ERTEC Experience

*David Bridges*

### The Context of Consortium Collaboration

In many respects higher education institutions operate in conditions closer to the market place than do schools. Their main sources of income are: the fees which students bring with them if they choose a particular institution and are acceptable to that institution; contracts with private and public agencies for research and developmental work won normally on the basis of competitive tendering in which considerations of quality and cost have been weighed; and research income from government based on an independent assessment of the quality and productivity of individual departments in comparison with others working in the same subject area. In each of these areas, universities are in competitive relations with each other:

- they compete to attract students at home and overseas — and to this end increasingly tailor what they offer to students' demands and interests, target niche markets, cultivate local and regional support, offer compacted two-year degrees to cut down the cost to students (while all the time adjusting to government interventions in the market aimed at rewarding financially, for example, those universities which achieve growth in numbers in science and engineering rather than in the humanities and social sciences);
- they compete for contracts for research and developmental work in the private and public sector in much the same way as, and often in competition with, private companies;
- they compete for the inclusion of their research products in the programmes of international research conferences or the pages of the more prestigious research journals, for research council funding and hence for high ratings in the research assessment exercise and the income that this brings.

Most of these conditions apply equally in the context of teacher education. There is however some central government control in this context over the supply side of teacher education: over the curriculum which is offered in initial teacher training and over its mode of delivery. Initial training courses have to satisfy criteria laid down in Department for Education (DFE) Circulars 9/92 and 14/93 defining, for example, the competences to be achieved among its trainees and the period of time that they spend in training in school, and these criteria are backed up by OFSTED inspections. The DFE also exercises considerable control on the demand side of the market by setting limits on the total number of students who may be admitted to training and by allocating target numbers of students to individual training institutions (though these have themselves been in part a function of previous success in recruitment and the cost and quality of training provided) and by control over the rate of payment in the funding which universities receive per student.

Notwithstanding the increasingly competitive climate in higher education more generally and in teacher education more specifically, there remains here as in the school context, a continuing disposition towards professional and inter-institutional collaboration. Teacher educators in different higher education settings sometimes identify more strongly with each other than with colleagues working under very different conditions and perhaps within a different cultural mould in different departments. It is after all not so long ago that many of those currently teaching in university departments were college of education tutors meeting in subject boards under their area training organization. If those occasions seemed tedious and time-consuming at the time, the passing years have left a sense of nostalgia for a more collegial style of working. In any case in a period of time in which teacher educators have been the butt of quite vicious, systematic and explicitly politically motivated attacks from government, its members have drawn some support from each other and from their recognition that it was they as a community who were under attack and not just themselves as individuals.

## The Establishment of the Eastern Region Teacher Education Consortium

These conditions of both competitiveness and collegiality provide the backdrop against which I want to explore the experience of consortium working of the six initial teacher training institutions in East Anglia. At the time at which this particular initiative began in 1987 these were, with their current names in italics where these have changed:

- Anglia College of Higher Education School of Education
  *Anglia Polytechnic University Faculty of Education*
- Bedford College of Higher Education
  *De Montfort University Bedford*
- Hatfield Polytechnic School of Education
  *University of Hertfordshire School of Humanities and Education*
- Homerton College Cambridge
- University of Cambridge Department of Education
- University of East Anglia School of Education

and they were joined for this initiative with The Engineering Council to form the Eastern Region Teacher Education Consortium (ERTEC).

What had brought this very disparate collection of institutions together and with The Engineering Council in the first place was a small-scale initiative in 1986 under the title Industry Matters in Initial Teacher Education (IMITE) which had provided the opportunity for teacher-education staff to get some first-hand experience in industrial settings and to explore its relevance to their work in initial teacher training. However a much more substantial opportunity for collaborative working under a related agenda arose when the Manpower Services Commission (as it was then called) invited bids for a five-year programme of staff and curriculum development under its Enterprise in Higher Education initiative. This invitation was primarily directed at whole higher education institutions, but the group that was already meeting under the umbrella of IMITE saw the potential for an innovative proposal from a consortium of teacher-education institutions linked to The Engineering Council.

To cut a long story short (see Bridges, 1994 for a fuller account), the group was eventually successful in its bid and it received funding first for a development year (1989) and then for a subsequent five years (1990–4 inclusive). ERTEC defined a framework of objectives (see Appendix A) and a five-year strategy for their achievement was drawn up in the form of individual plans for each institution and an overall plan for cross-institutional or consortium working (e.g., in the form of joint conferences, workshops and publications). Each institution had its own ERTEC institutional coordinator and these together with the consortium director constituted the management committee responsible for the day-to-day working of the programme. The management committee was answerable to a steering committee chaired for most of this period by Denis Filer, the Director General of The Engineering Council and comprising the management committee plus heads of member institutions, representatives of industry, the Employment Department, headteachers and education–industry related bodies.

It is worth stressing, perhaps, that the consortium was set up to achieve the objectives of a project in a finite time, not as a permanent institution. The central consortium function was to stimulate and support an agenda of change across the participating institutions. It was a means to this end not an end in itself.

Not all the activity falling under the project involved the consortium acting in concert — though it was all guided by the strategic objectives and by annual action plans originated independently but agreed collectively. The following range of 'consortium' activity was evident in each of the five years of the initiative:

- representatives of member institutions acting together to organize e.g., a conference or workshop for the benefit of all institutions;
- the director, institutional coordinators or other members acting on behalf of the consortium as a whole — e.g., publishing a consortium newsletter or representing the consortium at a national event;
- bilateral collaborations, including collaborative development projects and exchanges of expertise between consortium member institutions;

- activity unique to one institution which was however reported, disseminated or distributed across the consortium e.g., Anglia's CD ROM products; and
- activity unique to one institution which although it was within the overall project framework fails even to be reported outside the institution.

In their discussion of consortium collaboration institutional coordinators have seen these distinctions as representing a spectrum moving from a strong to a weak sense of consortium collaboration.

### Evaluation, Self-evaluation and Evidence from Other Sources

The consortium was subject to several layers of external evaluation in the form of:

- annual submission of measures against performance indicators;
- visits by Employment Department higher education advisers and an annual review meeting with Employment Department officers to confirm, among other things, that activity which members had contracted to undertake had in fact taken place; and
- a national evaluation of the Enterprise in Higher Education initiative by the National Foundation for Educational Research — an attempted quantitative evaluation of the overall achievement of the initiative after one year.

In addition the Employment Department established an expectation of local self-evaluation and hired the Tavistock Institute to provide a national framework of training and support.

One of the areas the consortium focused on in its own local-evaluation work was its experience of consortium working. This evaluation included:

- employing an internal/external evaluator to interview participants and report on their perceptions (see Whittaker, 1991 and 1993);
- reflective discussion within consortium management committee;
- two joint seminars with representatives of the Scottish Enterprise Consortium, in which consortium collaboration was a central focus;
- two consortium evaluation workshops (the first in November 1990 facilitated by Elliott Stern of the Tavistock Institute and the second in July 1991) in which sessions were devoted to generating data on consortium working;
- annual reports by each institution on progress against targets;
- a commissioned report focusing on cross-institutional collaboration in resource development to support student learning (Wheeler, 1993); and
- a commissioned study on cultural change (Hyland, 1994).

All this activity was designed primarily to support ongoing evaluation by key participants in the consortium rather than the production of a report for an outside audience. Not that all those responsible for carrying forward the work of the consortium were terribly interested in this evaluation work or in reflection on the reports which issued from it. (They were downright hostile to the more bureaucratic external forms of evaluation sponsored by the Employment Department.) 'Evaluation', said one colleague, 'is for parasites who live off people who get things done!' Nevertheless it provides the evidential basis for most of the following observations.

Reference will also be made, however, to some of the (limited) existing literature on consortium working, which carries interesting echoes of some of ERTEC's own experience. The establishment of consortia of higher education institutions is a recent phenomenon in the UK, unless one takes the Oxbridge collegiate system or perhaps the constituent elements of the University of Wales or of London as examples. Neal (1988) describes however a history of consortium collaboration in the United States which goes back to the establishment of the Claremont Colleges in 1925, grew slowly until after World War II, but expanded rapidly in the 1960s as both private and public financial support looked favourably on the notion.

In the educational context of England and Wales, schools and colleges have had more experience of consortium working — certainly in the field of staff development — than higher education institutions. Bridgwood (1989) has pointed out that the Certificate of Pre-Vocational Education initiative was often organized on a consortium basis, with students taking some modules in school and others in college and schools have collaborated for some time in the organization of careers conventions or the provision of Advanced Level courses for 16–18 year-olds (Dean *et al.*, 1979). But under the local education authority (LEA) training-grants scheme many LEAs deliberately organized schools into 'clusters' sometimes 'pyramids' (involving the different phases of schooling within a locality) for the provision by the LEA or themselves of staff development. These sometimes, but not always, coincided with the consortia which were established for the local provision of staff and curriculum development under the Training Agency's Technical and Vocational Education Initiative (TVEI). The criteria laid down for the extension phase of TVEI specified that: 'each authority's extension plan . . . should normally include the arrangements for grouping of schools/colleges in ways appropriate to each area' (quoted in Bridgwood, 1989, p. 1). Bridgwood observes in her introduction to the report on consortium collaboration in TVEI the particular interest, which is also a theme of this chapter, of the phenomenon of consortium collaboration in a world otherwise marked by increased competitiveness between institutions, which are enjoying increased independence as they have the opportunity to opt out of local authorities and increasing autonomy in local management.

There are other interesting parallels between the US higher education experience, the UK school experience and ERTEC's experience of consortium working which will be referred to in the observations which follow.

## The Perceived Benefits of Consortium Working

The benefits of consortium working, as recorded by ERTEC participants, include the following (Whittaker, 1991).

Members recognized the *greater pulling power* of the consortium with sponsoring and funding agencies. It was quite explicitly acknowledged by both the Training Agency and by a representative of The Engineering Council that the cross-institutional character ERTEC was crucial to their support (see Neal, 1988, 'The solidarity that stems from a consortial approach should attract funders who want to concentrate their impact', p. 13).

Similarly the consortium felt itself to have *greater political weight* in, for example, making representations to national bodies and senior industrialists than single institutions might have carried. It is interesting to compare the college head of department reported in the TVEI evaluation: 'the consortium gives us a power base which the authority ignores at its peril' (Bridgwood, 1989, p. 27). Neal argues similarly: 'colleges and universities . . . have more leverage when they address common issues and concerns together. They can deliver a more comprehensive, more accurate, and thus more persuasive picture of higher education's importance than individual institutions can alone' (Neal, 1988, p. 15). The wealth of human and other resources available to the consortium as a whole has been an acknowledged advantage when members have bid for research and developmental contract work nationally.

The consortium served to provide *support for innovators* professionally and in their own institutions. It functioned especially in this way in the management committee at which institutional coordinators could voice their frustrations and ask for and receive moral support and practical help whether it was in the form of advice on strategy, technical assistance with the word processor, help in organizing a conference or a letter to their institutional head supporting the case for more secretarial assistance or promotion. 'The supportive function was brought out very clearly when I talked with institutional co-ordinators about the functioning of the Management Committee . . . It is clear that mutual support can be and is given. There are also opportunities to vent frustrations and to bounce ideas off a critical and supportive group of colleagues. The "College of Institutional Co-ordinators" is a valuable agency reducing co-ordinators' feelings of isolation . . .' (Whittaker, 1991, p. 9). The consortium also ran for the particular benefit of its management group workshops on management, on evaluation and on strategies for change.

The consortium found very practical utility in having *a structure which facilitated and legitimated the networking of experience, bilateral collaboration and economies of staff effort* e.g., by collaborating in developing a profiling scheme or an information-technology guide rather than replicating much of the same work in separate institutions (see Neal's argument re US consortia: 'by co-operating with other similar or dissimilar colleges and universities, an institution can achieve more, do something better, or reduce the cost of an activity', Neal, 1988, p. 3).

A particular benefit of a cross-institutional consortium which brought together teacher educators in the region has been the welcome these have given to the *re-affirmation of their professional identity as teacher educators* across higher education institutions in which this identity had been blurred and in a political context in which they felt collectively beleaguered. (The school coordinator reported in the TVEI evaluation: 'interaction with other institutions has created a community identity instead of a school identity.', Bridgwood, 1989, p. 44.)

These kinds of benefits were anticipated in early planning and provided then the motivation for the formation of the consortium. Experience delivered them in sufficient quantity to sustain that motivation into the sixth year of the programme.

## Issues Raised about Consortium Working

The issues which the experience of consortium working has raised are however an antidote to complacency and are in many ways more interesting than the perceived benefits because they are less predictable.

### 1 Who experiences the consortium?

Institutional coordinators (i.e., the management committee) experienced it pretty intensively (see The TVEI evaluation report which points out that the benefits of consortium working 'were particularly appreciated by school and college co-ordinators and by members of curriculum working parties', Bridgwood, 1989, p. 25). Clusters of staff experienced it episodically when they participated in consortium-wide conferences; a few others recognized it as the source of support for some pet project; for many others the consortium newsletter in their pigeon hole may have been the only — and that momentary — reminder of their association with ERTEC. In only two of the member institutions did ERTEC matters feature *routinely* in the committee responsible for initial training. Students were almost totally unaware of ERTEC as such, though they were aware of initiatives bearing on their experience which in fact had their origins or support in the consortium.

Perhaps this did not matter *providing* the shared objectives were being achieved at institutional level. The consortium was, after all, a means to an end and not an end in itself. As one contributor to the local evaluation put it: '... the drive of Enterprise in Higher Education is into transforming institutions, it is not towards setting up a successful consortium' (Whittaker, 1991, p. 14).

The concern has been voiced, however, that the consortium apparatus might come to serve 'an ERTEC elite' rather than the full population of its member institutions — and this has been reinforced by the perceived level of patronage which those in key positions in the consortium have been able to wield.

### 2 Consortium activity as a substitute for institutional activity

One acknowledged risk is that far from supporting would-be innovators in their drive for institutional change, the consortium provides them with the less threatening and risky alternative of a safe haven of like-minded colleagues located at a geographical, psychological and political remove from the site of conflict. In other words, activity in the context of consortium committees and working groups becomes a substitute for activity in the less hospitable surrounding of the institution.

ERTEC was under increasing pressure from its Employment Department advisers to demonstrate collective consortium activity — but also to ensure that the EHE initiative was 'embedded' in its member institutions. There are some indications, however, that the first of these demands may undermine the second. Francis (1992) has argued:

> The evidence is that such are the demands of the external bodies which fund enterprise projects, that process innovators are becoming progressively detached from their host institutions. The 'real' work of the enterprise project may displace the 'busy' work of the institution. (Francis, 1992, pp. 143–4)

What of course can be even worse is the situation in which it is the 'busy' work of the enterprise project which displaces the 'real' work inside the institution.

### 3 The consortium as a prop to institutional circumvention

This is an extension of the last hypothesis but one for which there is rather more evidence. ERTEC's six institutional coordinators have varied enormously in the extent to which they have worked to achieve change through the mainstream committees and structures of their institutions or by circumventing them. When asked to give their own crude estimation of how much of their efforts were of one sort or another they gave responses which indicated anything from 90–10 per cent mainstream working and from 10–90 per cent through their own informal structures which Francis (1992) analyses in terms of Knowles *et al.*' model of 'unplanned change' (Knowles *et al.*, 1988). A feature of those operating programmes of unplanned change, is that they are unaccountable to internal management systems dealing with policy issues. Applying the model to her own enterprise project, Francis observed that 'their process of accountability was recognised as being through the funding bodies external to the institution. The point of contact internally was generally the finance department. This practice affected the sphere of influence within the institution. Reports from funded projects would be described to the academic board in general terms by a director and information from the coordinator would be communicated through the medium of the college news and the annual report. While this had promotional effect, it did not engage staff or management in the discussion of substantive issues' (Francis, 1992, p. 145).

The informal structures promoting change in ERTEC institutions and the individual coordinators maintaining them relied heavily on the consortium for their support. The finance and other privileges which sustained them came from the consortium, though to these were added the enthusiasm, inventiveness, energy and perhaps 'enterprise' of those who managed them.

It is possible to offer alternative perspectives on the significance of these informal structures. On an interpretation dear to more than one ERTEC institutional coordinator these informal structures were the work of heroic innovators struggling against moribund and bureaucratic systems of management. They could be and were portrayed, alternatively, as systems of patronage run by semi-feudal barons unwilling to submit to obstructive but legitimate democratic procedures or a recalcitrant management, whichever threatened to frustrate the ambitions of their project.

The consortium, it appears, had the function or effect of supporting such structures. Whether this was to its credit or discredit is open to different evaluation.

What is perhaps significant however is the question of how sustainable these circumventing structures are if, as has been suggested, they rely on the combination of consortium support, financial patronage and a fairly elaborate structure of personal ties and obligations sustained by personal dynamism. Take the individual away (early retirement, promotion outside the institution, etc.) take away the funding support — and how much will keep running? 'The enterprise coordinator . . . may be able to influence the involvement of individual members of staff through the building of project systems, but will be unable to embed these developments within the institution without the commitment and involvement of the management team' (Francis, 1992, p. 151).

*4   The sustainable consortium*

The consortium had to consider what would happen to its initiative after Employment Department funding ended in 1994. The three alternatives which first occurred to us were:

- that the developmental processes have been sufficiently achieved or internalized in individual institutions and that there would be further need for consortium activity;
- that some consortium activity would continue but under the direct responsibility of participating institutions (perhaps taking it in turn to provide light servicing support); and
- that the institutions would see value in sustaining some central extra- or supra-institutional apparatus.

The third of these alternatives was always an unlikely outcome. Higher educational institutions are fairly possessive about their own funds, carry elaborate super-structures of their own and are ill-disposed to passing funds on to external organizations outside their direct control. There is all the difference in the world between persuading an HE institution to agree to a deal which puts some funding into an external overarching body as part of a package which brings income into the institution and persuading it to accept a net financial loss for the sake of such superstructure. The rationale of the project in any case supported the first of these alternatives. The consortium was after all set up as a project with a finite life to support institutional change. If it was successful then it would have rendered itself superfluous: the changes which it sought would have become mainstreamed in the institutions. To a considerable extent the reports by heads of institutions in ERTEC's final or 'Quinquennial' Report (Bridges, 1994) confirm that this was indeed what happened.

Besides, after seven years of sustained collaboration, the strength of commitment of the central players in the consortium was being eroded in a variety of ways. Two long-standing institutional coordinators had taken early retirement and a third was contemplating the same route. Another was preoccupied with a highly successful career which he had already for some time struggled to combine with his ERTEC responsibilities. The ERTEC Director was under heavy pressure to focus on internal priorities within his institution including a new role as dean of school and The Engineering Council coordinator was himself simultaneously directing a multi-million pound five-year national project.

And yet the value which was attributed to consortium working (see section 4 above) went beyond its purely instrumental part in achieving project objectives, and there remains a commitment to sustaining some of its activity. At the time of writing the probability is that four of the focus groups which have been especially appreciated as part of the consortium working will continue to meet at least for the following year. These include both a primary and a secondary course coordinators network, technical resource staff network and a network of administrative and academic staff concerned with admissions and access.

But other groups are already establishing themselves in different formations across the institutions. The continuing education sections of the universities in the eastern region have now established a credit accumulation and transfer agreement. The Employment Department research project on competence-based assessment, though based at the University of East Anglia, has drawn colleagues from Anglia Polytechnic University and Bedford College onto its steering committee. An Essex-based project on the profiling of teacher competence brings together the initial training departments of Homerton, Anglia Polytechnic University and Bedford. Perhaps when some new initiative which calls for a broader base of cooperation the practice of mutual collaboration, which ERTEC made routine, will enable ERTEC institutions to compete successfully once again on a national scale and play a leading role in continuing innovation.

## Competition and Collaboration in Higher Education: The Future

And indeed there are a number of good reasons to think that this willingness and capacity to develop collaborative inter-institutional relations will be an important condition for the success of higher education in the coming decade. In their report to the Committee of Vice-Chancellors and Principals on *Longer term prospects for British higher education* Williams and Fry (1994) present a picture of higher education in 2004 which will have expanded to about one and a half million students (compared with one million today); in which the modularization of first degrees and taught postgraduate degrees will be almost universal; and in which there will be considerable institutional differentiation — all of which, they suggest, will have far-reaching implications for relations between higher education institutions and between higher education and further education.

Quite what these implications are will depend on whether HE institutions respond competitively or collaboratively. On the competitive scenario all higher education institutions will try to compete over the whole range of teaching and research. This will have the attraction to purchasers that it will keep prices down, but it has a number of risks. One is that price competition will be at the cost of quality across the board or in particular sections of the market. Market conditions, after all, produce Ratners as well as Cartiers. Perhaps more seriously, the further development of competitive relations will seriously erode the academic and social role of universities in putting knowledge and understanding 'in the public domain'. Traditionally, research has advanced on the basis of the free and open sharing of work in a collegial but critical forum which has broken the bounds of the nation state let alone those imposed by an individual university. Advances in information technology have now created the conditions which allow the freest and fastest possible exchange between scholars located all over the world. It would be a disaster both for the academic vitality of the country and for the cultivation of an informed democratic citizenry if competition between universities was to foster their increasing tendency to regard research as a commodity whose secrets have to be guarded like the recipe for Coca-Cola in order that their full financial potential can be exploited in the market.

Williams and Fry indicate, however, an alternative scenario based on more collaborative relationships. The condition which would permit this would be increasing institutional differentiation: for example, some universities concentrating on undergraduate teaching and some on higher degrees and research; specialization in subject areas (especially those requiring very expensive equipment or those for which there is a restrictive market); specialization of client groups (with some serving a largely home-based regional population and others a wider national or international community). In these conditions collaborative relations between largely complementary institutions will seem a natural alternative. Williams and Fry suggest that 'a preference for collaboration rather than competition was clearly expressed by most of those whom we consulted at all stages' and that one form of collaboration which was felt to be particularly attractive by many of their respondents was 'regional and local consortia of complementary institutions' (Williams and Fry, 1994, p. 29). They continue: 'These might be an extension of existing franchising arrangements and it is not difficult to conceive of the evolution by 2004 of a national network of consortia of universities and colleges in major cities and discrete geographical regions linked by credit transfer schemes, each offering the whole range of higher education provision from foundation courses to research degrees.' (ibid., pp. 29–30).

On this scenario, the ERTEC experience may reflect not the last throes of nostalgia for a departed age of collegiality, but the first light of a new phase in the development of higher education in which it is recognized that providing for the highest quality as well as the widest extent of higher education provision will depend on collaborative relations between higher education institutions which support each other from their complementary skills and talents.

For some, newly espoused of the market language, such collaborative relations are a condition for the successful delivery of higher education: the collaboration is a technical requirement of the project. For others, steeped still in a sense that there is an intrinsic rather than an instrumental connection between education and collaborative interpersonal relations (see Fielding's chapter in this volume), the educative community is one which seeks constantly the project which will warrant and give expression to its collaborative spirit. The first of these relationships has provided the public justification for ERTEC; the second expresses the more private aspirations of many of its participants.

### Appendix A

## Eastern Region Teacher Education Consortium
*Original statement of objectives*

### Pedagogy

- To encourage and enable teachers and student teachers to be enterprising people (by which we mean creative, adventurous, ready to take initiative and shoulder responsibility, forward looking, proactive, dynamic, and effective communicators of their ideas and achievements).
- To give more place in our programmes to educational processes which shift the emphasis from teaching to learning and encourage students' responsibility for their own learning, through for example: resource based learning, experiential learning including learning in the work situation; collaborative learning and team work; independent study; student self evaluation, including participation in the production of a record of achievement which acknowledges enterprising capabilities developed outside as well as inside the formal course.

### Access

- To remove irrelevant obstacles to capable students' participation in our courses and entry into teaching, especially those rooted in ethnicity, gender and unconventional educational or career patterns.
- To widen admission to initial teacher training by seeking new clients and providing new types of courses.

### Economic and industrial awareness

- To enable staff and students to have a better understanding of the national economy, of the economic interdependence of nations, of the function of different sectors of industry, commerce, finance and public services within a national economy; and of the way in which companies and public service organisations (including schools) operate to a budget and manage employer/employee relations.
- To ensure that at least some of this understanding is derived from first hand experience in a real economic setting.

### Enterprising Institutions

- To learn, in particular from all kinds of industry, how to make our own institutions more enterprising in home and overseas' markets and how to manage enterprise successfully.
- To take advantage specifically of the opportunities opened by the developments in the European Community for new initiatives in teacher training.

### Preparing students to handle enterprising initiatives in schools

- To enable students to take their own enterprising capability into their future workplaces.
- To enable students to handle in schools the range of initiatives (e.g., TVEI,

school industry links, project and cross-curricular work, Young Enterprise and Mini Enterprise) which parallel those which the Employment Department is addressing in higher education.

## References

BRIDGES, D. (Ed) (1994) *ERTEC: The Quinquennial Report*, Norwich, ERTEC.

BRIDGWOOD, A. (1989) *Working Together: Consortium Links in TVEI*, Moorfoot, NEFR/ Training Agency.

DEAN, J., BRADLEY, K., CHOPPIN, B. and VINCENT, D. (1979) *The Sixth Form and its Alternatives*, Windsor, NFER.

ERTEC (1991) *Continuing Self-Evaluation*: a report of 12 July Workshop, Norwich, ERTEC.

FRANCIS, E. (1992) 'Change agents, glass ceilings and EATE', in *Journal of Assessment and Evaluation in Higher Education*, 17, 2, pp. 139–52.

HYLAND, R. (1994) *ERTEC, Enterprise and Cultural Change: Beyond the Performance Indicator*, Norwich, ERTEC.

KNOWLES, H.P. and SAXBERG, B.O. (1988) *Organisational Leadership of Planned and Unplanned Change*, Butterworth USA, Futures.

NEAL, D.C. (Ed) (1988) *Consortia and Inter-institutional Co-operation*, Riverside, NJ, ACE/ Macmillan.

WHEELER, R. (1993) 'The potential for cross-institutional collaboration in the development of resources to support school-based training', a report to ERTEC, mimeo.

WHITTAKER, R. (1991) *Consortium Collaboration in Higher Education: Benefits and Drawbacks of Consortium Working*, ERTEC Occasional Paper number 2, Norwich, ERTEC.

WHITTAKER, R. (1993) 'Consortium evaluation in higher education', in *Assessment and Evaluation in Higher Education*, 18, 3, 1993.

WILLIAMS, G. and FRY, H. (1994) *Longer Term Prospects for British Higher Education: A Report to the Committee of Vice-Chancellors and Principals*, London, University of London Institute of Education.

*Chapter 12*

# Collaboration through Networking: The Collaborative Action Research Network

*Bridget Somekh*

A spider's web is as strong as steel and as flexible as nylon.

There are 180 names listed in the 1994–5 directory of members of the Collaborative Action Research Network. They come from over twenty countries. In the introduction to the directory I likened these individuals to the canopy of a rain forest, because the full list of those connected to the network over the years — and, in my experience, quite likely to re-emerge and rejoin when they have the need — is very much larger. CARN's silent partners and labyrinthine inter-connections, like the roots and successive layers of the rain forest, are the source of its strength. We (CARN is very much about 'we') are personally linked, either because in many cases we have worked together, met at conferences, or written letters to each other, or because our CARN membership acts as a 'passport' guaranteeing our commitment to a shared set of educational values. We all believe in the possibility of improving educational practice through practitioners' participation in research. So, we meet each other, even for the first time, as friends and trusted colleagues.

A spider's web seems a rather obvious metaphor for a network since a network is made up of many individuals linked by apparently flimsy, almost invisible bonds. It depends for its existence on the individuals who, though attached to many different organizations, reach out lines of communication to each other. The network exists in the personal links, not in any formal organization. Individuals can find a respite in the network from the otherwise continuous need in their professional lives to develop and maintain their roles (values and functionality) in the context of organizational politics. At least to an extent, if individuals have particular needs the network has the flexibility to move to accommodate them — by providing personal support and practical assistance. In other ways the metaphor of a spider's web is useful in warning against the dangers which, as coordinator of CARN, I have tried to avoid. An educational network exists for its members, not for the coordinator. It is created by the members' efforts, not by an all-powerful central figure. Its purpose is certainly not to establish a powerbase to entrap or ensnare those who approach from outside.

**The Origins and Ideals of CARN**

CARN was founded by John Elliott in 1976, with a small grant from the Ford Foundation, to enable continuing support for the teacher-researchers who had worked in the Ford Teaching Project. In 'Ford T' a group of teachers, led by John Elliott and Clem Adelman of the University of East Anglia, had carried out action research into the practice and development of enquiry/discovery learning. The first CARN Bulletin was published in January 1977 by the Cambridge Institute of Education, where Elliott had just been appointed tutor in curriculum studies. It set out the following rationale for the network:

> To date much conventional Education Research seems divorced from everyday teaching situations, and teachers have been researched *on*, rather than researched *with*. Professional researchers rarely research into the practical problems as they are experienced by the teacher. We feel that more meaningful research into these everyday situations can be initiated and developed far more effectively, either by teachers themselves, or by teachers and researchers working as equal partners. This method by which teachers actively participate in investigating their own classroom situations is termed *action research*. (CARN, 1977, p. 5)

There were 145 members listed in the first CARN Bulletin, of whom thirty-two came from outside the UK (mainly from Australia, the USA, Canada and Germany). The bulletin also included information about current research activities of members, details of the specialist help members could offer each other through the members' advisory service, lists of publications and recommended reading, information on available conferences and courses, and a membership form for joining CARN. In Bulletin number 2, published in January 1978, a five-page article outlined the plans for the first CARN conference to be held in Cambridge in July 1978. Since that time there have been altogether thirteen of these international gatherings usually attended by between 100 and 150 people. They are held in the UK (in recent years at different venues every eighteen months) and are events which greatly nourish the networking. The third CARN Bulletin, published in Spring 1979, included three papers from the first conference conceptualizing issues relating to action research (Elliott, 1978; Harlen, 1978; and Simons, 1978), a report on the conference itself, and critiques of working papers produced by small groups. It also contained case studies of seven schools written by members of their staffs. When the funding from the Ford Foundation came to an end in 1979, a steering group was set up comprising John Elliott as coordinator, his secretary at the Cambridge Institute Dido Whitehead, eleven teachers (including myself), two leaders of teachers' centres, and four lecturers/researchers from higher education institutions. This was the only organizational structure. Steering-group members were invited not elected and there were no elected officers.

This early structure signalled the values of CARN as it was conceived by its founder. It should not be controlled by academics in Higher Education, but should belong equally to all those with educational interests (in the early days attendance at conferences was also managed on a quota system to ensure one-third teachers, one-third local education authority advisers or teachers' centre leaders, and one-third higher education people). Nevertheless, the motivating force behind CARN membership was always more than that of advocacy for action research and the educational values it espoused, such as autonomy, equality, reflexivity (self-monitoring) and openness. CARN members, particularly steering-group members, were motivated also by the opportunities CARN offered for personal–professional links with its founder John Elliott and with each other. Particularly for those of us who were teachers, the professional dialogue we became part of through CARN took away the sense of isolation in our work (e.g., Nias, 1989; Somekh, 1991a). CARN also gave us a sense of control and empowerment through access to informed debate on matters of educational policy and practice. Our own places of work — whether schools, county halls, teachers' centres, teacher training colleges or university departments — fell into place as part of a larger educational system, rising above the petty politics of institutions, that was dedicated to educating children and young people. But the paradox was that, at the beginning, CARN depended to promote its egalitarian values and empower its members upon the patronage of a strong, dynamic leader, John Elliott. I will return to this paradox later in the chapter.

Ten years later, after I became coordinator, a subgroup of the CARN Steering Group drew up a policy document to promote CARN's work within the UK. This was then endorsed by the whole steering group and used by local groups to gain support for their work. It builds on the original statement of CARN's Bulletin No. 7, demonstrating the continuity in CARN's aims and educational values over ten years. The document begins with a statement of aims:

*The Classroom Action Research Network*

CARN sets out to promote:

- recognition that action research provides a powerful means of bringing about effective curriculum development and teacher professional development through a single process;
- support for teachers in carrying out action research in their schools and classrooms;
- encouragement for pupils' participation with teachers in researching the process of learning;
- support for schools in setting up action-research activities as part of their in-service programme for teachers;
- opportunities for professional development through action-research at all stages of teacher education;
- collaboration between teachers in higher education institutions, colleges and schools, and LEA advisory staff, in developing research-based practice;

- funding for the publication of research reports by teachers at all levels of the service; and
- funding for local and regional conferences to disseminate teachers' research.

*CARN: A Network for Success*

The policy document was written at a time when CARN's educational values — and those of the education system as a whole — seemed to be under threat. The relatively closed education system was being challenged from outside in a deliberate attempt to undermine the authority of professionals and open up 'the secret garden of the curriculum' to public scrutiny. Politicians and policy-makers were engaged in introducing a centralized curriculum in which teachers would 'deliver' lessons as 'products' to 'customers' (conceived of largely as tax payers rather than children or sometimes even their parents). Following the initial statement of aims, the policy document expands upon a clear set of values embedded in CARN's activities. The document had a political purpose for Steering Group members at the time, who saw CARN as a possible lever in the political process at a time of great stress for the profession as a whole. A short extract serves to illustrate this point:

Currently there is great interest in achieving quality in education through importing ideas from the world of industry and commerce. But, there are dangers in adopting a model for education where pupils might be seen as products. What is applicable in manufacturing a commercial product is not relevant to the development of a human being. We must be careful about importing wholesale the language and practices of industry. It is a simplification to view the outcomes of schooling merely as the attainment of targets, or to believe that the curriculum is a package that can be delivered following closely defined objectives. On the contrary, we need to teach learners how to learn, so they can take full advantage of the changes that lie ahead of them. Children as learners require teachers committed to asking questions, exploring new ideas and risking some uncertainty. Beyond the core of any prescribed curriculum, teachers must have the autonomy to develop curricula according to the needs of individual pupils. A research-based approach to teaching provides the means of bringing this about.

Teachers who are researchers work on problems they have helped to identify. They develop commitment through lively involvement. Their teaching becomes more than a job. A prescribed curriculum will inhibit this process, albeit unintentionally, by removing from teachers any major responsibility for curriculum development and decision-making. It is difficult for teachers to develop a curriculum which is already prescribed.

We believe that it is important that the voice of the teaching profession should be heard through the publication of detailed reports of research carried out by teachers in schools and classrooms. Educational policy making can be kept in touch with practice if it draws directly on research reports of this kind. There should be no gulf between policy and practice. (CARN, undated)

The CARN policy document was written in 1989 as a response to the changing values in UK society in general, and education policy in particular. The burgeoning market ideology was shocking to many of us who had always subscribed to the democratic values of child-centred education and the empowerment of teachers as individuals and professionals. I remember spending time when drafting the document debating whether it would be too confrontational — and therefore counterproductive in a document designed to promote action research — to state that we rejected the idea that children's education in schools could be compared with the production of a can of baked beans in a factory. Nevertheless, although the document was useful for individuals and institutions wanting to promote action-research locally, it would be hard to identify any significant initiative which resulted from its production. The issue of CARN's political function — or lack of it — is another to which I will return later in the chapter.

The concerns of, CARN members in a changing educational and political context and the extent to which these have challenged and contested CARN's fundamental educational values, is indicated by issues which have come up for debate at the thrice-yearly Steering-Group meetings and (in the last two years) the mini conferences which take place on the morning of the same day. These have included, for example:

1 Classroom issues
   • How best to help a teacher in teaching reading using a 'real books' approach (at a time when methods of teaching reading had become a hot political issue) (June 1991).
   • How to promote teacher reflection and help teachers to theorize at a deeper level about their teaching in order to 'de-mystify theory' (at a time when, as a result of the introduction of a specified centralized curriculum, teachers were in danger of becoming locked too completely into a 'practical culture', and the Secretary of State for Education had gone on record blaming HE institutions for undermining good teaching practice by promoting 'barmy theory') (January 1992).
2 School issues
   • How an in-school coordinator of in-service training could best support colleagues undertaking action research for a part-time Masters degree that, at the same time, was contributing to their school-development plan (June 1991).
3 LEA issues
   • How an LEA advisor could best maintain an action-research group for teachers when funds for research and development within the LEA were shrinking (June 1991).

4  Issues relating to local action-research groups
  • How to maintain interest in, and support for, a local action-research group over a period of time, given the pressures on teachers and schools caused by innovation overload (January 1992).
5  Higher education issues
  • The need for those of us who are lecturers in HE to research our own practice as well as facilitating other people's research into their practice (May 1993).
  • How to respond to the growing interest in action-research among nurses but still maintain support for teachers (at a time when major changes in education policy and particularly funding mechanisms were reducing opportunities for teachers, while changes in the policy and practice of nurse education were enabling action research to flourish) (October 1994).
6  Methodological issues
  • Ways of critiquing and presenting action research (May 1993).
  • The role of feeling in action research, for the researcher and other participants (May 1993).
7  CARN organizational issues
  • Whether to set up a 'Young CARN' group for students in FE, under-16s and children, and, if so, what would be the best way of going about it (November 1992).

**Democratic Change**

A number of changes have taken place since I became coordinator of CARN in 1987. The first, was a significant enlargement of the steering group. Instead of being a small group of individuals selected because of their known interest or practical experience in action research, the steering group was opened up to all those who had a role in supporting action-research in their local area, or a special interest of some kind in action-research. Instead of being invited, individuals involved in leading action-research had a 'right' to be members. In practice this means that when I am approached by anyone who appears to come into the category of 'leading action-research' I suggest he or she might like to join. The list of UK members of the steering group more than doubled within a year and then remained more or less stable — it seems that there is a natural ceiling to the size of the group as individuals drop out and others join (in 1993 there were forty-three UK and twenty-eight overseas steering-group members). This new openness has had the advantage of allowing the steering group to develop the function of a support group for participants in addition to its administrative 'steering' function. However, once the group became less exclusive it arguably became more difficult to obtain release from school for teacher members to attend meetings (in practice this was always difficult, however).

The steering group meets three times a year. In the early days it met at the

Cambridge Institute of Education but since 1987 it meets at venues which rotate around the country to distribute the travel demands fairly. Attendance is entirely voluntary (apologies are sufficient to signal the continuing interest of those unable to attend a particular meeting). Including visitors, there are normally between ten and twenty people at a meeting. Until the mini conferences were instituted in February 1993 (these are held in the morning before the steering group meeting in the afternoon) the item 'Report from Local and Regional Groups — Discussion of Issues' was always placed first on the agenda and normally took up half to two-thirds of the meeting time. This ensured that individuals went away feeling that their time had not been wasted on too much discussion of administrative items. Nevertheless, an examination of the extended notes ('minutes') kept by our secretary Claire Burge (in post since 1987) reveals that the CARN Steering Group has fulfilled the following administrative and organizational functions:

- responding to requests for help in emergencies (e.g., if not enough people have enrolled for a conference to ensure a worthwhile event);
- taking major decisions (e.g., to move to a system of membership by subscription, to establish a new journal, to appoint development coordinators);
- endorsing — or commenting upon — more minor decisions made by the coordinator (e.g., endorsing my action in signing a statement on the Education Bill (HL) 1993 drawn up by BERA, and questioning my action in joining the campaigning group, the Council for Educational Advance, with the result that this decision was reversed.); and
- monitoring the coordinator's procedures and actions and keeping oversight of the finances of CARN, albeit rather remotely (e.g., reviewing CARN's structure, requesting fuller information on membership numbers at the next meeting, requesting a fuller financial statement at the next meeting).

Another change in the organization of CARN took place in October 1991. This was the introduction of membership by paid subscriptions. Up till that time membership of CARN was linked to the purchase of the CARN Bulletin. It was a simple system: the name and address of everyone who purchased a bulletin was entered on a card and henceforward all these individuals received all CARN mailings. It guaranteed the development of an ever-extending network — no one dropped out, not even the dead! It worked well for ten years, at a time when partnerships between higher education and schools were often informal and partnership costs were seen as part of the legitimate business of higher education. Then, as the culture and ethos of higher education in the UK changed, the cost of CARN's mailings and other administrative functions became prohibitive. The new subscription system has eased the administrative problems while challenging us to ensure value for money for our members. It also has the disadvantage of drawing a line between those who are 'members' or 'non-members' which I find a very uneasy distinction in a network. In practice I think of the paid-up members as those within the larger network who are currently active and in close communication; while all those whose 'cards' still lurk in our archive but have not been in touch recently or taken out membership are still, in my mind, part of the larger network. The benefits of belonging to CARN have kept everyone involved in some way, and many of us strongly committed, but it has to be said that this commitment has been squeezed by difficulties in getting support from our institutions (e.g., for travel costs to meetings or travel/subsistence fees to attend conferences).

One of the most contentious changes was the alteration of the name of CARN, in 1993, from the Classroom Action Research Network to the *Collaborative* Action Research Network. This first came up for discussion at the meetings of the Health Care Action Researchers Group which was founded in 1991 by Lynne Batehup and Julienne Mayer of Kings College, London; Alison Binnie of the John Radcliffe Hospital, Oxford; and, Angie Titchen of the Institute of Nursing, Oxford. For the first two years I attended meetings as the group's facilitator and felt the need to respond when nurses and other health practitioners expressed the view that the word 'classroom' seemed to exclude them. Although at first the idea of a change of name was unthinkable, over the next two years my ever more frequent need, as coordinator, to explain the word 'classroom' to members of other professional groups (police officers, social workers, personnel managers), and reassure them that CARN was as much for them as it was for teachers, brought home the serious-ness of the discourse problem. Finally, at the CARN Steering Group meeting in November 1992, a range of suggestions for changing the name were put forward and the decision was taken to put it to vote by the whole membership of CARN. Although words such as 'practitioner' were given consideration, in the end it was decided that the acronym CARN must remain unchanged and four alternatives for words beginning with C were voted on: 'Critical', 'Collaborative', 'Classroom' or 'Change through'. Ballot papers were mailed to 150 members and forty replies were received. Of these twenty-two voted for 'Collaborative', eleven for 'Change through', five to keep 'Classroom', and two for 'Critical'. The decision to change the name to Collaborative Action Research Network was taken at the meeting in February 1993.

The deeply felt outrage of some of the founding members of CARN at the change of name was an expression of the values which CARN embodies, and which they felt were rejected by the change from Classroom to Collaborative. Classroom signified the 'chalk-face' roots of CARN in practitioner's understandings, as well as the educational purposes of the network. Perhaps, too, it underlined the intended subversiveness of CARN in claiming control of research for teachers, in defiance of the hegemony of the academy. Worse, from the point-of-view of those who argued against it, 'collaborative' suggested a rather particular, and narrow definition of action research. It seemed to imply that CARN was buying into the definition of action-research embodied in the work of Carr and Kemmis (1983) and others who saw action-research as a means of empowering teachers through creat-ing a collaborative community. It has to be said that the loudest complainants were academics not practitioners, but the founder of CARN, John Elliott, was among them and over the next year the change of name came up for comment at every meeting as part of 'matters arising' from the minutes of the previous meeting. As coordinator presiding over this change I felt a twinge of guilt!

## Promoting Educational Discourse through Publications

In my view, the great achievement of CARN — over and above the extraordinary but elusive benefits of networking which I will attempt to define a little more closely later in the chapter — has been its publications. These have sprung from the networking since many of the published papers were first presented at CARN conferences. In his editorial to CARN Bulletin no. 4 (1980), John Elliott wrote: 'One of CARN's aspirations is to facilitate a free and open exchange of ideas and to allow those on the receiving end to assess their merits for themselves.' (Elliott, 1980) Ten years later, in my own opening address to the 1989 conference held at the University of East Anglia, I quoted Elliott and argued that 'the writing and reading of our publications . . . constitutes the core of our whole network organisation . . . (they) spring directly from continuing research activities, carried out by individuals or small groups and reported at local or international conferences. The publications are records of the research process which broaden and publicise the private discourse of individuals.' (Somekh, 1991b, p. 7)

Despite, perhaps even because of, their centrality to CARN's purposes and development, the nature of the CARN publications has also changed over the years. In part this has been an outcome of the move towards a market ideology in HE institutions in the UK. A network conceived at a time when the dominant culture valued 'give-and-take' and 'partnership' found costs escalating as the years passed and the dominant culture became one of 'seeking competitive advantage'. The publications always sold out eventually at a profit, but CARN found itself having to invest large sums of money in production costs and recouping these only slowly over a period of two to three years. But that is all the negative side. On the positive side, the new educational ethos of enterprise, coming at the same time as the advent of new technology, raised all our expectations of quality. In 1993 CARN published its first three professionally produced books, *The CARN Critical Conversations Trilogy* (Ghaye and Wakefield, 1993a; Plummer and Edwards, 1993; Ghaye and Wakefield, 1993b) through Hyde publications. Also in 1993, CARN launched the new international journal, *Educational Action Research*, published by Triangle. And in 1994, CARN began working with Jean McNiff of Hyde Publications to support the launch of a new magazine, *Action Researcher*, with a pull-out section devoted to CARN. These three separate ventures provide CARN with a much more adventurous range of publications than was ever possible with in-house publications. With at least twenty papers published in the EARJ alone each year, there has been an increase in the number of papers published under CARN's wider auspices. The net is being spread further and, judging by the number of papers offered at the conference and the ever-increasing number submitted to EARJ, it appears that CARN has become more effective in acting as an incentive for action researchers to write.

The move into commercial publishing challenged CARN to review and develop its editorial policy. From the beginning, in the spirit of Elliott's 'free and open exchange of ideas' (op.cit.) we had resisted notions of selection and control, so that, almost invariably, papers presented at the conferences were published in the bulletins with only the lightest editing. Introducing a system for reviewing and selecting papers was a contentious step. We worried that it smacked of academic control and as a result in 1992/3 the CARN Publications Committee, under the leadership of Tony Ghaye, designed the *Critical Conversations* so that each paper was responded to by a critical friend and the author was then given the opportunity to respond to the response. Although papers were subjected to selection and editorial control, this three-part presentation at its best promoted a feeling of exploration and informality. It broke down the authority of the texts and therefore, we hoped, made them more approachable to a wide-ranging audience of academics and practitioners.

The editors of Educational Action Research (John Elliott, Chris Day, Richard Winter and myself), elected by the CARN Steering Group members, faced exactly the same dilemma in developing a policy for selecting and editing articles. In response, we developed a combined strategy:

1   Firstly, we adopted an action-research approach to the process of *selecting what counts as quality*, saying only in our call for papers: 'Readability and honest engagement with problematic issues will be among the criteria against which contributions will be judged. The journal can be construed as carrying out — through its contributors and reviewers — action-research on the characteristics of effective reporting and the editors will, therefore, welcome exploratory forms of presentation.'

2   Secondly, we adopted a relatively tight set of criteria for *selecting the kinds of papers* to be included in each issue. These, as set out in the Editorial to volume 1, no. 1, (EARJ, 1993) are:
   • contributions that address the relationship between action-research and the political context of practice;
   • accounts of fairly large-scale development programmes that are grounded in practitioners' action research;
   • practitioners' own accounts of action-research they have carried out or generally participated in;
   • papers addressing major theoretical and methodological issues;
   • papers reflecting work carried out in a range of countries; and
   • papers by practitioners from a range of professional groups.

This combined strategy has had the effect of encouraging debate, both within the journal (Clarke *et al.*, 1993; Lomax, 1994) and between the editors, about what might be appropriate criteria for judging action-research and related articles; while ensuring that the pursuit of quality is not used — intentionally or unintentionally — to privilege one kind of article or one kind of educational group over another (e.g., higher education lecturers over school teachers or nurses).

### The Process of Networking and its Benefits

In some senses networking is part of every individual's normal, day-to-day living and working practices. We interact with others to whom we are linked by common purposes, and who, in their turn, are linked to others by common purposes. However, the key concept in networking, as I am defining the term, is that of power relations. In all human interactions there are issues of power and control, which determine among other things whose purposes are prioritised, who is allowed to speak, what can be said, and whose influence will hold greatest sway in determining action (I am assuming here Foucault's [1974] analysis of power as a means of structuring knowledge and social processes). CARN is a network which attempts to reduce the power differential between individuals as much as it is possible to do so, while recognising that we need to remain politically aware and use power relations positively where necessary, rather than acting upon the naive belief that they can ever be entirely removed.

Peter Posch (1994) distinguishes between 'hierarchical networks . . . with a pyramidal relationship of super — and — sub-ordination with ranked (sets of) elements and lines of communication between them,' and 'dynamic networks' such as one in Vienna (Schneck, 1989) 'set up by the teachers themselves . . . unbureaucratically supported (but not taken over) by the regional teacher centre.' According to Posch, 'The essential feature of dynamic networks is the autonomous and flexible establishment of relationships to assist responsible action in the face of complexity and uncertainty.' He, thus, links the notion of a hierarchical network with technical rationality, and dynamic networks with 'reflective rationality', building upon Schön's (1983) analysis of 'reflective practice' as the distinguishing feature of good professionals. To a large extent CARN is similar to the Environment in School Initiatives (ENSI) network that Posch describes later in his paper, in that CARN members have strong interests in 'external support' (they interact with open and knowledgeable partners outside their own institutions), 'legitimation' (they develop and consolidate their educational values through these interactions with 'external' individuals and groups) and 'political impact' (they aspire to making a difference to the educational experiences of students, whether the latter be children in school, adults starting out in higher education, or adults engaging in some form of on-going professional development). However, in his analysis of ENSI Posch distinguishes only two kinds of dynamic network: the school-mediated dynamic network and the broker-mediated dynamic network. In my analysis of CARN I want to make use of Posch's two categories (replacing 'school-mediated' with 'self-generating') and add a third: the loosely coordinated umbrella network.

In my personal experience over fifteen years CARN incorporates all three of these network types. They are not separate but inter-related. Individuals may engage in only one of the three kinds at some times, and in two, or all three, of the kinds at other times.

## The Self-generating Dynamic Network

This kind of network in some ways represents the height of CARN's aspirations but is necessarily the least common. It is generated by participants with a shared concern who have broadly similar status one with another. It is autonomous, self-financing, and egalitarian. From the start the network will depend upon one or two individuals taking some leadership in running meetings and handling communications. The minimal level of organisation dictates that the locally-mediated dynamic network is normally small and highly dependent upon personal contacts. The pay-offs to participants are often high because the network has come together in response to a clearly-defined mutual need. One of the best examples of this kind of network in CARN in recent years has been the Health Care Action Researchers group. Particularly in its first three years, the Health Care group was vibrant and energetic, holding regular meetings, drawing in new participants from across the country, sharing knowledge about action research, and providing mutual support through discussion of action research issues and practical problems, all in a highly effective manner. In my view, a significant indicator of the empowerment of this group is that it became the driving force behind CARN's change of name by democratic vote of the membership as a whole.

### The Broker-mediated Dynamic Network

Posch defines a 'broker' as 'a manager of interfaces between schools and from schools to other institutions.' He therefore sees himself in the role of a broker as leader of the ENSI project within Austria. An example of a broker-mediated dynamic network within CARN was the Pupil Autonomy in Learning with Micro-computers Project (PALM), funded by the National Council for Educational Technology in association with Cambridgeshire, Essex and Norfolk LEAs, 1988–90, of which I was the Coordinator. PALM, like ENSI in Austria, brought together a group of people with a common purpose (developing more effective use of computers as tools for students' autonomous learning), with funding for local activities and central facilitation. PALM became a constituent part of CARN through PALM teachers presenting papers at CARN conferences and publishing through CARN. Nevertheless, PALM remained a separate broker-mediated network in its own right. Inevitably, this kind of network exists for a limited time, though like the Ford Teaching Project itself, it may develop into a different kind of network — or merge with and re-shape an existing network — and thereby continue to exist in the longer term.

This kind of network is difficult to establish — witness the many occasions when individuals within LEAs or Higher Education institutions have been given funding to get such an initiative off the ground and, after an initial spate of activity, have found that participation at meetings reduces, and those who were intended to find new opportunities through participation in the network are obviously not experiencing it in that way! Where, as in PALM, an institution such as a school has made a commitment to working with a project the broker-mediated network may be artificially held together through individuals' sense of responsibility to a commitment, but in that case it will no longer be functioning as a broker-mediated dynamic network, but will have become something other.

In my experience, the key to successful broker-mediated networks lies in the broker's understanding of the power-relations involved, and his or her willingness to give equal priority to the needs and purposes of all members of the network. Where funding has been given to the group by a sponsor this means that the broker must exercise considerable skill in negotiating purposes with individuals and groups which are broadly consistent with the sponsor's purposes. My check-list for successful brokerhood would include:

> allowing each individual or group to determine the main focus of their time and energy within the network;
> making a habit of listening and being ready to change direction when someone else's idea is better than one's own;
> personalising the relationship (e.g. by adding hand-written notes to otherwise impersonal communications such as letters addressed to all participants);
> ensuring that meetings are professionally-fulfilling for all concerned, and if possible fun;
> providing all those services which it is easy to provide and which are consonant with your own purposes — and making sure that people know that this is an expected part of your role and does not demand any particular loyalty or 'pay-back' later (it may of course have this effect if the effect is not sought!);
> keeping in regular, purposeful contact with everyone so that the network maintains a high profile;
> pacing the work, negotiating deadlines, keeping the sponsor happy, and ensuring that there are positive outcomes — products perhaps — as these serve as pay-offs for all participants.

**The Loosely Coordinated Umbrella Network**

Since I became coordinator in 1987, CARN has uniquely come to be a loosely coordinated umbrella network, as well as incorporating both the other kinds of dynamic network. John Elliott has called it 'a network of networks'. As Coordinator of CARN my main role has been to relate to the leaders of the many and varied action research groups around Britain and throughout the world and keep everyone talking to each other. This is what I have attempted, but of course with varying degrees of success.

It is a continuing paradox that although action-research espouses egalitarian values, CARN is subject to a constant political process which serves to fragment action researchers into camps or power bases with their own brand of action-research (including often a brand name!). Prominent action-researchers become established figures with national or international reputations, and generate allegiance from an identifiable group of supporters. The inter-personal motivation which lies at the core of networking, and the importance for those who perceive themselves as powerless of forging alliances with the powerful, provide a context in which individuals can develop personal networks as a power base. As coordinator of CARN I have tried to identify all these established or emerging groups and link them to CARN — or CARN to them.

The concept has been of CARN as a network which links with all action-researchers, whether or not they are formally members, and whether or not they go under the banner of CARN. I have seen CARN as an umbrella network which links all those personalized networks (some small, some much larger) which depend for their existence upon the energy and initiative of key personalities who are leaders in the field of action-research. It has not been easy to achieve, particularly as, since I became coordinator in 1987, I have been based at the University of East Anglia where John Elliott, himself one of these key personalities, is professor of education. I have tried to prevent CARN from being seen to belong to either myself or John (e.g., by rotating the venues of steering group meetings and conferences). But I have not always succeeded: for example, in Jean McNiff's book (McNiff, 1988) CARN is wrongly named in one place as the Cambridge Action Research Network. CARN belongs to the whole membership and not to me personally — yet I would be naive if I did not recognize that I have become identified with CARN and have inevitably shaped its development — if for no other reason than that I am the only member who has attended every steering-group meeting and every conference since 1987. Like all other members I pay a subscription, conference fees and travel costs. But in other ways I am not like other members. All CARN mail passes through my hands, and I have paid part-time secretarial support from Claire Burge to manage the day-to-day administration of CARN, including answering the many letters and queries that come in from all over the world.

Inevitably, CARN is part of a political process. Arguably, if it were not seen by its members as a lever for power that would indicate its failure at a fundamental level. But, as coordinator, it has been my role to keep a balance between the interests of individuals and the interests of all the members of the network as a whole. A good example of the operation of this kind of political balancing act has been the development of the CARN publications policy that I have already described. In the old 'free and open forum for debate' afforded by the CARN Bulletins, people in higher education published alongside teachers. By 1990, as a result of the increased commodification of academic knowledge within a 'market place' culture which had begun to allocate funding to institutions on the basis of the prestige of their publications, it was unrealistic to ask academics to submit publications to CARN Bulletins in preference to refereed journals (the former counting lowest and the latter highest in the system used to rate academic publications). Hence the birth of CARN's refereed journal, *Educational Action Research*. EARJ, as well as all the other things it aspires to be, is a means for CARN to claim prestige for publications which meet action-research criteria for excellence rather than the criteria of more traditional research paradigms. It recognizes the need for CARN members in higher education to trade in their writing as a commodity, and also ensures that papers by practitioners are accorded the same prestige of publication in a refereed journal.

Another paradox springs from CARN's inability, because of its entirely loose organizational structure and shoe-string funding arrangements, to take much organized action, despite the strong educational values of many of its members which leads them to aspire to shape educational policy. It may even be that CARN's strength depends upon this very failure to take effective organized action. It is frustrating that many good ideas are put forward and only a few are acted upon. But the reality is that individuals who spend much of their time organizing initiatives for their own institutions cannot expend the same kind of energy on organizing initiatives for CARN. In a competitive market place, some initiatives — such as providing schools with support to set up action-research groups — might place individuals in a position of conflicting interests (CARN's purposes to provide low-cost support conflicting with their own institution's purpose to provide support at a fair but fully costed market price). Where the two sets of purposes come together, for example in launching a new journal, CARN takes action very effectively and rapidly because everyone can be relied upon to contribute time and energy. The same calculation of 'exchange theory' (Homans, 1958) applies to any wider political action that CARN might perhaps have taken over the years, but in fact has not. Nearly always I have resisted allying CARN with any political party or pressure group, on the basis that as a network rather than an organization we do not have a mandate to represent our members interests. On the one occasion when I took a decision to affiliate CARN to the CEA (an educational lobbying group whose values mirror many of those in the CARN policy document) the steering group voted within six months that we should withdraw. Individuals appear to see CARN as a source of intellectual stimulus and a haven for engaging in professional dialogue free from institutional or wider political pressures.

### Collaboration on the Fringe: Strengths and Weaknesses

In terms of the theme of this book, CARN is engaged in consorting and collaboration *on the edge of* the educational market place. It was founded in the mid 1970s (arguably the only time when 1960s values were at the forefront of education policy in the UK) and has had to adapt in order to thrive in the context of the market place values of the 1990s. It *has* adapted and it *has* thrived — but only by remaining on the fringe. Consciously, the strategy has been to maintain CARN's bedrock educational values of professional exploration, personal reflection and collaborative partnership, while adapting enough to ensure that the work individuals do for CARN will gain them the credit they need within their own organizations. For teachers this means carrying out practically orientated research on their students' learning; for HE lecturers it means organizing conferences, being on the editorial board of journals, and writing articles for professionally produced books and journals.

As I see it, the major strength and the main weakness of CARN are interlinked, both resulting from its being a network and not an organization. The weakness is its lack of a formal structure and inadequate financial resources — both of which make it difficult to get routine and mundane things done. The need for a more formal structure was raised by Chris Day at the steering-group meeting in October 1991. But the inter-linked strength is that CARN is freer from organizational politics than any other organization I know, and this means that it is easy to get a major initiative off the ground if a sufficient number of members care about it and want to see it happen. Following Chris's request, there was a full discussion of the need for a more formal structure for CARN at the steering-group meeting in January 1992. I pointed out that the role of coordinator might be better fulfilled if it were undertaken by more than one person, and that this change would also address the ethical problem of 'sole-power' being vested in one person. But those present decided against appointing an elected coordinator, treasurer and secretary for a fixed term of office because, in the words of one member as stated in the minutes: 'Gill said she for one liked the informality, and had always trusted Bridget to manage CARN for the good — she feared the politicking and private agendas that can surface in more formal groups' (CARN SG minutes, January 20, 1992, p. 4, item 4).

I quote this extract from the steering-group minutes, not in order to claim credit for myself, but to indicate the generous trust and powerful sense of shared endeavour which characterizes CARN at its best. I would argue that a coordinator who is extremely busy doing other things, and has only a minimum of administrative support because of shoe-string resources, is actually unable to exercise autocratic control — and that, this being so in the case of CARN, I have encouraged the efforts of others with gratitude. (This construction is, of course, necessarily partial, but represents my aspiration, at least.) They, meanwhile, have given of their time — e.g., to attend meetings, to assist in organizing conferences, to edit publications, to serve on the editorial board of the journal — freely and willingly, according to their own inclination and energy at the time. There will often be substantial fluctuations in the numbers attending meetings, and although sometimes this will be due to the flagging energies of the coordinator, most often it seems to be due to random change or some seasonal effect such as the timing of teaching practice. And you can't plan for it — one year a huge turn-out in February will be put down to the meeting falling in school half term, so you plan for the same week in February next year and get the lowest turn-out ever! The level of endeavour in a network fluctuates naturally. People make differential contributions depending upon their other commitments, the state of their psyche and the stage of their career. When one falls away another will be coming to the fore. As far as possible, I have tried to ensure that they do not feel any obligation (out of any spurious sense of guilt) to continue their efforts when they have run out of steam. What has to be done has to be shared; and what doesn't get done because there aren't enough volunteers available, doesn't get done — that's it!

### References

CARR, W. and KEMMIS, S. (1983) *Becoming Critical: Knowing through Action Research*, Victoria, Deakin University Press.

CARN (1977) *Classroom Action Research Network, Bulletin No. 1,* Cambridge Institute of Education.

CARN (undated) 'In Need of Action and Research: New Directions for Education', CARN leaflet, CARE, Norwich, University of East Anglia.

CLARKE, J., DUDLEY, P., EDWARDS, A., ROWLAND, W., RYAN, C. and WINTER, R. (1993) *Educational Action Research,* 1, 3, pp. 490–2.

EARJ (1993) *Educational Action Research,* 1, 1, Oxford, Triangle Journals, pp. 5–6.

ELLIOTT, J. (1978) 'The self-assessment of teacher performance', *School-based Evaluation, CARN Bulletin No. 3,* pp. 46–8.

ELLIOTT, J. (1980) *The Theory and Practice of Educational Action Research, CARN Bulletin No. 4,* Cambridge Institute of Education.

GHAYE. T. and WAKEFIELD, P. (1993a) *The Role of Self in Action Research,* Hyde Publications, Bournemouth.

GHAYE, T. and WAKEFIELD, P. (1993b) *Creating Cultures for Improvement: Dialogues, Decisions and Dilemmas,* Hyde Publications, Bournemouth.

HARLEN, W. (1978) 'Pupil assessment', *School-based Evaluation, CARN Bulletin No. 3,* Cambridge Institute of Education, pp. 40–5.

HOMANS, G.C. (1958) 'Social behavior as exchange', *American Journal of Sociology,* 63, 6, pp. 597–606.

LOMAX, P. (1994) 'Standards, criteria and the problematic of action research within an award bearing course', *Educational Action Research,* 2, 1, pp. 113–26.

McNIFF, J. (1988) *Action Research: Principles and Practices,* Macmillan, London.

NIAS, J. (1989) *Primary Teachers Talking: A Study of Teaching as Work,* Routledge, London and New York.

PLUMMER, G. and EDWARDS, G. (1993) *Dimensions of Action Research: People, Practice and Power,* Bournemouth, Hyde Publications.

SIMONS, H. (1978) 'Suggestions for a school self-evaluation based on democratic principles', *School-based Evaluation, CARN Bulletin No. 3,* Cambridge Institute of Education, pp. 49–55.

SOMEKH, B. (1991a) 'Collaborative action research: Working together towards professional development', in BIOTT, C. (Ed) *Semi-detached Teachers: Building Support and Advisory Relationships in Classrooms,* London, Falmer Press, pp. 67–84.

SOMEKH, B. (1991b) 'Opening the discourse', in O'HANLON, C. (Ed) *Participatory Enquiry in Action, CARN Publication 10A,* Norwich, University of East Anglia.

*Chapter 13*

# Beyond Collaboration: On the Importance of Community

*Mike Fielding*

## Introduction

Unless collaboration is seen as, in an important sense, separate from the market place; unless it is motivated by a personal and professional impulse utterly at variance with the market; and unless the collaboration is radically incomplete then consorting and collaborating in the education market place will more often than not be at best a diversion and at worst a betrayal of the central purpose of schools and colleges — namely the education of the pupils/students for whom they have responsibility.

Whilst it is important to acknowledge the potential of consortia and of collaborative professional arrangements in the brave new world of the market, it is also important to raise questions about the adequacy of either as means to specifically educational ends. This volume's rich and varied examples of schools and other educational institutions working together, forming consortia, and getting involved in a whole range of collaborative arrangements with each other and with parents, communities, and businesses will, I am sure, be both reassuring and exciting for many who feared the worst with the advent of 'the education market place', whether interpreted as education affected by the market place or, more seriously, as education reconstructed in the image and likeness of a market place. The degree to which they are reassuring will have a great deal to do with whether or not the exchange of goods and services in the market place has been of benefit to the educational experience of pupils and students. The degree to which they are exciting will have much to do with the capacity of these new forms and examples of collaboration to fire imagination and enrich understanding of what the practice of education for human being and becoming might look like.

Collaboration and consortium arrangements are not of themselves good. We can, after all, collaborate for all sorts of reasons, in all sorts of ways, with all sorts of ends in view which may or may not be shared by those involved. We are still near enough to World War II for the word 'collaboration' to remind us that its apparently neutral procedural characteristics have an inescapable moral resonance which bring us properly and inescapably back to values and purposes. Consortia can exist for reasons which may not be universally welcomed. The emergence of

*149*

the Consortium of Selective Schools in Essex is as likely to be as contentious as their recent decision to use thirty-minute tests in maths and English alongside a forty-five minute verbal reasoning test.

Put more positively, I will argue that if collaborative and consortia arrangements are to succeed as part of an educational undertaking they need to be viewed and understood as part of a wider, more inclusive intention which sees education as fundamentally about community. Community is not a cuddly afterthought or a convenient compensation for those who dislike the anomic rigours of the market or those who are damaged by them. It is prior to the market both in terms of importance and purpose (Macmurray, 1961) and is implacably antithetical to it (Cohen, 1994). Community is both the condition and the means of educational and human fulfilment.

## Changing Our Theory of Schooling: Sergiovanni on Schooling and Community

One of the most thorough and interesting books to explore the importance of community in education is Thomas Sergiovanni's *Building Community in Schools* (Sergiovanni, 1994) which offers a rich tapestry of practical examples interwoven with an informed and imaginative grasp of the philosophical issues which help us to understand what community is, why it is important and how it might be developed. As a scholar whose previous work lies mainly in the area of educational management, focusing in particular on the nature of leadership (Sergiovanni, 1990, 1991, 1992), it is interesting and reassuring to see him exploring the limitations of management with an intensity and conviction that also gives us a more authentic sense of its possibilities.

At the heart of Sergiovanni's argument is the strong conviction that contemporary social and political dilemmas facing the United States (and by implication and to a significant degree many other western nation states such as the UK) have their roots in a continuing and intensifying tension between the individual's desire for independence, autonomy, the opportunity to pursue things in their own way and a contrasting desire for belonging, for connectedness, for something which gives meaning to the fragmentation, loneliness and isolation which so often attends too fierce an emphasis on individualism. In one sense, of course, none of this is new: these dilemmas are at the very heart of much of western culture since the break up of the Middle Ages and are currently at the centre of debates in social and political philosophy. His suggestion that the key factor preventing us from making educational and social progress lies in the demise of community is in line with a long and respected tradition and many will warm to his suggestion that 'to enable good schools to flourish, we need to rebuild community. Community building must become the heart of any school improvement effort. Whatever else is involved . . . it must rest on a foundation of community building' (Sergiovanni, 1994, p. xi). What is new is not only his capacity to give a whole range of illustrations and examples of what that means in practice, but also, and equally importantly, Sergiovanni's argument that a reassessment of these cultural dilemmas requires us to change our theory of schooling from one which sees schools primarily as organizations to one which instead sees schools as communities. His affirmation that 'If we view schools as communities rather than organisations, the practices that make sense in schools as organisations just don't fit' (Sergiovanni, 1994, p. 4) is an inviting preface to much that is fresh and challenging in his unfolding argument.

Before going on to look at some of the consequences of such a change it is important to get a more substantial feel for the philosophical basis of Sergiovanni's conviction. It is here that the strengths and, as I shall argue later, the limitations of his model lie. The main source of Sergiovanni's model is the work of the nineteenth-century German sociologist Ferdinand Tonnies whose book *Community and Association* (*Gemeinschaft und Gesellschaft*) (Tonnies, 1955, [1887]) had a significant impact on subsequent sociological studies of society, the state and community.

Following Tonnies's notion of *Gemeinschaft*, Sergiovanni's working definition of community suggests that:

> communities are collections of individuals who are bonded together by natural will and who are together binded to a shared set of ideas and ideals. This binding and bonding is tight enough to transform them from a collection of 'I's' into a collective 'we'. As a 'we' members are part of a tightly knit web of meaningful relationships. This 'we' usually shares a common place and over time comes to share common sentiments and traditions that are sustaining. When describing community it is helpful to speak of community by kinship, of mind, of place, and of memory. (Sergiovanni, 1994, p. xvi)

In contrast, *Gesellschaft* is more typical of modern society. Community values are superseded by contractual ones and life takes on a much more impersonal feel. Achieving a sense of meaning becomes more elusive and more problematic. Applying the notion of *Gesellschaft* to the modern corporation Sergiovanni suggests that:

> In the corporation, relationships are formal and distant, having been prescribed by roles and role expectations. Circumstances are evaluated by universal criteria as embodied in policies, rules, and protocols. Acceptance is conditional. The more a person co-operates with the organisation and achieves for the organisation, the more likely will he or she be accepted. Relationships are competitive. Not all concerns of members are legitimate. Legitimate concerns are bounded by roles rather than needs. Subjectivity is frowned upon. Rationality is prized. Self-interest prevails. These characteristics seem all too familiar in our schools. (Sergiovanni, 1994, p. 10)

This last comment is indicative of Sergiovanni's own preferences. Whilst acknowledging that *Gemeinschaft* and *Gesellschaft* are ideal types which don't actually exist, he suggests they do help us categorize and explain opposites and plot movement between them. His main argument in the book is that schools have overemphasized *Gesellschaft* to the detriment of *Gemeinschaft*. 'In modern times the school has been solidly ensconced in the *Gesellschaft* camp . . . with unhappy results. It is time the school was moved from the *Gesellschaft* side of the ledger to the *Gemeinschaft* side. It is time that the metaphor of the school was changed from formal organisation to community.' (Sergiovanni, 1994, p. 14).

What is involved in making that move provides the fascination and the practical value of the book. Although Sergiovanni does not explicitly address the issue of how a school or educational undertaking might relate to other schools and external bodies, there is an interesting chapter on 'Becoming a Professional Community' which seeks to redefine what we mean by professionalism and explore the subsequent effects such a redefinition has on notions of 'colleagueship'.

The redefinition of professionalism starts with a robust rejection of too close an association with models from the medical profession. Whilst some parallels are appropriate, the suggestion is that the parallel has led us down a path which is too technicist in its feel and its focus.

> It encourages us to view professionalism primarily as a technical activity involving the delivery of expert services to clients. This view shapes how we view teaching practice. We come to believe, for example, that professionals enjoy a knowledge and skill monopoly. Teaching comes to be viewed as instruction involving delivery of expert knowledge to students. During the transition process the teacher's role is active and the student's role is passive. A contract is implied: the teacher gives expert service, the student gives submission. The teacher has the power to do, decide and direct, and the students are expected to follow. (Sergiovanni, 1994, p. 140)

The pursuit of this kind of professionalism tends to emphasize impersonal, *Gesellschaft* relationships. Drawing on the work of MacIntyre (MacIntyre, 1981), Flores (Flores, 1988), and Noddings (Noddings, 1986), Sergiovanni argues for a professional ideal which is made up of four different dimensions which sit more comfortably in the move towards *Gemeinschaft*. These are:

1  a commitment to practice in an exemplary way;
2  a commitment to practice toward valued social ends;
3  a commitment to the ethic of caring; and
4  a commitment, not only to one's own practice, but to the practice of teaching itself.

The commitment to practice in an exemplary way is basically about helping the school to become a learning community, where adults see themselves and are seen as learners and where pupils/students see themselves as teachers as well as learners. There is a move away from 'the *Gesellschaft* transmission model, where experts create instructional delivery systems as a way to transmit their expertness to clients' (Sergiovanni, 1994, p. 143) to something which is much more reflexive, much more informing of, and informed by, relationships. There is also a commitment to action-research and an insistence that where the school is involved with outside experts the brief is about empowerment of those within the school to take forward change rather than the application of external solutions.

The second dimension — a commitment to practice towards values social ends — is about committing yourself to your students, their parents and the school's aspirations and values. It is, Sergiovanni argues, about stewardship and the transformation of teaching from an occupation to a calling.

The third ideal — that of caring — is in many respects the most important. It is argued that caring which is 'demonstrated in substantive ways that lead to learning' (Sergiovanni, 1994, p. 145) is fundamentally about relationships. Citing an inspirational passage from Nell Noddings (Noddings, 1986) the technicist argument that caring gets in the way of effective teaching is eloquently answered:

> Fidelity to persons does not imply that academic excellence, the acquisition of skills, or the needs of contemporary society should be of no concern. To suppose, for example, that attention to affective needs necessarily implies less time for arithmetic is simply a mistake. Such tasks can be accomplished simultaneously, but the one is undertaken in the light of the other. We do not ask how we must treat children in order to get them to learn arithmetic but, rather, what effect each instructional move we consider has on the development of good persons. Our guiding principles for teaching arithmetic, or any other subject, are derived from our primary concern for the persons whom we teach, and methods of teaching are chosen in consonance with these derived principles. An ethic of caring guides us to ask: What effect will this have on the person I teach? What effect will it have on the caring community we are trying to build? (Noddings, 1986, p. 499)

The fourth and last dimension concerns a commitment, not just to the development of one's own practice, but to the development of teaching as a practice as such. This final concern transforms teaching from an individual to a collective practice. Success is collective success, about teaching and learning in a school, about teaching as a professional activity.

This revised notion of professionalism which goes well beyond bare requirements of competence to embrace what might be called professional virtue has a knock-on effect on how we conceive of what Sergiovanni calls 'colleagueship'. Colleagueship for Sergiovanni involves a firm commitment to exploring a more collective practice and more collegial ways of working, whilst acknowledging the dangers that too heavy an emphasis on community might pose for the significance of the individual voice.

## On the Dangers of Marginalizing Difference

Sergiovanni's book is a good one: it is imaginative, ambitious and impressive in its scope. It is largely stimulating to read and full of practical examples which help us not only get to grips with a new and much needed alternative perspective on schooling in barren times, but also move our own thinking on in ways which are likely to impact on practice. The nature of the questions it raises for consortium and collaborative undertakings are at once properly disturbing as well as creatively reassuring and provide a first line of defence against the insinuations of dubious compromise and the imperatives of the cash nexus to which we are all susceptible.

However, it is also a flawed book, though not in the sense that its central messages are invalid or unimportant. Rather it is flawed in the double sense that, firstly, key issues in the debate about community are not adequately addressed and, secondly, its philosophical limitations parallel a tendency to remain on the surface of testimony rather than dive into the murkier, less congenial depths of complex and contested experience. The strength of its advocacy and the urgency of its narrative give too little sense of what is puzzling or problematic about the concept and the reality of community in postmodern times.

The absence of any reference in Sergiovanni's text to post-modern writers for whom notions like 'community' and 'justice' are problematic is a serious omission. The difficulty for postmoderns arises largely because these grand 'totalizing' notions like 'community' suppress differences which are centrally significant in our struggle to make sense of who we are and who we might become. They also do nothing to challenge dominant notions of rationality which privilege a, usually white, western, male perspective. Notions like 'community' are seen to presume a degree of homogeneity which runs counter to the keen and complex sense of difference which feminist postmodernists in particular have been exploring (see Young, 1986).

Sergiovanni's unwillingness to engage with these issues is as consistent as it is regrettable. There is one occasion on which he acknowledges the general area of concern which the post-moderns typically pursue. But he does so in a way which does not do justice to the importance of the issues. Rounding off a section on the importance of collective practice and collegiality, Sergiovanni remarks that 'It does appear that when we develop conceptions of the common good and wrap them in the norms of *Gemeinschaft*, the values of individuality and freedom are compromised' (Sergiovanni, 1994, p. 150). There follows a page or so of discussion and examples of possible safeguards, but the length of treatment is inversely related to its quite clear importance both in academic debate and the realities of daily life. One reason for this surprising lacuna may well have its origins in the philosophical inadequacy of Tonnies's account of community and it is to this issue which I now wish to turn.

## On the Limitations of an Organic Conception of Community

This substantial weakness in Sergiovanni's work is both surprising and predictable. It is surprising in the sense that the postmodern challenge to community is something which is unambivalently present in our experience of daily life and increasingly prominent in debate within social and political philosophy. It is predictable in the sense that the philosophical roots of his understanding of community push him towards a position which, in its quite proper desire to emphasize the importance of belonging, too often ends up suffocating the very fulfilment it is trying to promote.

The major frustration and limitation of Sergiovanni's understanding of community lies in his adoption of a perspective that is a prisoner of the intellectual climate of its birth. Tonnies's work, whilst hugely significant, remains a product of late nineteenth-century thought. Dominated by the idea of organism, its understanding of human society and individual flourishing represented a considerable advance on the mechanistic thinking of the previous era. But it does not provide an adequate account of community for the twentieth century and beyond.

The view of community which Tonnies's organic, *Gemeinschaft* account replaced was the atomistic or contractarian, *Gesellschaft* model typified by Thomas Hobbes, Adam Smith and Jeremy Bentham in the seventeenth, eighteenth and nineteenth centuries and by thinkers like F.A. Hayek, John Rawls, and Robert Nozick in our own. Fundamentally, the view of human nature represented by what Kirkpatrick in his outstanding work on community (Kirkpatrick, 1986) calls the contractarian model suggests that human beings exist in their own right prior to society and that society and other forms of association come about because people decide, from the standpoint of self-interest, to make contracts with others for their own benefit. It is no accident that this view emerged pre-eminently in the sixteenth and seventeenth centuries which saw the break up of the medieval *Gemeinschaft* and the emergence of capitalism and the market society. Community on this account is prudential, contractual, wary, conditional on the interests of the individual being met. The dominant image is that of a machine comprised of what Tonnies himself referred to as 'atom like units'.

The atomistic, contract form of community linked to an individualistic, typically capitalist market-oriented view of society is deeply and destructively flawed. Whilst it adequately describes certain forms of human unity which are important, they are typically contractual and impersonal. The account of community it offers is partial, particular and parsimonious. It has little time, place or understanding of much of what is best in human endeavour and an ideological antipathy towards notions like service which see people in ways which have no necessary connection with self-interest or profit. Some, like Gerry Cohen (Cohen, 1994), argue that it is very difficult to make much sense of the notion of community in the context of the market place. Community is essentially 'the anti-market principle according to which I serve you not because of what I can get out of doing so but because you need my service. That is anti-market because the market motivates productive contribution not on the basis of commitment to one's fellow human beings and a desire to serve them while being served *by* them, but on the basis of impersonal cash reward' (Cohen, 1994, p. 9).

The organic, *Gemeinschaft* notion of community rests on very different assumptions about human beings and the kinds of unity which enable them to flourish. Whilst *Gesellschaft* is clearly a feature of the modern era and initially was a necessary and important liberation from the bonds of tradition, it is only able to express an aspect of our human being and one which is frequently as destructive as it is partial. In contrast to the individual's grudging and often apprehensive surrender of freedom for the sake of usually temporary, self-interested alliances of

*Gesellschaft*, those like G.W.F. Hegel and Tonnies who advocate an organic view of community, argue that human beings can only achieve fulfilment in and through community. The individual and the community are organically related: the one is not opposed or antagonistic towards the other; they are better understood as an interdependent, living unity. Hegel illustrates the point by reference to the limbs of a body: 'the limbs and organs ... of an organic body are merely parts of it: it is only in their unity that they are what they are, and they are unquestionably affected by that unity, as they also in turn affect it. These limbs and organs become mere parts, only when they pass under the hands of the anatomist, whose occupation, be it remembered, is not with the living body but with the corpse' (Hegel, 1975 [1830], pp. 191–2). The organic relations between people which are characteristic of *Gemeinschaft* or community are, for Tonnies, more fundamental and more natural than those of *Gesellschaft* or society. It is *Gemeinschaft* which 'is the lasting and genuine form of living together ... [whereas] *Gesellschaft* (society) is transitory and superficial. Accordingly, *Gemeinschaft* (community) should be understood as a living organism, *Gesellschaft* (society) as a mechanical aggregate and artefact' (Tonnies, 1955 [1887], p. 39).

The strength of the organic view of community lies in its capacity to capture the importance of forms of relationship and unity which acknowledge the essentially fulfilling nature of human interdependence. There is much that is attractive about such a position, whether the *Gemeinschaft* of Tonnies which he argues is the only 'lasting and genuine form of living together' (Tonnies, 1955 [1887], p. 39) or the eventual communist society of Marx where he argues 'only in community ... is personal freedom possible ... In a real community the individuals obtain their freedom in and through their association' (Marx, 1970 [1846], p. 83). The organic view is especially attractive at a time when the ravages of the market are destroying communities and the texture of the social fabric is becoming increasingly threadbare. There are, however, substantial worries which need to be acknowledged. Firstly, many would argue that the overriding weakness, both philosophically and in lived experience, is that despite repeated assertions of the individual's importance, in the end that importance is subservient to the good of the whole. In other words, an individual is only of functional importance; their significance is related to whatever it is they contribute to the community or, in some versions, the state. Secondly, Tonnies's conservative grieving for the loss of aspects of pre-capitalist community is too narrow and too strongly tied to particularities over which we have too little control — place, time and kinship. Thirdly, the bonding of *Gemeinschaft* has too much about it which serves to suffocate rather than enable human flourishing.

### On the Need for a New Model of Community: Community as a Unity of Persons

If both the contract and the organic models of community have significant dangers and if they only partially capture what is important in human flourishing, what might a third model look like? How might it articulate what the others have only been able to hint at or grasp inadequately? The most compelling attempt to grapple with this challenge is to be found in the work of John Macmurray, one of the most important and most neglected British philosophers of the century.

Macmurray argues that neither the contract nor the organic models are able to express the fundamental nature of community. Both are, in fact, more properly understood as forms of society rather than community. Both have their place, both may contribute towards community, but both fall short of an adequate expression of its true nature. Their inadequacy lies in their characteristically instrumental nature. Cooperation (and collaboration), which are typical of these forms of unity, are essentially functional relations. There are common purposes which bring people together and those purposes shape the way in which people relate to each other:

> Each member has his place in the group by reason of what he contributes, in co-operation, to the pursuit of the common end. He is a member in virtue of the function he performs in the group; and the association itself is an organisation of functions. Thus, though the members are persons, and the group is an association of persons, the members are not associated *as persons*, but only in virtue of the special functions they perform in relation to the purpose which constitutes the group; and the society is an organic unity, not a personal one. (Macmurray, 1950, pp. 54–5)

For Macmurray there is another form of human unity — community proper — in which we are uniquely able to express ourselves as persons. Such relationships go beyond our functional interdependence, whether it be grudging and prudential or more welcoming and fulfilling.

> A community . . . rests upon a different principle of unity. It is not constituted by a common purpose. No doubt its members will share common purposes and co-operate for their realisation. But these common purposes merely *express*, they do not *constitute* the unity of the association; for they can be changed freely without any effect upon the unity of the group. Indeed it is characteristic of communities that they create common purposes for the sake of co-operation instead of creating co-operation for the sake of common purposes . . . It is not functional. It is not organic. Its principle of unity is personal. It is constituted by the sharing of a common life . . . It is the sharing of a common life which constitutes individual personality. (Macmurray, 1950, pp. 55–6)

Community, then, is a personal not a functional mode of unity. It is fundamentally important because, Macmurray argues, it is only in community that we are able to be and become more fully ourselves. Community is about the reciprocal caring for, and enjoying, someone for their own sake; it is not about using others to achieve one's own fulfilment.

Macmurray has a great deal more of interest to say about the nature of community, particularly with regard to its constitutive principles of freedom and equality which he explores in an admirably clear and accessible way in his short book *Conditions of Freedom* (Macmurray, 1950). The exclusive, inward and objectionable nature of traditional notions of community are addressed by the double insistence on these two principles.

He illustrates the point with reference to the example of friendship. Taking the principle of equality first, Macmurray argues that:

> Friendship is essentially a relation between equals . . . (which) is not to say that they are equally clever, or equally strong, or equally good. Personal equality does not ignore the natural differences between individuals, nor their functional differences of capacity. It overrides them. It means that any two human beings, whatever their individual differences, can recognise and treat one another as equal, and so be friends. (Macmurray, 1950, p. 73)

This insistence on personal equality is partnered by the second constitutive principle of friendship which is freedom. Two significant things follow from this. Firstly, 'the unity between friends cannot be imposed' and, secondly, 'it provides for a complete self-expression and self-revelation which is mutual and unconstrained . . . It provides the only conditions which release the whole of the self into activity and so enable a man to be wholly himself without constraint' (ibid). Whilst these conditions are never fully realized, particularly in communities struggling to exist in unpropitious times, 'It is the mutual intention to treat one another as equals and to be free in relationship that makes us friends' (ibid.).

Finally, it is important to point out that these two principles condition each other reciprocally.

> Equality is a condition of freedom in human relations. For if we do not treat one another as equals, we exclude freedom from the relationship. Freedom, too, conditions equality. For if there is a constraint between us then there is fear; and to counter that fear we must seek control over its object, and attempt to subordinate the other person to our own power. Any attempt to achieve freedom without equality, or to achieve equality without freedom, must, therefore, be self-defeating. (Macmurray, 1950, p. 74)

This is a compelling account of community which with elegance and conviction delineates principles which enable us to see our way more clearly towards forms of human relation which regard individuality and community as interdependent rather than contradictory. It is also a powerful account, not just of community but of democracy. Indeed, Macmurray goes on to suggest that 'The democratic slogan — liberty, equality, fraternity — embodies correctly the principles of human fellowship. To achieve freedom and equality is to create friendship, to constitute community between men' (Macmurray, 1950, pp. 74–5).

In making that essential link with democracy Macmurray also makes a further important point about community which is particularly pertinent in the context of Sergiovanni's bold and insightful distinction between schools as communities and schools as organizations. Community is not only an essentially voluntary mode of human unity it is also not amenable to organization. 'It is characteristic of communities that they create common purposes for the sake of co-operation instead of creating co-operation for the sake of common purposes. It follows from this that a community cannot be brought into existence by organisation' (Macmurray, 1950, pp. 55–6). The most that organization can do is provide appropriate material conditions which will enable community or fellowship to flourish.

This last point about organization is difficult to grasp in our current understanding of schools which is so heavily dominated by managerial modes of thought. It also leaves unanswered two of the most fundamental questions of social and political philosophy which is of direct concern to teachers and others who wish to see schools become more like communities and less like commercial organizations. Firstly, 'What is the relation between community and society, between fellowship and politics, between personal unity and functional unity, between schools as communities and schools as organisations?' Secondly, 'How might we encourage community if organisational and political means constantly stand in tension with it?'

With regard to the first question about the relationship between community and society, between the personal and the political, Macmurray is quite clear that the former is prior to the latter:

> Community is prior to society . . . Personal freedom . . . can be achieved only in fellowship. Indeed, the extent and quality of such political freedom as we can achieve depends in the last resort upon the extent and quality of the fellowship which is available to sustain it. Conversely, the unity of co-operation which is the care of politics, has significance only through the human fellowship which it makes possible; and by this its validity and its success must be judged. (Macmurray, 1950, pp. 56, 69–70)

As he cogently remarked in his later Gifford Lectures, 'the economic is for the sake of the personal . . . an economic efficiency which is achieved at the expense of the personal is self-condemned, and in the end self-frustrating' (Macmurray, 1961, pp. 188, 187).

With regard to the second question about how we create community if not by organization Macmurray's answer is both profound and simple and has a direct bearing on the issue of 'collaborating and consorting in the market place'.

> The functional life is *for* the personal life; the personal life is *through* the functional life. This means that a man's working life is for the sake of his personal life; that the meaning and purpose of life in the factory or office is to be found in the home life; that men are not to be used for labour, but labour to be used for men; that people are more important than the jobs they do . . . (However) it is not possible in practice to keep the two lives

separate. The kind of working life a man has to live decides the kind of personal life he can have . . . The personal life needs cultivation and that means time and resources. We cannot keep the two lives in watertight compartments because the shape of one decides the outlines of the other. (Macmurray, 1941)

If schools are to be and become communities their organizational structures and processes must enhance rather than inhibit the opportunities and the desire of those within it to relate to each other as persons, not just as occupants of roles or fulfillers of functions. They must also reaffirm their sense that what they are about is framed firmly within the context of educational purposes, not just the purposes of schooling.

If we transfer this perspective to the circumstance of the education market place it seems that whilst it is true that consorting and collaborating (the functional) is for the sake of education (the personal), it is also true that the nature of that collaboration enhances or diminishes the possibility of its educational fulfilment.

One particularly striking example of a form of collaboration which in its structures and in its intention moves its members constantly in the direction of community and away from the merely functional exchange of ideas is IADAS (International Association for the Development of Adolescent Schooling). This international network, set up with the intention of encouraging the development of exploratory educational practice within and between schools who have a broadly similar approach to education, has met once a year for over twenty years in different host institutions and explored jointly negotiated themes through the perspectives and practices of the participating schools. There are many reasons why this international partnership has continued to flourish and grow since its inception in 1974, but among them those that have to do with the close interrelationship between its purposes, structures and practices are particularly significant.

Three strands of IADAS which strike me as especially important are, firstly, its capacity to encourage and celebrate diversity; secondly, its insistence that those who participate do so as professional equals; and thirdly, that the reciprocal commitment to the principles of freedom and equality, which the espousal and nurturing of diversity and equal value proclaim, combine to create community within a framework of values and intentions that speak of interest in and care for the plurality of each other as educators and as persons.

The nurturing and celebration of diversity expresses itself in a number of ways. Schools bring to the conference something from their institution that they are proud of which they can share via a workshop or presentation. The particular examples fall within the ambit of an agreed theme that participating schools had a hand in negotiating at the previous year's conference.

The equal-value principle is expressed not only through the allocation of time and opportunity to articulate what each country wishes to explore, but also in the attitudes and dispositions which inform the responses and the dialogue which ensue. Different participants pick up on different aspects of conversation and debate according to their own interests and preoccupations, but no country is demeaned, attacked or marginalized. Interest in, and curiosity about, the ways in which themes work themselves through in different national contexts provide the stimulus and inform the humility of response. Here challenge is a consequence rather than a forerunner of diversity, and growth the outcome of juxtaposition, reframing and dialogue rather than the measured and often muted response often found in the context of a procrustean framework such as OFSTED.

The principle of community is articulated in action in two ways; through the manner and form of dialogue and debate, and through the personal contact amongst participants. With regard to the first of these, prior to the conference each country produces a short paper sketching out some of its practical explorations of the previously agreed theme. The host country goes through the reports and picks out contrasting and similar strands which then form the basis of cross-cultural discussion. At its best this kind of debate helps participants to try to come to terms with their own understandings of themselves as teachers with regard to their own practice and aspirations by encountering how those ideas and values are enacted in other circumstances in other contexts.

The fact that these encounters are often deeply felt in intellectual, practical and emotional senses points to the second strand of community which participants invariably experience. A great deal of attention is given to domestic and social arrangements, particularly by the host country. All participants stay with host families and during the three days of the conference the practical activities and experiences which are shared serve to bind and deepen relationships and understandings. Community, then, has practical expression within a broad framework of shared values which inform the exploration of difference and diversity in personal and professional circumstances where participants are valued equally and uniquely. Human development is an essentially reciprocal, interactive process in which diversity and commonality are interdependent. The richness of our difference depends on the richness of what we share; individuality is the product and not the precursor of community. The richness of what we share depends upon the richness of what makes us unique; the vibrancy of community depends upon the degree to which it encourages and celebrates difference (Fielding, 1994b, p. 411).

### Education, Community and the Market Place

What I have argued thus far has focused largely on the importance of schools regarding themselves not just as organizations, but as communities. My view is that their life as communities is more important, more fundamental and more quintessentially educational than their life as organization; their purpose as educational institutions, not just schools, requires that their organizational arrangements are conceived of as functional means towards personal ends — namely, the education of those for whom they care and have responsibility. Implicit in this is the view that education is essentially a personal and not a technical process.

Again, Macmurray's writing is particularly helpful in deepening our understanding of the nature of education as a personal process at a time when the ludicrous contradictions, reversals and re-reversals of a barren, technical approach to curriculum in particular and schooling in general have done so much to impoverish and dishearten teachers and students alike. His refreshingly radical, but largely unpublished, work on education is unambiguous in its affirmation of the centrality of community. Writing in the late 1950s in his Moray House Lecture 'Learning to be Human' Macmurray relates his views on the nature of human flourishing to the context of education and argues that community — 'entering into fully personal relations with others' — is central because education is essentially about being and becoming more fully human.

> (The) principle, that we live by entering into relations with one another, provides the basic structure within which all human experience and activity falls, whether individual or social. For this reason the first priority in education — if by education we mean learning to be human — is learning to live in personal relation to other people. Let us call it learning to live in community. I call this the first priority because failure in this is fundamental failure, which cannot be compensated for by success in other fields; because our ability to enter into fully personal relations with others is the measure of our humanity. For inhumanity is precisely the perversion of human relations. (Macmurray, 1958)

Later on in the same paper he turns his attention to the technicist fallacy which has grown rather than diminished in the intervening decades.

> No technical training in educational methods can ever be (sufficient), however unexceptionable the methods may be in themselves. Education is not and cannot ever be a technical activity. The attempt to turn would be teachers into technicians by teaching them classroom tricks is as stupid as it is ineffective . . . Here, I believe, is the greatest threat to education in our own society. We are becoming more and more technically minded: gradually we are falling victim to the illusion that all problems can be solved by proper organisation: that when we fail it is because we are doing the job in the wrong way, and that all that is needed is the 'know-how'. To think thus in education is to pervert education. It is not an engineering job. It is personal and human. (Macmurray, 1958)

At the heart of the educational process lie not only the relationships between the staff and the pupils, but also between the staff themselves.

> Community . . . is the condition of success in (the school's) educational function. Only in a community can a living culture be developed . . . If the staff is a community, the school will be a community. If the staff is a mere society of functional co-operation nothing will make a community of the school. (Macmurray, 1949)

How then does this relate to the range of cooperative activities and alliances in the 'education market place' which have been outlined in this book? In broad terms it means, firstly, that we need to remind ourselves, in ways which help us to look with honesty and insight at the real nature of our increasingly pressured daily work, what the collaboration is for. We need to remind ourselves that consorting and collaborating (the functional) is for the sake of education (the personal) and distinguish between the functions of schools that are educational and those that are not. Secondly, it means that we should also take care to remind ourselves that the nature of the collaboration and consortia with which we choose to get involved affects whether or not our purposes can be realized. We need to ask ourselves whether the particular alliances and conjunctions we form enhance rather than diminish the possibility of education and of community for our pupils and ourselves.

## Taking Stock: Asking Difficult Questions of Ourselves and Others

Looking back at the kind of issues Sergiovanni and Macmurray have raised about education, schooling and the nature of community, what might be a series of starter questions we might ask ourselves to help us make judgments about whether or not the particular instances of collaboration we are contemplating are ones which sit comfortably with what we believe education to be about?

In all, I suggest thirteen points which may be helpful to consider. From Macmurray we might take four broad questions which bring us back to those fundamental distinctions between community and society, the personal and the functional which have so much purchase on whether or not education is best served by what we intend to do.

1   Why are we doing this?
What are the reasons for us entering this collaborative arrangement? Is our involvement demonstrably and authentically to do with the specifically educational aspects of our work as a community?

2   How will it help to develop community amongst us?
In what ways will this cooperative undertaking help to further the specifically educational work of the school as a community?

3   Can we shape or transform it appropriately?
How might we shape or transform the way in which we work in this collaboration so that the functional might lead to the personal, so that cooperation might lead to community?

4   Will it extend community?
Will involvement offer opportunities to widen and strengthen community amongst those involved?

From Sergiovanni we might take nine points which help us to focus our thinking:

5   Beyond the poverty of delivery

Will this encourage the move away from teaching as a dominantly instrumental, delivery activity to clients to one which is more widely conceived, more reflexive and more inclusive of teachers and students as persons?

6  Teachers as learners

Will it encourage teachers to see themselves as learners who have the capacity to develop their practice together rather than see themselves as individual or aggregated recipients of external 'solutions'?

7  Means integral to ends

How will it encourage a view of processes which suggests that means are not distinct from ends rather than a narrower view which sees process as important and significant only insofar as it achieves particular results?

8  Valuing others unconditionally

Will this collaboration encourage the valuing of others for who and what they are regardless of achievement, rather than making that valuing of others, apportioning of respect or help conditional on results or status?

9  Teachers as persons

How will it encourage colleagues to view each other in less defined ways which encompass broad interaction, wide concern and a sense of each other as people rather than the occupants of rôles?

10  Educational stewardship

Will it encourage the nurturing of stewardship and the commitment of teachers to the wider, enduring aspects of education which reinforce the sense of teaching as a calling rather than an occupation?

11  Education as personal process

Will it encourage teachers' commitment to education as a fundamentally personal process in which the proper and exciting demands of technique are placed in the overarching and overriding context of the well-being and flourishing of persons?

12  Concern for education as professional practice

Will it encourage the sharing of good practice and the development of our collective knowledge, understanding and practice of teaching and not foster an unremitting vigilance which constrains giving as guarded, partial, reserved or conditional?

13  Towards common purposes

How will it encourage and reinforce our shared obligations and commitments to common purposes which transcend particular, transient agreements?

These questions are not offered as a new series of imperatives which must always apply in all cases. Rather they are offered as a series of questions which may help to orient thinking in the direction of schools as communities at a time when the pressures of the market are operating in entirely the opposite direction. Of course, not everything one does or considers will be approached from these standpoints; some may not apply, some may conflict with each other, some may not sit well with legitimately different positions one could take on the pursuit of education as it is conceived of, and argued for, in this chapter. However, my hope is that amongst them there is much that rings true and much that gives pause for thought amongst those who are committed to education in, through and for community.

### Language, Community and the Poverty of the Market

In drawing this chapter to a close it is important to acknowledge considerable difficulty finding language appropriate to the task in hand. There are three aspects to the difficulty. Firstly, it is partly to do with the importance of articulating concerns and exploring ideas in ways which challenge the impoverished and impoverishing language of the market (Fielding, 1994a). Secondly, it is also to do with the particularly problematic nature of community. Not only is community a contested concept about which different traditions of social and political thought argue with considerable fervour, it is an 'essentially contested concept' i.e., a concept where those disputes are inevitably and unresolvably present.

Thirdly, and equally significantly for those wrestling with issues of human identity and social cohesion in western society as the new millennium approaches, there is an acknowledged difficulty with a term like community which carries with it so much of the baggage of the past. The point is put with characteristic eloquence and insight by Michael Ignatieff who argues that

> Words like fraternity, belonging and community are so soaked with nostalgia and utopianism that they are nearly useless as guides to the real possibilities of solidarity in modern society. Modern life has changed the possibilities of civic solidarity, and our language stumbles behind like an overburdened porter with a mountain of old cases . . . Modernity is changing the locus of our belonging; our language of attachments limps suspiciously behind, doubting that our needs could ever find larger attachments . . . . Our task is to find a language for our need for belonging which is not just a way of expressing nostalgia, fear and estrangement from modernity. . . . (We need), as much as anything else, language adequate to the times we live in. *We need to see how we live now and we can only see with words and images which leave us no escape into nostalgia for some other time or place.* (Ignatieff, 1984, pp. 138, 139, 141 my emphasis)

Ignatieff's final point is salutary, not just in its warning that our language must transcribe the melody and cacophony of postmodernity, but also in his deeply felt reminder that language shapes our world just as it is shaped by it. 'Our needs are made of words: they come to us in speech, and they can die for lack of expression. Without a public language to help us find our words, our needs will dry up in silence' (Ignatieff, 1984, p. 142).

I am not sure that, say, Giddens, is right when he opts for 'cosmopolitanism' rather than 'community', arguing that 'We must work with different models of social cohesion than the notion of community today' (Giddens, 1994, p. 38) because it is too inward, too excluding of others and too divisive. Nor am I sure that, say, Young, is right in her suggestion that 'it is less confusing to use a term other than community rather than redefine the term' (Young, 1986, p. 23). Neither am I convinced that the quest for new words, such as 'heteromity', moves us any further on (Stone, 1992). Nonetheless, I would applaud the attempt and would wish to

*165*

reaffirm the importance of words which guard against the possibility that 'our needs will dry up in silence'.

What is vital in all this is that we listen with care to the susurrus of values that speaks beneath the surface of the words we use. The patterns they create affect the nature of the dialogue we can have about the kind of human being and becoming to which we aspire. The market has no place for, or understanding of, community in its organic or its personal senses. Like Tonnies, I would argue that 'even though a certain familiarity and *Gemeinschaft* (community) may exist amongst business partners, one could indeed hardly speak of commercial *Gemeinschaft* (community). To make the word combination, "joint-stock *Gemeinschaft*", would be abominable' (Tonnies, 1955 [1887], p. 38). Like Cohen I would affirm that 'The immediate motive to productive activity in a market society is typically some mixture of greed and fear, in proportions that vary with the details of a person's market position and personal character. In greed, other people are seen as possible sources of enrichment, and in fear they are seen as threats.' (Cohen, 1994, p. 9).

Not only are these 'horrible ways of seeing people' (ibid.), they are utterly inappropriate within the context of an educational undertaking. Insofar as the market imprints its moral, psychological and procedural imperatives on the work of schools and colleges it constantly threatens to undermine what is specifically educational in it. Whilst consorting and collaborating in the education market place holds the possibility of being creative, exciting and enabling of the learning of staff and students, it will only be so insofar as it leads to the nurturing of community in general and an educational community in particular. In the end the answer lies in whether or not the market motives of greed and fear can be increasingly driven to the margins of our professional life by those of service and care for and of others as persons. What we are collaborating for and how we intend to go about it will determine whether or not the nature of that collaboration is likely to enhance the possibility of educating each other in and through community.

### References

COHEN, G.A. (1994) 'Back to socialist basics', *New Left Review*, 207, September/October, pp. 3–16.

FIELDING, M. (1994a) 'Delivery, packages and the denial of learning', in BRADLEY, H., CONNER, C. and SOUTHWORTH, G. (Eds) *Developing Teachers Developing Schools*, London, Fulton, pp. 18–33.

FIELDING, M. (1994b) 'Valuing difference in teachers and learners: Building on Kolb's learning styles to develop a language of teaching and learning', *Curriculum Journal*, 5, 3, pp. 393–417.

FLORES, A. (Ed) (1988) *Professional Ideals*, Belmont, California, Wadsworth.

GIDDENS, A. (1994) 'What's Left for Labour?', *New Statesman & Society*, 30, September, pp. 37–40.

HEGEL, G.W.F. (1975) [1830] *Logic* (Wallace, W. trans.), Oxford, Clarendon Press.

IGNATIEFF, M. (1984) *The Needs of Strangers*, London, Chatto and Windus.

KIRKPATRICK, F.G. (1986) *Community: A Trinity of Models*, Washington, Georgetown University Press.

MACINTYRE, A. (1981) *After Virtue*, London, Duckworth.

MACMURRAY, J. (1941) 'Two lives in one', *The Listener*, 36, 657, 18 December, p. 822.

MACMURRAY, J. (1949) 'Cultivation of the Personal (III)', The Payne Lectures on the philosophy of education, 29 November, Unpublished.

MACMURRAY, J. (1950) *Conditions of Freedom*, London, Faber.

MACMURRAY, J. (1958) 'Learning to be Human', Moray House Annual Public Lecture, 5 May, Unpublished.

MACMURRAY, J. (1961) *Persons in Relation*, London, Faber.

MARX, K. (1970) [1846] *The German Ideology — Part One*, Arthur, C.J. (Ed), London, Lawrence and Wishart.

NODDINGS, N. (1986) 'Fidelity in teaching, teacher education and research for teaching', *Harvard Educational Review*, 56, 4, pp. 496–510.

SERGIOVANNI, T.J. (1990) *Value-Added Leadership*, Orlando, Florida, Harcourt Brace Jovanovich.

SERGIOVANNI, T.J. (1991) *The Principalship: A Reflective Practice Perspective*, (2nd ed), Needham Heights, Massachusetts, Allyn and Bacon.

SERGIOVANNI, T.J. (1992) *Moral Leadership*, San Fransisco, Jossey Bass.

SERGIOVANNI, T.J. (1994) *Building Community in Schools*, San Fransisco, Jossey Bass.

STONE, L. (1992) 'Disavowing community', *Proceedings of the Philosophy of Education Society*, 48, pp. 93–101.

TONNIES, F. (1955) [1887] *Community and association (Gemeinschaft und Gesellschaft)* Loomis, C.P. (Ed), London, Routledge and Kegan Paul.

YOUNG, I.M. (1986) 'The ideal of community and the politics of difference', *Social Theory and Practice*, 12, 1, pp. 1–26, also in NICHOLSON, L.J. (Ed) (1990) *Feminism/ Postmodernism*, London, Routledge and Kegan Paul, pp. 300–23.

*Chapter 14*

# Theories of Association: The Social Psychology of Working Together in Educational Consortia

*Harry Gray*

### Historic Influences

Historically, British education has for the most part been characterized by the autonomy of institutions. All schools whether public or private used to be more or less responsible for their own curriculum, further-education colleges tried to meet locally determined demand and universities pursued a path of collegial individualism. Nowadays the picture is very different. Even in higher education there is a great move to collaboration rather than competition. Schools vie for customers but collaborate for staff development. FE colleges — though independent corporations — find they have to collaborate with other bodies (such as TECs and LECs) to deliver their mission, and universities uneasily join in consortia to carve up their dominance in the world of high-level skills. Undoubtedly, the greatest contributor to these new and novel forms of cooperation has been the British Government since 1979 with its legislation about education and targeted funding — mainly from the Employment Department, especially in its erstwhile personifications as the Manpower Services Commission (MSC) and Training Agency(TA), with its TVEI (Technical and Vocational Education Initiative), Work Related Further Education (WRFE) and Enterprise in Higher Education (EHE). The relationships which FE and HE continue to develop with the Training and Enterprise Councils (TECs) will require a great deal of collaborative working and there will undoubtedly be more such demands as educational institutions work with government bodies and agencies.

### Divergent Cultures

The purpose of this chapter is to reflect on the working of educational consortia as they are most commonly encountered in their working with government agencies. The basis for this reflection is my recent work as an education adviser to the Employment Department (and more particularly a review I undertook of consortium working in higher education) and some of the relevant literature in social psychology.

On the whole, government departments — both local and national — function in a bureaucratic way which means they assume that other organizations are also bureaucracies or organized as simple administrative systems. Such is seldom the case with non-government organizations and certainly not so in education. Organizational cultures in education tend to be more individually orientated than in almost any other form of business largely because they serve a multitude of purposes. Non-educators often find educational institutions maddeningly obscure and enigmatic but it has to be realized that schools, colleges and universities have a multitude of stakeholders (SEC, 1990). They have to try to be all things to all men and women and they are remarkably successful at it. But it does make for a complication of relationships with funders — particularly those that are not government departments — who believe their simple insights to be more clearly focused than the confused perspectives of the practitioners.

## Government Initiatives

The impetus towards collaborative working since the late 1970s has come from the Government rather than the institutions themselves and there can be little doubt that there is an element of direction and control involved. Consortial working may become even more important now that many educational institutions are private corporations — a move apparently against the present policy of the Department for Education (DfE). TVEI, WRFE and EHE were designed to direct education towards a more carefully focused concern with preparation for working life and often worked through various forms of inter-organizational cooperation. The persuasive factor was the making available of money to responsive institutions and there seem to have been remarkably few complaints about the forms of encouragement and the kinds of demand compliance made on institutional organization and management. Here and there moral, ethical and political objections were raised but they proved insubstantial overall and all three major initiatives and many more minor ones have been pronounced to be generally successful.

Nevertheless, the process of persuasion is not unproblematical and the assumptions about how easy it is for individuals and organizations to work together have often been simplistic. For this reason, it is worth trying to look at the underlying principles of collaboration to see if there are any lessons to be learned from practice and to see if ideas fit together into a reasonably coherent theory. In this way there can be an opportunity for future partners to benefit from learning. The normal instrument by which government departments confer funds on clients is through a contract. A contract is a legal agreement through which a client agrees to deliver certain outcomes under certain conditions for the benefit of the funding agency but compatible with the wishes of the client. It must be obvious that a government contract has the function of delivering outcomes that are consistent with government policy. Invariably government interests are paramount and

whether the interests of other parties are consistent may be of secondary importance. There is nothing amiss with such a situation; it is a perfectly normal
commercial relationship.

The sums of money available for educational consortia have often been quite
small — in the region of £10K or £20K or even less. Such sums often appeared
large to schools and colleges because they were unused to additional funding of this
nature but as the projects worked through, the money available was often discovered to be insufficient for a thorough job, particularly with regard to central administration. This has certainly been the case with many higher education projects,
where institutional overheads were frequently underestimated. Many members not
involved in the original financial negotiations tend to have an unrealistic attitude to
spending money and often assume that additional funds will be made available
'because the funders will want to see the project as a success'. In practice funders
are often unable or reluctant to provide additional funding believing that contractual matters are at issue (Whitaker, 1991).

### Basic Contractual Issues

The problem, however, is that not all contracts are of such a nature that desire (both
on the part of funders and fundees) and compliance (on the part of the fundees) are
identical or even compatible. Contracts over quantifiable matters often provide
problems of assessment and evaluation but contracts that are over ideological
or qualitative matters invariably lead to conflict. Fortunately, the kinds of contract
the MSC (Manpower Services Commission) and, to a lesser extent its successor the
Employment Department, has used have not been highly compliance dependent.
There has often been a great deal of negotiation over the manner of delivery and
its content and it can be argued that some of the contracts were over indulgent to
the client, but, nevertheless, these educational contracts have invariably worked
because there was a general will on both sides that they should work. And because
there was this common will, it came to be overlooked that there were a lot of
problems for the client groups among themselves. For example, few consortia are
made up of the initial principal negotiators so that the continuing partners are often
unclear about the original aims and agreements. A united front to work with a
government department has often obscured the difficulties individuals and their
institutions have in working together. We need, therefore, to look at some of the
issues that arise from association, collaboration and consortial working.

### Group Theory

To understand how institutions collaborate, it is useful to have a theory of group
behaviour. Such a theory may be social, psychological, economic, political or whatever but it must offer a systematic view of how and why people work together and
what contributes to success or failure. The organizational view used for analysis

here derives from social psychology and group dynamics and relates to the ways in which temporary organizations or groups function (for example, Schein, 1966; Sims *et al.*, 1993; Whitaker, 1985). As a starting point, clearly, commonality of purpose is critical but such commonality is often more apparent than real and easily slips away when a group gets into difficulties. Schools, colleges, universities, government departments and agencies do not relate to one another as monolithic, objective entities, they relate through individuals who have greater or lesser autonomy in how they relate to other people. Being a representative is quite difficult and there is often confusion over the roles of representative, delegate and plenipotentiary. There is an added complication when an additional layer is interposed and a steering committee is set up. Often the members of the steering committee have no previous association with either the negotiation process or the institutions represented.

On the whole, the common characteristic of representatives is that they have the same or a congruent value system as their parent organization — at least when operating in a work environment. Civil servants tend to have the values of civil servants, teachers of the kind of school they work in and university lecturers generally sound like university lecturers when they talk to other people. It is in the general value system of their organization or profession that most representation occurs but it does so entirely through individual people as they themselves are and not as 'the organization' from which they come. This means that individual personality is by far and away the strongest factor in association, and individuals will almost certainly experience conflict between personal and professional values. It is individuals who work together not institutions or organizations. As a new form of organization materializes — the consortium — a fresh set of organizational values grows in place which adds yet one more dimension to values conflict and compatibility. When one looks at a single group of people, they tend to show their individuality; when their group comes into association with another there tends to be a bonding within each group. When there is a common object, if it is perceived as an enemy, there is a closing of ranks and a simplifying of identity. When the object is perceived friendly, there is a fragmentation or differentiation among the membership.

This makes it quite difficult for a paymaster or sponsor to work with a group or groups because there is a constant interplay between individuals (when the environment is perceived to be safe) and subgroups when the environment is perceived to be hostile (Gray, 1976). In many cases there is an '*éminence grise*' in the background that embodies the partisan interest of represented bodies and institutions. Many psychologists who look at groups are interested in the interplay of individuals with individuals and pairings of individuals against other pairings. Few group psychologists would believe that formal groups lose their personal constituency just because the situations in which they perform are designated as formal. That means that if government departments believe that the people they relate to are objective and impersonal representatives of the institutions, they are mistaken. Members of temporary groups (consortia etc) have many personal concerns and anxieties which influence their interpretation of what is going on in the consortium and hence their behaviour as well.

### Problems of Representation

Because groups are made up of individuals, it is difficult to come to a contract that is actually binding on each member. Indeed, the very fact that members are 'representative' in some way yet often not legally bound into the organization means that much formal contracting is void and certainly imaginary. A good example of this is the EHE contract which was usually signed by the vice-chancellor. Many civil servants thought that such an agreement would be binding on all the members of the university and there was some consternation when it was discovered that by and large university teachers do not feel themselves bound by any agreement their vice-chancellor might make on their behalf! In the case of schools, it is usual to find that agreements made with teachers in a workshop or development group meeting outside the school or extra-institutional are of little interest to teachers who have not been involved in the process.

This is a universal problem with all consortial working; working members of a consortium seldom represent sufficiently fully the interests and commitment of those they represent. And there are no sanctions in law that can coerce behaviour; indeed coercion would be counterproductive. However, what usually happens is that the issues are fudged. Knowing that agreement is unlikely or problematic, delegates look for forms of wording that suggest that representation has been effective and by broadening the terms of reference produce statements that can be taken as broadly subject to general agreement.

### Institutional Tension

Consortia tend to have shorter life spans than they are often credited with. Members join with some eagerness and perhaps high commitment and expectations but quickly realize that however lofty the purposes of the association, very quickly the group has to contend with a lot of low-level interaction between individuals. During the early stages of a group's life, there is a great deal of work to be done not only on sorting out whether there are common values but whether membership will be rewarding and comfortable. Most people join a consortium because they have a fairly high personal ambition, often and most usually one that has an extra-institutional dimension. In short, most people join for promotion purposes. This means they are torn between loyalty to their parent organization and the seeking of new credentials that will serve them in good stead for internal or external advancement.

In small group theory, this can be easily observed as people jostle for power, leadership, influence, and allies; and as they seek positions for themselves that meet their psychological needs for safety, comfort, risk or danger. Sometimes, organizations behave much as individuals and their representatives bring with them the culture of the parent organization and its pathology, *i.e.*, what one might think of as the dark side of interpersonal and personal, group and intergroup relations. Hence representatives of some organizations appear dominating and aggressive and it is recognized that this is how the organization appears to behave to outsiders. Equally, some institutions that have the reputation for being somewhat ineffective often produce representatives who characterize the common view.


## Membership

Membership of a consortium is usually of a temporary nature. Consortia are frequently pump-priming exercises and have a built-in lifespan sometimes as little as one year and seldom more than five. This means that personnel are recruited or appointed with a terminal point in mind from the very beginning and though the excitement of joining a new venture often makes five years look a long way ahead, it is not long before the mind begins to look more cautious at the finishing point. Because the consortium is also often experimental, — indeed, this is most probably more often the case than not — the resources (both in demand and on offer) are marginal to the parent organizations and the people chosen for involvement must be recruited out of the 'organizational slack'; people whose organizational position is in some way uncertain or free-standing. Although there may be some representation from a high level, the actual hard work will be done by members who are below the top ranks or whose position is in process of marginalization. For every member there will be a tension about loyalty — to the parent organization or the consortium. And for some members the consortium will replace the home organization as the more salient concern, displacing former loyalties and perhaps creating some confusion back home. Some members will quite deliberately use the period of their membership as a mechanism for transition from one position or organization to another — a matter of which their colleagues may be quite unaware.


## Objectives and Purposes

Consortia are usually formed in order to achieve certain fairly clear objectives. It is usually a condition of membership that two or three requirements are fulfilled. One is that there be a benefit to the participating institutions; the second is that there will be made no demand on resources that is unacceptable to the participating institutions; and the third is that there is a clear definition of activity in which the consortium will engage. Funding bodies like clear objectives because they are measurable in quantifiable terms (usually numbers of people and pounds sterling). But there is often an attempt to express outcomes in qualitative terms. When this occurs there are problems of ambiguity and interpretation which cannot always be resolved. It is also generally believed that if objectives are stated clearly and unambiguously, their achievement will be largely a matter of course. Unfortunately this is too simple a view since interpretations vary so widely.

For one thing, as has just been explained, individuals have a complexity of reasons for being members of the consortia and many of them are concerned with the consortium as a vehicle for personal returns (rewards) rather than identification with institutional needs. But objectives are a problem on other counts too. Object-ives are tied to the time at which they are conceived and may not relate to future con-ditions. Objectives denote past history rather than the reality of future achievement. That is why, for example, EHE contracts were consistently negotiable according to contemporary institutional needs and opportunities. For another thing, organiza-tions cannot have objectives, only their members can, and the forms of language used for agreement at one time may turn out with the passage of time not to fit the perceived circumstance of the current state of affairs (Reynolds, 1994). Further-more, the criteria (even the highly quantifiable ones) that appeared to be relevant when the objectives were written down may not be relevant when time has come for the assessment of achievement. These may be small matters when the issue has to be negotiated by only two partners but when the negotiation is between several people, several groups and several represented institutions, the nonsense of setting precise objectives is apparent.

### Personal Energy

Because consortia function through individuals and individuals have their own personal life scenarios, consortia are more vulnerable to personal failure than their parent institutions. By their very nature consortia tend to be ephemeral. They are set up for specific purposes and for a predetermined period of time. They are only loosely attached to institutions. Individuals join looking for optimization of per-sonal outcomes rather than expenditure of effort. There are, of course, from the outset always enthusiasts and willing leaders; also the indifferent and the spoilers. It is often a surprise to find how many disaffected people join new enterprises. Yet for many people who cannot find a comfortable central position in their organiza-tion, an extra-institutional body is a useful escape channel.

The key issues in the management of a consortium probably centre more around individual needs and individual personality than around matters of task management. Because they are so dependent on people who are detached from their normal working environment consortia are very vulnerable in many respects. For one thing, there will always be a tension between the consortium and the home organization. Members will be looking over their shoulders much of the time to see what is happening at home and assessing whether it is wise to continue membership and on what terms. For a variety of reasons, some members — e.g., paid leader-ship or secretariat — will be more committed to success than others — and it will be 'success' as nebulously defined rather than successful attainment of concrete objectives. Some will join for short-term gain because they are looking for quick rewards. There will be many promises and avowals of assistance but many will be short-lived and many unredeemed. The fundamental life-dynamic is not the consor-tium (except for delegated full-time members) but the home organization. Most people find it difficult to live in two organizations at the same time particularly when the relationship is not well articulated. And if there are strong values differ-ences (personal and organizational), the level of discomfort will be high.

### Marginality

Consortia are — again by their very nature — marginal to the parent organizations unless the consortium be captive to a single institution. That means they are vulnerable to withdrawal of support both financial and moral. They are also at risk from senior managers in the parent organizations who may have surrogate needs to be satisfied. Marginal units can serve very useful purposes for an institution because they help to span the boundary with the outside world without too much disturbance to the host. In a period of new development in the world at large, consortia can be a comparatively non-threatening means of access to ideas and funds. But they can also facilitate closure of an activity without much pain to the parent organization as well. Organizations tend to protect themselves from too much outside influence by setting up marginal units to develop 'new' ideas or poach them from other places. In fact, these units serve the purpose of modifying outside influence and turning it into ideas that are more manageable. For the funder, they provide clear terminal mechanisms. At the end of funding (or whatever) these units can be closed down completely, or used to foster desired reforms in an acceptable and manageable way. Consortia are a sort of halfway house to marginality. They can be drawn in or expelled without much disturbance or concern.

### Creativity

Although consortia are generally set up to develop new ideas, they are seldom as creative as is expected. Some of the reasons have already been given — self-interest, institutional marginality, complexity of objectives and conflicting purposes. They are also easily influenced by maverick members. They absorb a lot of energy without necessarily producing anything outstanding or substantial. They tend to be arenas of compromise. Members tend to want their say and if they feel unheard elsewhere they will try to use the consortium as their mouth piece. If they have to produce a report it may well be obviously composite, full of compromise and accommodation to disparate individual interests and bear little relationship to the original supposed clarity of purpose. Much depends on how the work of the consortium is managed (including the relationship with any steering or supervisory body) and how responsibility is apportioned and accountability delegated. Consortia of equal partners are most likely to be unsuccessful because there is too much vying for leadership and control. Probably the most successful consortial groups are those which have a preappointed leader or rapporteur and a clear senior organizational partner. But in such cases the success is that of the writer of the report and the satisfaction of the needs of the senior partner not of the group as a whole.

Consortia that have a predetermined lifespan always begin to run down just after the midway point in their life. It is easy to see why this should be the case — the same sort of thing happens with holidays — because at some point members begin to look to their own future after the consortium. Since the other world is the more important, the consortium becomes less significant for all but those whose *raison d'être* is completion of the original task. This second half may be the most creative period but the membership will already be falling off and the energy to complete will depend on a small band of the most committed. Of course once the midway period is past there can be no renewal. There is little point in more funds being made available because the spirit of the group has been broken. Personal time spans are not easily changed because they are complex creations of a multitude of personal needs and desires. Membership of the consortium almost certainly depends on release or secondment from one of the parent organizations and individuals fear a loss of connection if they continue to work outside their original place of employment. One of the problems with consortia is that they tend to have quite specific business to do and it is difficult to augment that artificially, by importing an extension of work, unless of course all the organizations concerned see it as a priority need.

### Evaluation

It is almost impossible to evaluate what a consortium does as, for example, the NFER experience with evaluation of TVEI confirms (Bridgwood, 1989). Of course, there are traditional measures of assessment (formative, summative and impressionistic) but consortia do not really exist for their declared purposes; they are vehicles for the attainment of other ambitions, many personal and peculiar and some deriving from the activities of the consortium itself and so unanticipated. Many members will declare that the consortium of which they were a member achieved other things than those intended. Sponsors may be happy with a quantitative assessment and are in any case seldom eager to be seen to have financed a failure. Consortia will always tend to break up into smaller units once the purposes of solidarity have been achieved. Each supporting institution will have discovered some of the consortial activities that it can now better do on its own. Consortia have such uncertain identity and such tenuous relationships with parent bodies that their lives are fragile. In fact, few parent organizations want a successful consortium because that implies some lack on their own part. So in some ways, consortia are on a hiding for nothing from the very start and the real wonder is that they achieve the success that they often demonstrably do.

### Positive Advantages

It may sound from what has been written so far that consortia are too liable to produce problems to be very useful. This is not quite the case. The basic problem is that too much is expected of them and they are often not well understood by those who relate to them — especially those who are outside since the insiders get totally caught up in their dynamic processes. The main considerations for successful consortia are not to expect too much, to go for simple but almost infinitely negotiable objectives, to allow them to perform as a vehicle for personal need as much as is compatible with funder's aims, and to clarify the supporting relationship with parent bodies at the outset. Consortia exhibit the characteristics of ordinary organizations but in a rather exaggerated and attenuated (even etiolated) form. Funders should realize that they have greater vested interest in what the consortia does than any of the members and this means there can be no hands-off relationship that might encourage recrimination. No one can compel consortia members to remain enthusiastic until the end but funders can begin to take up some of the organizational strain towards the middle of the life cycle. It is also worth examining the hidden agendas that appear when consortia are formed. No one is free from ulterior motives and sometimes it is the funders who are most dishonest about their real intentions.

## Acknowledgment

My thanks are due to Howard Andrew of Glasgow Caledonian University who shared his valuable insights into consortia and made helpful comments on earlier drafts. Also to Jim Shaw, policy manager for TVEI, Employment Department who helped me to clarify some ambiguities and oversimplifications.

## References

BRIDGWOOD, A. (1989) *Working Together: Consortium Links in TVEI*, NFER/Training Agency.

GRAY, H. (1976) *Exchange and Conflict in the School*, in HOUGHTON, V., McHUGH, R. and MORGAN, C. *Management in Education*, Milton Keynes, Ward Lock/Open University.

REYNOLDS, M. (1994) *Group Work in Education and Training*, London, Kogan Page.

SCHEIN, E. (1966) *Organizational Psychology*, Englewood Cliffs, New Jersey, Prentice Hall.

SCOTTISH ENTERPRISE CONSORTIUM (SEC) (1990) *Evaluation Report (inc Appendices)*, Stirling, Scottish Enterprise Consortium, University of Stirling.

SIMS, D., FINEMAN, S. and YIANNIS, G. (1993) *Organizing and Organizations*, London, Sage.

WHITAKES, D.S. (1985) *Using Groups to Help People*, London, Routledge and Kegan Paul.

WHITAKER, R. (1991) *Consortium Collaboration in Higher Education: Benefits and Drawbacks of Consortium Working*, ERTEC Occasional Paper No. 2, Norwich, University of East Anglia.

# Notes on Contributors

**Michael Barber** is professor of education at Keele University and director of its Centre for Successful Schools. His work on urban education, includes *Education in the Capital* (1992), a briefing for the National Commission on Education on *Raising Standards in Deprived Urban Areas* (1993) and, with others, two reports for OFSTED on *Urban Education Initiatives* (1994).

**David Bridges** is professor of education at the University of East Anglia. Between 1989 and 1994 he was director of the Eastern Region Teacher Education Consortium. He was editor, with Terry McLaughlin of *Education in the Marketplace* (1994).

**Ann Bridgwood** works with the Office for Population Censuses and Surveys, and previously evaluated the Technical and Vocational Education Initiative for NFER. She is the author of *Working Together: Consortium Links in TVEI* (NFER/Training Agency, 1989).

**Mike Fielding** is tutor in education at the Cambridge University Institute of Education.

**Harry Gray** works at the University of Salford, and is higher education adviser to the Employment Department.

**Mike Harbour** is warden of Medina High School on the Isle of Wight. Between 1989 and 1994 he was headteacher of Benjamin Britten High School, Lowestoft. The school is a member of the North Lowestoft Schools Network. Mike Harbour has interests in initial teacher education, community education, educational management and the development of collaborative approaches to educational change.

**Linda Hargreaves** is lecturer in education at the University of Leicester. She became involved in research on small schools as a PhD student on the DES-funded 'Curriculum Provision in Small Primary Schools' Project (1983–6) and was co-director of the 'Implementation of the National Curriculum in Small Schools' Project.

**Chris Husbands** is reader in education at the University of Warwick. Between 1990 and 1995 he was lecturer and then senior lecturer in education at the University of East Anglia, Norwich, and previously taught in comprehensive schools in London, Norwich and Hertfordshire. He has written extensively on new teachers' professional learning.

**Michael Johnson** is senior research fellow in the Centre for Successful Schools at Keele University. He was coordinator of the 'Two Towns' Project from 1990–4. He is co-author of a number of publications on urban education including *Urban Education Initiatives* (1994) for OFSTED.

**Lynne Monck** has been headteacher of Fearnhill School, Letchworth, one of the pilot Education 2000 schools since 1988. She is an external examiner to the University of Cambridge school-based teacher-education programme, and has previously taught in Norfolk.

**Bridget Somekh** has been depute director of the Scottish Council for Research in Education since February 1995. She was previously lecturer in education at the Centre for Applied Research in Education at the University of East Anglia and between 1987 and 1995 was coordinator of the Collaborative Action Research Network.

**Peter Upton** is principal of Tavistock College, Devon and **Phil Cozens** is head of learning needs at Audley Park, Devon. Upton has carried out research in Europe and the USA on school culture and bullying, lecturing both in the UK and abroad. He is a Churchill Fellow and a Fellow of the Royal Society of Arts.

**Ron Wallace** is an independent education consultant and OFSTED inspector. He taught for eleven years in London grammar and comprehensive schools, was for twelve years headteacher of The Bedwell School in Stevenage and was subsequently Hertfordshire's director of TVEI and chief adviser. He is the author of *Introducing Technical and Vocational Education* (Basingstoke, Macmillan Education, 1985) and of 'The Act and Local Authorities' in Flude and Hammer *The Education Reform Act* 1988 (Basingstoke, Falmer Press, 1990).

**Sylvia West** is warden of Impington Village College, Cambridgeshire and author of *Educational Values for School Leadership* (1993).

# Index

Classroom Action Research Network *see*
CARN
clustering
small rural schools *see* rural schools:
cluster development
Cohen, Gerry A. 150, 155, 166
collaboration *see also* consortia
collegiality and 68, 71, 81
community involvement 59–61
community values *see* community
values
competition and 2–3, 19
critical evaluation 163–4
cross-phase *see* cross-phase liaison
higher education institutions 123,
128–9
instability 18
limitations of 149–50
partnership development 15, 17–18
professional interchange 15, 16–17,
37–8
purchasing consortia 15–16, 19
small rural schools *see* rural schools
staff development *see* staff development
Technical and Vocational Education
Initiative *see* TVEI
Collaborative Action Research Network
*see* CARN
colleges of further education
collaboration with other bodies 168
incorporation 111
collegiality 68, 71, 81
community involvement 59–61
community values
contractual model 155
diversity 160
equality 158, 160–1
in schools 159–60, 161–4
market principles and 149–50, 155,
165–6
organic model 156
reciprocity 160, 161
theories of T.J. Sergiovanni 150–4
unity of persons 156–61
use of language 165–6
competition 9, 10
collaboration and 2–3, 19
higher education 2, 119, 128–9
recruitment of pupils 1, 10, 12, 38, 168
service providers 1, 12
tendering 19
wastefulness 16
comprehensive education 11
computer-literacy 63

consortia *see also* collaboration
advantages 176–7
contractual issues 170
creativity 175–6
divergent cultures 168–9
evaluation 176
government initiatives 169–70
group behaviour 170–71
higher education 123, 128–9, 168
historic influences 168
institutional tension 172–3
life spans 172, 174, 175–6
marginality 175
membership 173
objectives and purposes 173–4
personal energy 174
purchasing 15–16, 19
representation of members 172
vulnerability 174
consumer choice 10, 11, 12
autonomy and self-interest 87
children as consumers 134
silent manipulation 86–7
Cook, Peter 60
Cook, P. and Dalton, R. 58
cooperation *see* collaboration
Coopers and Lybrand 50
Cordingley, P. and Kogan, M. 11, 16,
18
Coulthard, Nigel 4
*Critical Conversations* 140, 141
cross-phase liaison 36–7
curriculum continuity 37, 40, 50–51
governors 43–4
INSET 40, 42
Key Stage 3 science 45
marketing 45–6
management and support structures
41–3, 48
middle- and high-school 38–41
primary schools 40–41, 44
professional distrust 37
school improvement 99
top-down approach 40
curriculum
cross-phase continuity 37, 40, 50–51
Education 2000 63–4
Information Technology 62–3
small rural schools *see* rural schools:
curriculum support
teacher autonomy 135–6
TVEI 110
working parties 112–13
Curriculum Council for Wales 21